Pro Spring Security

Securing Spring Framework 6 and Boot 3-based Java Applications

Third Edition

Massimo Nardone
Carlo Scarioni

Apress®

Pro Spring Security: Securing Spring Framework 6 and Boot 3–based Java Applications, Third Edition

Massimo Nardone
HELSINKI, Finland

Carlo Scarioni
Surbiton, UK

ISBN-13 (pbk): 979-8-8688-0034-4
https://doi.org/10.1007/979-8-8688-0035-1

ISBN-13 (electronic): 979-8-8688-0035-1

Managing Director, Apress Media LLC: Welmoed Spahr
Acquisitions Editor: Melissa Duffy
Development Editor: Laura Berendson
Coordinating Editor: Gryffin Winkler
Copy Editor: Kim Burton

Cover designed by eStudioCalamar

Cover image by Manuel Torres Garcia from Pixabay

Distributed to the book trade worldwide by Apress Media, LLC, 1 New York Plaza, New York, NY 10004, U.S.A. Phone 1-800-SPRINGER, fax (201) 348-4505, e-mail orders-ny@springer-sbm.com, or visit www.springeronline.com. Apress Media, LLC is a California LLC and the sole member (owner) is Springer Science + Business Media Finance Inc (SSBM Finance Inc). SSBM Finance Inc is a **Delaware** corporation.

For information on translations, please e-mail booktranslations@springernature.com; for reprint, paperback, or audio rights, please e-mail bookpermissions@springernature.com.

Apress titles may be purchased in bulk for academic, corporate, or promotional use. eBook versions and licenses are also available for most titles. For more information, reference our Print and eBook Bulk Sales web page at http://www.apress.com/bulk-sales.

Any source code or other supplementary material referenced by the author in this book is available to readers on GitHub (https://github.com/Apress). For more detailed information, please visit https://www.apress.com/gp/services/source-code.

Paper in this product is recyclable

I would like to dedicate this book to the memory of my beloved late mother, Maria Augusta Ciniglio. Thanks, Mom, for all the great things you have taught me, for making me a good person, for making me study to become a computing scientist, and for the great memories you left me. You will be loved and missed forever. I love you, Mom. RIP.

—Massimo

Table of Contents

About the Authors... ix

About the Technical Reviewer xi

Acknowledgments xiii

Introduction xv

Chapter 1: The Scope of Security 1

The Network Security Layer... 4

The Operating System Layer 5

The Application Layer.. 5

    Authentication 6

    Authorization 7

    ACLs 9

Authentication and Authorization: General Concepts 9

What to Secure.. 14

Additional Security Concerns... 15

Java Options for Security 17

Summary... 19

Chapter 2: Introducing Spring Security 21

What Is Spring Security?... 21

Where Does Spring Security Fit In? 23

Spring Security Overview.. 26

    What Is Spring Boot? 28

Spring Framework 6: A Quick Overview... 29

    JDK 17+ and Jakarta EE 9+ Baseline 30

    General Core Revision 30

Core Container...30

Data Access and Transactions...31

Spring Messaging..32

General Web Revision..32

Spring MVC...32

Spring WebFlux...32

Observability...33

Pattern Matching...33

Testing...34

Dependency Injection..34

Aspect-Oriented Programming...36

What's New in Spring Security 6?..38

Summary..44

Chapter 3: Setting up the Scene 45

Setting up the Development Environment 45

Creating a New Java Web Application Project 52

Adding Spring Security 6 to the Java Project..57

Spring Security 6 Source...58

Configuring the Spring Security 6 Web Project...65

Summary..74

Chapter 4: Spring Security Architecture and Design.................75

What Components Make up Spring Security?...75

The 10,000-Foot View...75

The 1,000-Foot View...76

The 100-Foot View..77

Good Design and Patterns in Spring Security 116

Strategy Pattern 117

Decorator Pattern 117

SRP..118

DI...118

Summary..118

Chapter 5: Web Security **121**

Configuring the new Spring Security 6 Project 126

The Special URLs 142

    Custom Login Form 143

    Basic HTTP Authentication 150

    Digest Authentication 152

    Remember-Me Authentication 155

    Logging Out 158

    Session Management 161

Summary 167

Chapter 6: Configuring Alternative Authentication Providers **169**

LDAP Authentication 185

    Using an Embedded LDAP 186

X.509 Authentication 198

OAuth 2.0 200

JSON Web Token 201

Spring WebSocket 202

Java Authentication and Authorization Service 203

Central Authentication Service 203

Summary 204

Chapter 7: Business Object Security with ACLs **205**

ACL Key Concepts 205

Summary 210

Chapter 8: Open Authorization 2.0 (OAuth 2.0) and Spring Security **211**

An Introduction to OAuth 2.0 211

    OAuth 2.0 Security 213

    Integrating OAuth 2.0 with Spring Security 214

    OAuth 2.0 Login 217

Summary 238

Chapter 9: JSON Web Token (JWT) Authentication **239**

The REST API 239

Introduction to JSON Web Token 242

Summary 279

Index **281**

About the Authors

 **Massimo Nardone** has more than 27 years of experience in information and cybersecurity for IT/OT/IoT/IIoT, web/mobile development, cloud, and IT architecture. His true IT passions are security and Android. He has been programming and teaching how to program with Android, Perl, PHP, Java, VB, Python, C/C++, and MySQL for more than 27 years. He holds an MSc degree in computing science from the University of Salerno, Italy. Throughout his working career, he has held various positions, starting as a programming developer, then security teacher, PCI QSA, auditor, assessor, lead IT/OT/SCADA/SCADA/ cloud architect, CISO, BISO, executive, program director, and OT/IoT/IIoT security competence leader.

In his last working engagement, he worked as a seasoned cyber and information security executive, CISO and OT, IoT and IIoT Security competence Leader, helping many clients to develop and implement Cyber, Information, OT, and IoT security activities.

His technical skills include security, OT/IoT/IIoT, Android, cloud, Java, MySQL, Drupal, Cobol, Perl, web and mobile development, MongoDB, D3, Joomla!, Couchbase, C/C++, WebGL, Python, Pro Rails, Django CMS, Jekyll, and Scratch. He has served as a visiting lecturer and exercises supervisor at the Helsinki University of Technology (Aalto University) Networking Laboratory.

He stays current with industry and security trends and is a board member of the ISACA Finland chapter, ISF, the Nordic CISO Forum, and the Android Global Forum.

He holds four international patents (PKI, SIP, SAML, and Proxy areas). He currently works as a cybersecurity freelancer for IT/OT and IoT. Massimo has reviewed more than 55 IT books for different publishers and has coauthored *Pro JPA 2 in Java EE 8* (Apress, 2018), *Beginning EJB in Java EE 8* (Apress, 2018), and *Pro Android Games* (Apress, 2015).

Carlo Scarioni is a passionate software developer, motivated by learning and applying innovative and interesting software development tools, techniques, and methodologies. He has worked in the field for more than 18 years and moved across multiple languages, paradigms, and subject areas. He also has many years of experience working with Java and its ecosystem. He has been in love with Spring since the beginning, and he is fascinated by how Spring allows building complex applications out of discrete, focused modules and by the clever use of decorators to add cross-cutting functionalities. He has worked mostly with data engineering solutions in the last few years. He has been creating solutions around the use of modern data stack components in cloud environments while at the same time developing software using technologies such as Spark, Python, and others.

About the Technical Reviewer

Mario Faliero is a telecommunication engineer and entrepreneur. He has more than ten years of experience in radio frequency hardware engineering. Mario has extensive experience in numerical coding, using scripting languages (MatLab, Python) and compiled languages (C/C++, Java). He has been responsible for developing electromagnetic assessment tools for space and commercial applications. Mario received his master's degree from the University of Siena.

Acknowledgments

Many thanks go to my wonderful family for supporting me while I was working on this book. Luna, Leo, and Neve, you are the most beautiful reason of my life.

I want to thank my beloved late mother, Maria Augusta Ciniglio, who always supported and loved me so much. I will love and miss you forever, my dearest mom.

Thanks to my beloved father, Giuseppe, and my brothers, Mario and Roberto, for your endless love and for being the best dad and brothers in the world.

Many thanks to Melissa Duffy for giving me the opportunity to work as a writer on this book, Shonmirin P. A. for doing such a great job during the editorial process and supporting me, and Laura Berendson, development editor, for helping me to make it a better book.

—Massimo Nardone

Introduction

Denying the impact of the Spring Framework in the Java world would be simply impossible. Spring has brought so many advantages to Java developers that we could say it has made us all better developers.

The previous version of this book utilized Spring Security 5. Therefore, in this new edition of the book, it is very important to note the most important changes from version 5 to version 6.

Spring Framework 6.0 was released on November 16, 2022. It came with a Java 17+ baseline and a move to Jakarta EE 9+ (in the Jakarta namespace), focusing on the recently released Jakarta EE 10 APIs such as Servlet 6.0 and JPA 3.1. Spring's current version's core building blocks of dependency injection and aspect-oriented programming widely apply to many business and infrastructure concerns. Certainly, application security can benefit from these core functionalities. Even in version 6, Spring Security is an application-level security framework built on top of the powerful Spring Framework that deals mainly with the core security concepts of *authentication* and *authorization*, which, also in version 6, are some of the fundamental functionalities of Spring Security.

Spring Security aims to be a full-featured security solution for your Java applications. Although its focus is on web applications and the Java programming language, you will see that it goes beyond these two domains.

Because there are new things in the version, the baseline for Spring Boot 3 and Spring Security 6 is Java 17.

Also, the WebSecurityConfigurerAdapter class to configure security settings was deprecated in version 6, using a more component-based approach and creating a bean of type SecurityFilterChain.

AuthorizeRequests was also deprecated and replaced with authorizeHttpRequests, and in Spring Security 6, AntMatcher, MvcMatcher, and RegexMatcher were deprecated and replaced by requestMatchers or securityMatchers for path-based access control.

Also, in version 6, some updates were done using OAuth 2.0 and SAML 2.0.

In writing this book, we wanted to expose some of Spring Security's internal works along with standard explanations of how to use certain features. The idea is to teach beyond the basics of how to do something in particular and instead focus on the plumbing inside the framework. This is the best way to learn something: seeing how it is built in the core. That's not to say that the book doesn't cover basic setups and gives quick, practical advice on using the framework because it certainly does. The point is that instead of saying, "Use this to do that," we say, "This works like this... and this allows you to...." This is a point of view that only tools like Spring can afford (because they are open source).

With that said, we suggest that the best way to use this book is to have the Spring Security source code checked out on your computer and go through the examples with both the code from the book and the code from Spring Security itself. This will help you understand each concept as it is introduced and teach more than one good programming trick and good practice. We recommend this approach for studying any software whenever you have the chance. If the source code is out there, grab it. Sometimes, a couple of lines of code teach more than a thousand words. This book primarily introduces Spring Boot 3, analyzes Spring Framework, and develops Java web applications with Spring Security 6 and Java 17/20.

Also, Spring Security 6 supports many different authentication mechanisms, which are introduced and developed in this book, including the H2 and PostgreSQL databases, LDAP, X.509, OAuth 2.0, JWT, JAAS, and CAS.

Who This Book Is For

This book is written mainly for Java developers who use Spring in their work and need to add security to their applications in a way that leverages Spring's proven concepts and techniques. The book will also be helpful to developers who want to add web-layer security to their applications, even if those applications are not fully Spring-powered at their core. The book assumes you have knowledge of Java and some of its tools and libraries, such as Servlet, Maven, OAuth 2.0, and JWT. It also assumes that you know what you want to use security for and in what context you want to use it. This means, for example, we won't explain protocols like LDAP in depth; instead, we'll concentrate on showing you how to integrate Spring Security with an LDAP user store. An in-depth knowledge of Spring is not essential because many of the concepts are introduced as we go along, but the more you understand about Spring, the more likely you are to get out of this book.

How This Book Is Structured

The book is divided into nine chapters that embody a progressive study of Spring Security. Starting from a summary of basic applications and an explanation of how the framework is structured, the content moves on to more advanced topics, such as using Spring Security in different JVM languages. The book follows a sequence corresponding to how this framework is normally used in real life.

The chapters in the book cover the following.

- **Chapter 1** introduces security in general and how to approach security problems at the application level.

- **Chapter 2** introduces Spring Security 6, how to use it, when to use it, and its security functionalities.

- **Chapter 3** introduces Spring Security with a simple example application that secures web access at the URL level.

- **Chapter 4** provides a full introduction to the architecture of Spring Security, including the main components and how they interact with each other.

- **Chapter 5** gives in-depth coverage of the web-layer security options available in Spring Security.

- **Chapter 6** covers a wide array of authentication providers, including H2 DB, LDAP, and JASS, which can be plugged into Spring Security.

- **Chapter 7** covers access control lists (ACLs), which are used to secure individual domain objects, and how they fit into the general security concerns.

- **Chapter 8** explains how to develop an application using Open Authorization 2.0 (OAuth 2.0) Login and Spring Security Customization.

- **Chapter 9** shows how to integrate Spring Security into JSON Web Token (JWT) authentication.

Prerequisites

The examples in this book are all built with Java 17 and Maven 3.9.2. The latest Spring versions are used if possible. Spring Security 6 is the version used throughout the book. Tomcat Web Server 10 is used for the different web applications in the book, mainly through its Maven plugin. The laptop is a ThinkPad Yoga 360 with 8 GB of RAM. All the projects were developed using IntelliJ IDEA Ultimate 2023.2.

You are free to use your own tools and operating system. Because everything is Java-based, you should be able to compile your programs on any platform without problems.

Downloading the Code

Any source code or other supplementary material referenced by the author in this book is available to readers on GitHub (`https://github.com/Apress`). For more detailed information, please visit `www.apress.com/gp/services/source-code`.

Contacting the Authors

You are more than welcome to send us any feedback regarding this book or any other subject we might help you with. You can contact Massimo Nardone via email at `massimonardonedevchannel@gmail.com` and Carlo Scarioni via his blog at `http://cscarioni.blogspot.com`, or you can send him email at `carlo.scarioni@gmail.com`.

CHAPTER 1

The Scope of Security

Security. It is an incredibly overloaded word in the IT, OT, and IoT world. It means so many different things in many different contexts, but in the end, it is all about protecting sensitive and valuable resources against malicious usage.

IT has many layers of infrastructure and code that can be subject to malicious attacks, and arguably, you should ensure that all these layers get the appropriate levels of protection.

In operational technology (OT), where generally the systems were isolated from the external networks and operated independently, the increasing connectivity and integration of OT systems with information technology (IT) networks and the Internet, the risk of cyberattacks targeting these systems has significantly grown. OT security aims to address these risks and protect against threats that could disrupt operations, cause physical damage, or impact public safety.

In the Internet of Things (IoT), security refers to the measures and practices implemented to protect the interconnected devices, networks, and data associated with IoT systems, such as networks of physical objects or "things" embedded with sensors, software, and connectivity to exchange data and perform various tasks. These objects range from household appliances and wearable devices to industrial machinery and infrastructure. Given the proliferation of IoT devices and their increasing integration into various domains, securing IoT systems is critical to mitigate potential risks and protect the privacy, integrity, and availability of their data and services.

The growth of the Internet and the pursuit of reaching more people with our applications have opened more doors to cyber criminals trying to access these applications illegitimately.

It is also true that good care is not always taken to ensure that a properly secured set of services is offered to the public. And sometimes, even when good care is taken, some hackers are still smart enough to overcome security barriers that, superficially, appear adequate.

The first step is to define a defense-in-depth strategy and security layers.

1

© Massimo Nardone, Carlo Scarioni 2024
M. Nardone and C. Scarioni, *Pro Spring Security*, https://doi.org/10.1007/979-8-8688-0035-1_1

Defense in depth (also known as DiD) is a security strategy that involves implementing multiple layers of defense to protect a system or network from potential threats. It aims to provide a comprehensive and resilient security posture by incorporating various security measures at different levels, such as physical, technical, and administrative controls.

The defense-in-depth concept recognizes that no single security measure is foolproof, and relying on a single layer of defense can leave vulnerabilities. By employing multiple layers, other layers can still provide protection even if one is breached or compromised.

In practice, a defense-in-depth strategy can include a combination of measures such as firewalls, intrusion detection systems, encryption, access controls, strong authentication mechanisms, security awareness training, regular system updates and patching, network segmentation, and physical security measures like locked doors and security cameras. These layers collectively create a more robust and resilient security infrastructure.

The goal of a defense-in-depth strategy is to increase the difficulty for attackers, making it harder for them to penetrate a system and move deeper into the network. Requiring attackers to overcome multiple barriers increases the likelihood of detection and mitigation, reducing the potential impact of a successful attack. Overall, it is a proactive approach to security that emphasizes multiple layers of protection, reducing the risk of successful attacks and minimizing the potential damage they can cause.

In general, a defense-in-depth strategy is a way to define how to develop the cybersecurity of the IT infrastructure by defining how all the defensive mechanisms are layered to protect and secure data and information. A failing or weak defense-in-depth strategy might result from a cybersecurity attack on the IT infrastructure.

Let's try to understand a bit more about defense-in-depth mechanisms. First, there are three major controls.

- **Physical controls** are security measures that aim to protect the physical infrastructure and assets. They include surveillance cameras, access controls (such as locks and biometric systems), perimeter fencing, security guards, and intrusion detection systems.

- **Perimeter security** focuses on securing the boundary between the internal network and the external environment. It involves firewalls, intrusion prevention systems (IPS), and demilitarized zones (DMZs) to filter and monitor network traffic, control access, and prevent unauthorized entry.

- **Network security** measures aim to protect the internal network infrastructure. They include technologies such as network segmentation, virtual private networks (VPNs), intrusion detection systems (IDS), and IPS to detect and prevent unauthorized access, monitor network traffic, and detect and respond to potential threats.

- **Identity and access management (IAM)** controls ensure that only authorized individuals can access systems and resources. This includes strong authentication mechanisms like passwords, two-factor authentication (2FA), multi-factor authentication, access control policies, and privilege management to enforce least privilege principles.

- **Application security** focuses on securing the software and applications used within an organization. This involves implementing secure coding practices, regular vulnerability assessments and penetration testing, web application firewalls (WAFs), and application-level authentication and authorization mechanisms.

- **Data encryption** protects data by transforming it into a secure format that can only be accessed with the correct decryption key. It is used to secure data at rest (stored data) and in transit (data transmitted over networks).

- **Security monitoring and incident response** involve continuous monitoring of systems and networks, which is crucial to detecting and responding to security incidents. This includes using security information and event management (SIEM) tools, log analysis, IDS, and incident response plans to promptly identify and mitigate potential threats.

- **Security awareness and training** includes educating employees and users about security best practices and potential threats is vital. Regular security awareness training helps individuals understand their role in maintaining a secure environment and enables them to identify and report suspicious activities.

By combining these major controls, organizations can establish a multi-layered defense-in-depth security approach that provides and increases overall resilience against various threats.

Figure 1-1 shows typical defense-in-depth mechanisms defining IT infrastructure security layers.

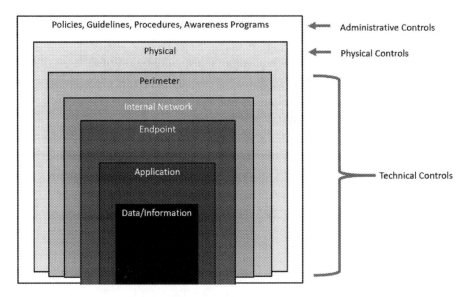

Figure 1-1. *Defense-in-depth mechanisms and IT infrastructure layers*

The three major security layers in an IT infrastructure are the network, the operating system (part of the endpoint security layer), and the application itself.

The Network Security Layer

The network security layer is probably the most familiar one in the IT world. When people talk about IT security, they normally think of network-level security—in particular, security that uses firewalls.

Even though people often associate security with the network level, this is only a very limited layer of protection against attackers. Generally speaking, it can do no more than defend IP addresses and filter network packets addressed to certain ports in certain machines in the network.

This is not enough in most cases, as traffic at this level is normally allowed to enter the publicly open ports of your various exposed services without restriction. Different attacks can be targeted at these open services, as attackers can execute arbitrary commands that could compromise your security constraints. Tools like the popular nmap (http://nmap.org/) can scan a machine to find open ports. Using such tools is an easy first step in preparing an attack because well-known attacks can be used against such open ports if they are not properly secured.

A very important part of the network-layer security, in the case of web applications, is the use of Secure Sockets Layer (SSL) to encode all sensitive information sent along the wire, but this is related more to the network protocol at the application level than to the network physical level at which firewalls operate.

The Operating System Layer

The operating system layer is probably the most important one in the whole security schema, as a properly secured operating system (OS) environment can at least prevent a whole host machine from going down if a particular application is compromised.

If an attacker is somehow allowed to have unsecured access to the operating system, they can basically do whatever they want—from spreading viruses to stealing passwords or deleting your whole server's data and making it unusable. Even worse, they could take control of your computer without you even noticing and use it to perform other malicious acts as part of a botnet. This layer can include the deployment model of the applications since you need to know your operating system's permission scheme to ensure that you don't give your applications unnecessary privileges over your machine. Applications should run as isolated as possible from the other components of the host machine.

The Application Layer

The primary focus of this book is on the application layer. The application security layer refers to all the constraints you establish in your applications to make sure that only the right people can do the right things when working through the application.

Applications, by default, are open to countless avenues of attack. An improperly secured application can allow an attacker to steal information from the application, impersonate other users, execute restricted operations, corrupt data, gain access to the operating system level, and perform many other malicious acts.

This book covers application-level security, which is the domain of Spring Security. Application-level security is achieved by implementing several techniques, and there are a few concepts that help you understand better what the book covers. They are the main concerns that Spring Security addresses to provide your applications with comprehensive protection against threats. The following three subsections introduce authentication, authorization, and ACLs.

Authentication

Authentication is the process of verifying the identity of a user or entity attempting to access an application. It ensures that the user is who they claim to be. Common authentication methods include the following.

- **Username and password**: Users provide a unique username and corresponding password.

- **Multi-factor authentication (MFA)**: Users provide multiple forms of identification, such as a password and a one-time verification code sent to their mobile device.

- **Biometric authentication**: Users verify their identity using unique physical characteristics, such as fingerprints, facial recognition, or iris scans.

The authentication process allows an application to validate that a particular user is who they claim they are. In the authentication process, a user presents the application with information about herself (normally, a username and a password) that no one else knows. The application takes this information and tries to match it against the information stored—normally, in a database or LDAP[1] (Lightweight Directory Access Protocol) server. If the information the user provides matches a record in the authentication server, the user is successfully authenticated. The application normally

---

[1] LDAP is explained in some detail in Chapter 8, where various authentication providers are covered.

creates an internal abstraction representing this authenticated user in the system. Figure 1-2 shows the authentication mechanism.

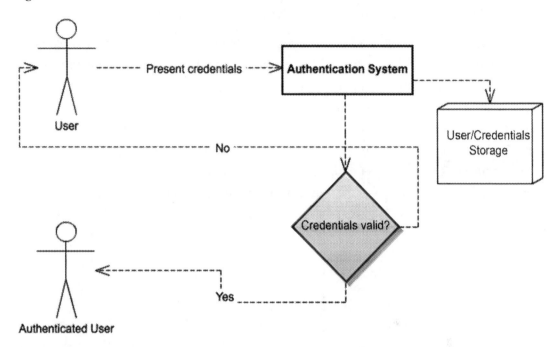

Figure 1-2. *Simple, standard authentication mechanism*

Authorization

Authorization determines what actions or resources a user can access within an application. Once a user is authenticated, authorization mechanisms control their permissions based on predefined rules and policies. This ensures that users can only access the features and data they are authorized to use. Authorization can be role-based, attribute-based, or rule-based.

- **Role-based access control (RBAC)**: Users are assigned roles, and permissions are granted based on those roles. For example, a manager role may access certain administrative features, while a regular user role may only access basic functionalities.

- **Attribute-based access control (ABAC)**: Access is granted based on specific attributes or characteristics of the user, such as job title, department, or location.

- **Rule-based access control**: Access control rules are defined based on predefined conditions or criteria. For example, granting access during specific timeframes or based on certain data conditions.

When a user is authenticated, that only means that the user is known to the system and has been recognized by it. It doesn't mean that the user is free to do whatever she wants in said system. The next logical step in securing an application is determining which actions the user can perform and which resources she can access. If the user doesn't have the proper permissions, she cannot carry out that particular action. This is the work of the authorization process. In the most common case, the authorization process compares the user's set of permissions against the permissions required to execute a particular action in the application, and if a match is found, access is granted. On the other hand, if no match is found, access is denied. Figure 1-3 shows the authorization mechanism.

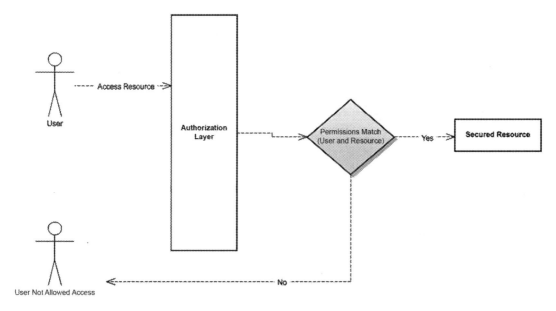

Figure 1-3. *Simple authorization process: the authenticated user tries to access a secured resource*

ACLs

An access control list (ACL) manages access rights and permissions to specific resources or objects within an application. It is typically used in conjunction with authorization. An ACL defines who has access to a particular resource and what actions they can perform on that resource. It consists of a list of users or groups and their corresponding permissions (read, write, execute, etc.) for specific resources.

ACLs are part of the authorization process explained in the previous section. The key difference is that ACLs normally work at a finer-grained level in the application. ACLs are a collection of mappings between resources, users, and permissions. With ACLs, you can establish rules like "User John has administrative permission on the blog post X" or "User Luis has read permission on blog post X." You can see the three elements: user, permission, and resource. Figure 1-3 shows how ACLs work; they are just a special case of the general authorization process.

Authentication and Authorization: General Concepts

This section introduces and explains fundamental security concepts that you will come across frequently in the book.

- **User**: The first step in securing a system from malicious attackers is identifying legitimate users and allowing access to them alone. User abstractions are created in the system and given their own identity. They are the users that are later allowed to use the system.

- **Credentials**: Credentials are the way a user proves who they are. Normally, in the shape of passwords (certificates are also a common way of presenting credentials), they are data that only the owner of it knows.

- **Role**: In an application security context, a role can be seen as a logical grouping of users. This logical grouping is normally done so the grouped users share a set of permissions in the application to access certain resources. For example, all users with the admin role have the same access and permissions to the same resources. Roles are a way to group permissions to execute determined actions, making users with those roles inherit such permissions.

- **Resource**: Any part of the application you want to access that needs to be properly secured against unauthorized access—for example, a URL, a business method, or a particular business object.

- **Permissions**: The access level needed to access a particular resource. For example, two users may be allowed to read a particular document, but only one can write to it. Permissions can apply to individual users or users that share a particular role.

- **Encryption**: It allows you to encrypt sensible information (normally passwords, but it can be something else, like cookies) to make it incomprehensible to attackers even if they get access to the encrypted version. The idea is that you never store the plain text version of a password but instead store an encrypted version so that nobody but the owner knows the original one.

The following describes types of encryption algorithms.

- **One-way encryption**: These algorithms, referred to as *hashing algorithms*, take an input string and generate an output number known as the *message digest*. This output number cannot be converted back into the original string. This is why the technique is referred to as *one-way encryption*.

  For example, let's suppose the requesting client encrypts a string and sends the encrypted string to the server. The server may have access to the original information from a previous registration process, for example, and if it does, it can apply the same hash function. Then, it compares the output from this hashing to the value sent by the client. If they match, the server validates the information.

  Figure 1-4 shows this scheme. Usually, the server doesn't even need the original data. It can simply store the hashed version and then compare it with the incoming hash from the client.

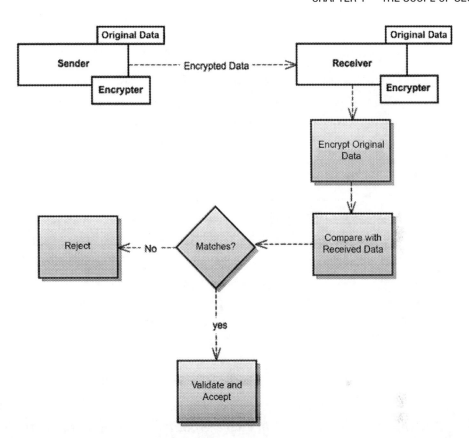

Figure 1-4. *One-way encryption or hashing*

- **Symmetric encryption**: These algorithms provide two functions:
  encrypt and decrypt. A string of text is converted into an encrypted
  form and then can be converted back to the original string. In this
  scheme, a sender and a receiver share the same keys to encrypt and
  decrypt messages on both ends of the communication. One problem
  with this scheme is how to share the key between the endpoints of
  the communication. A common approach is to use a parallel secure
  channel to send the keys.

  - **Key**: Symmetric encryption uses a single shared secret key for
    encryption and decryption. This means that both the sender and
    the recipient use the same key.

- **Speed**: Symmetric encryption algorithms are generally faster and more efficient than asymmetric encryption algorithms.

- **Use case**: Symmetric encryption is commonly used for securing large amounts of data, such as file encryption or secure communication between two parties who already share a secret key.

- Figure 1-5 shows symmetric encryption at work.

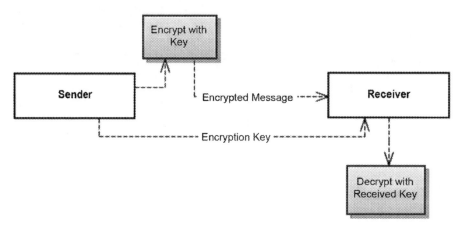

Figure 1-5. *Symmetric encryption: the two endpoints share the same encryption/ decryption key*

- **Public key cryptography**: These techniques are based on asymmetric cryptography. In this scheme, a different key is used for encryption than for decryption. These two keys are referred to as the *public key*, which is used to encrypt messages, and the *private key*, which is used to decrypt messages. The advantage of this approach over symmetric encryption is that there is no need to share the decryption key, so no one but the intended receiver of the information can decrypt the message. The following describes a normal scenario.

  - The intended recipient of messages shares her public key with everyone interested in sending information to her.

  - A sender encrypts the information with the receiver's public key and sends a message.

- The receiver uses her private key to decrypt the message.

- No one else can decrypt the message because they don't have the receiver's private key.

The following defines the key, speed, and use case for asymmetric or PKI encryption.

- **Key**: Asymmetric encryption uses a pair of keys—a public key and a private key. The public key is freely available to anyone, while the owner keeps the private key secret.

- **Encryption and decryption**: The public key is used for encryption, while the private key is used for decryption. This means the data encrypted with the public key can only be decrypted with the corresponding private key.

- **Security**: Asymmetric encryption provides a higher level of security because the private key is not shared or transmitted.

- **Use case**: Asymmetric encryption is commonly used for secure key exchange, digital signatures, and secure communication between parties who don't have a pre-shared secret key.

Figure 1-6 shows the public key cryptography scheme.

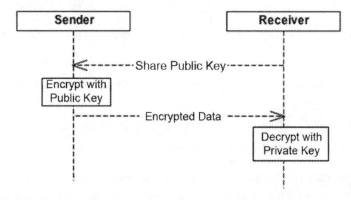

Figure 1-6. *Public key cryptography*

The use of encryption achieves, among other things, two other security goals.

- **Confidentiality**: Potentially sensitive information belonging to one user or group of users should be accessible only to this user or group. Encryption algorithms are the main helpers in achieving this goal.

- **Integrity**: Data sent by a valid user shouldn't be altered by a third entity on its way to the server or in its storage. This is normally accomplished through one-way cryptographic algorithms that make it almost impossible to alter an input and produce a corrupted message whose encrypted hash is the same as the original message (thus deceiving the receiver into thinking it is valid).

In practice, a combination of symmetric and asymmetric encryption is often used in *hybrid encryption.* In hybrid encryption, symmetric encryption encrypts the actual data, while the symmetric key is encrypted using the recipient's public key (asymmetric encryption). This approach combines the efficiency of symmetric encryption with the security and flexibility of asymmetric encryption.

What to Secure

Not every part of the application requires a strong security model or any security. If, for example, one part of your application is supposed to serve static content to everyone interested, you can simply serve this content. There probably are no security concerns to handle here.

Anyway, when starting to work on a new application, you should think about the security constraints that your application will have. You should think about concerns like those in the following list and whether they apply to your particular use case.

- **Identity management**: Your application will likely need to establish the users' identities. Usually, your application will do different things for different users, so you need a way to associate users with certain functionality. You also need to protect each user's identity information so it can't be compromised.

- **Secured connections**: In an Internet environment, where anyone in the world can potentially access your system and eavesdrop on other users accessing your system, you most likely want to secure the communication of sensitive data using some kind of transport layer security, such as SSL.

- **Sensitive data protection**: Sensitive data needs to be protected against malicious attacks. This applies to the communication layer, individual message transmission, and credentials data stores. Encryption should be used in different layers to achieve the most secure application possible.

Additional Security Concerns

There are many more security concerns than the ones explained so far. Because this is a Spring Security book and not a general application-security book, it covers only things related to Spring Security. However, we think it is important that you understand that there are many more security concerns than those addressed directly by Spring Security. The following is a quick overview of some of the most common ones. This is only intended to make you aware of their existence, and we recommend you consult a different source (such as a general software security textbook) to better understand all these concerns.

- **SQL (and other code) injection**: Validating user input is vital to application security. If data is not validated, an attacker could write any string as input (including SQL or server-side code) and send that information to the server. If the server code is not properly written, the attacker could wreak significant havoc because she could execute any arbitrary code on the server.

- **Denial-of-service attacks**: These attacks make the target system unresponsive to its intended users. This is normally done by saturating the server with requests to utilize all the server's resources and make it unresponsive to legitimate requests.

- **Cross-site scripting and output sanitation**: An injection can be done where the target is the client part of the application. The idea is that the attacker can make an application return malicious code inside the web pages returned and thus execute it in the user's browser. This way, the attacker invisibly executes actions using the real user's authenticated session.

- **Unauthorized access**: This occurs when an individual or entity gains unauthorized entry to a system, network, or data. It can result in data breaches, theft of sensitive information, or unauthorized manipulation of systems.

- **Malware and ransomware**: *Malware* refers to malicious software designed to disrupt, damage, or gain unauthorized access to systems. *Ransomware* is a specific type of malware that encrypts data and demands a ransom for its release. Both malware and ransomware can lead to data loss, financial loss, and operational disruptions.

- **Phishing and social engineering**: *Phishing* involves fraudulent attempts to obtain sensitive information, such as passwords or financial details, by disguising it as a trustworthy entity via emails, phone calls, or websites. *Social engineering* exploits human vulnerabilities to manipulate individuals into revealing confidential information or performing actions that can compromise security.

- **Data breaches**: These breaches occur when unauthorized individuals access sensitive or confidential data, such as personal information, credit card details, or intellectual property. Data breaches can result in financial loss, reputational damage, and legal consequences.

- **Insider threats**: These threats involve individuals with authorized access to systems or information who misuse their privileges for malicious purposes. This can include intentional data theft, sabotage, or unauthorized disclosure of sensitive information.

- **Weak authentication and password security**: Weak or easily guessable passwords, inadequate authentication mechanisms, and insufficient password management practices can leave systems vulnerable to unauthorized access and compromise.

- **Vulnerabilities and software exploits**: Software vulnerabilities, such as unpatched or outdated systems, can be exploited by attackers to gain unauthorized access, inject malware, or manipulate systems. It is crucial to promptly apply security patches and updates to mitigate these risks.

- **Cloud security**: Organizations utilizing cloud services must address specific security concerns, including data privacy, data segregation, access control, and cloud provider vulnerabilities.

- **IoT security**: The proliferation of IoT devices introduces new security challenges, including insecure device configurations, lack of encryption, and vulnerabilities in IoT networks. Compromised IoT devices can be used to launch attacks or gain unauthorized access to networks.

Addressing these IT security concerns requires a comprehensive and multi-layered approach, including implementing strong security controls, regular security assessments, user education and awareness, incident response planning, and adherence to security best practices.

Java Options for Security

Java and Java EE out-of-the-box security solutions are very comprehensive. They cover areas ranging from a low-level permission system through cryptography APIs to an authentication and authorization scheme.

The list of security APIs offered in Java is very extensive, as the following list of the main ones shows.

- **Java Cryptography Architecture (JCA)** supports cryptographic algorithms, including hash-digest and digital signature support.

- **Java Cryptographic Extensions (JCE)** mainly provides facilities for the encryption and decryption of strings and secret key generation for symmetric algorithms.

- **Java Certification Path API (CertPath)** provides comprehensive functionality for integrating the validation and verification of digital certificates into an application.

- **Java Secure Socket Extension (JSSE)** provides a standardized set of features to support SSL and TLS protocols, both client and server, in Java.

- **Java Authentication and Authorization Service (JAAS)** provides a service for authentication and authorization in Java applications. It provides a pluggable system where authentication mechanisms can be plugged in independently to applications.

- **Java Generic Security Services (Java GSS-API)** securely exchanges messages between communicating applications. "Introduction to JAAS and Java GSS-API Tutorials" is a series of tutorials demonstrating various aspects of using JAAS and Java GSS-API.

The JDK is divided into modules. The following modules contain security APIs.

- java.base

- java.security.jgss

- java.security.sasl

- java.smartcardio

- java.xml.crypto

- jdk.jartool

- jdk.security.auth

- jdk.security.jgss

For the entire list of Java release 20 security APIs, please refer to `https://docs.oracle.com/en/java/javase/20/security/security-api-specification1.html`. Figure 1-7 shows the Java platform security architecture and elements.

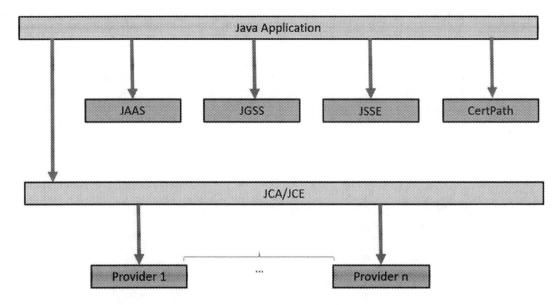

Figure 1-7. *Java platform security architecture and elements*

Spring Security's main concerns are in the authentication/authorization realm. So, it overlaps mainly with the JAAS Java API, although they can be used together, as you will see later in the book. Most of the other APIs are leveraged in Spring Security. For example, CertPath is used in X509AuthenticationFilter, and JCE is used in the spring-security-crypto module.

Summary

This chapter introduced security from a general point of view down to defense-in-depth mechanisms. It explained in a very abstract way the main concerns in IT security, especially from an application point of view. It also briefly described the main Java APIs that support security at different levels.

You can see that this chapter was a very quick overview of security concerns. It is beyond the scope of this book to go any further than this on general topics, although some of them are studied in more depth when they apply to Spring Security. This is nothing like a comprehensive software security guide, and if you are interested in learning more about software security in general, you should consult the specialized literature. The next chapter introduces Spring Security.

CHAPTER 2

Introducing Spring Security

In this chapter, you learn what Spring Security is and how to use it to address security concerns about your application.

We describe what's new in Spring Framework and Spring Security version 6. Using Spring Security 6 with authentication and authorization is discussed in detail.

Finally, you look at the framework's source code, how to build it, and the different modules forming the powerful Spring Security project.

What Is Spring Security?

Spring Security is a framework dedicated to providing a full array of security services to Java applications in a developer-friendly and flexible way. It adheres to the well-established practices introduced by the Spring Framework. Spring Security tries to address all the layers of security inside your application. In addition, it comes packed with an extensive array of configuration options that make it very flexible and powerful.

Recall from Chapter 1 that it can be said that Spring Security is simply a comprehensive authentication/authorization framework built on top of the Spring Framework. Although most applications that use the framework are web-based, Spring Security's core can also be used in stand-alone applications.

Many things make Spring Security immediately attractive to Java developers. To name just a few, consider the following list.

- **It's built on top of the successful Spring Framework.** This is an important strength of Spring Security. The Spring Framework has become "the way" to build enterprise Java applications, and with good reason. It is built around good practices and two simple yet

© Massimo Nardone, Carlo Scarioni 2024
M. Nardone and C. Scarioni, *Pro Spring Security*, https://doi.org/10.1007/979-8-8688-0035-1_2

powerful concepts: dependency injection (DI) and aspect-oriented programming (AOP). Also important is that many developers have experience with Spring, so they can leverage that experience when introducing Spring Security in their projects.

- **It provides out-of-the-box support for many authentication models.** Even more important than the previous point, Spring Security supports out-of-the-box integration with Lightweight Directory Access Protocol (LDAP), OpenID, SAML 2.0, form authentication, OAuth 2.0, Certificate X.509 authentication, database authentication, Jasypt cryptography, and lots more. All this support means that Spring Security adapts to your security needs—and not only that, it can change if your needs change, without much effort involved for the developer. More information on Jasypt cryptography is at `www.jasypt.org/`.

  This is also important from a business point of view because the application can either adapt to the corporate authentication services or implement its own, thus requiring only straightforward configuration changes.

  This also means that there is a lot less software for you to write, because you are using a great amount of ready-to-use code that has been written and tested by a large and active user community. To a certain point, you can trust that this code works and use it with confidence. And if it does not work, you can always fix it and send a patch to those in charge of maintaining the project.

- **It offers layered security services.** Spring Security allows you to secure your application at different levels, and to secure your web URLs, views, service methods, and domain model. You can pick and combine these features to achieve your security goals.

  It is very flexible in practice. Imagine, for instance, that you offer services exposed through RMI, the Web, JMS, and others. You could secure all these interfaces, but maybe it's better to secure just the business layer so that all requests are secured when they reach this layer. Also, maybe you don't care about securing individual business objects, so you can omit that module and use the functionality you need.

- **It is open source software.** As part of the Pivotal portfolio, Spring Security is an open source software tool. It also has a large community and user base dedicated to testing and improving the framework. Having the opportunity to work with open source software is an attractive feature for most developers. The ability to look into the source code of the tools you like and work with is an exciting prospect. Whether our goal is to improve the tools or simply to understand how they work internally, we developers love to read code and learn from it.

Where Does Spring Security Fit In?

Spring Security is without question a powerful and versatile tool. But like anything else, it is not a tool that adapts to everything you want to do. Its offerings have a defined scope.

Where and why would you use Spring Security? The following lists reasons and scenarios.

- **You need to develop web security.** Spring Security provides robust security features for web applications, including protection against common web vulnerabilities, such as cross-site scripting (XSS), cross-site request forgery (CSRF), and clickjacking.

- **You need strong mechanisms for securing URLs.** You want to restrict access to specific resources and enforce secure communication over HTTPS.

- **Your application is in Java, Groovy, or Kotlin.** The first thing to take into account is that Spring Security can be written in languages like Java, Groovy, or Kotlin and generally in any language supported by the JVM. So if you plan to work in a non-JVM language, Spring Security won't be useful.

- **You need role-based authentication/authorization.** This is the main use case of Spring Security. You have a list of users and resources and operations on those resources. You group the users into roles and allow certain roles to access certain operations on certain resources. That's the core functionality.

- **You want to secure a web application from malicious users.** Spring Security is mostly used in web application environments. When this is the case, the first thing to do is allow only the users you want to access your application, while forbidding all others from even reaching it.

- **You need to integrate with OpenID, LDAP, Active Directory, and databases as security providers.** If you need to integrate with a particular Users and Roles or Groups provider, you should look at the vast array of options Spring Security offers because integration might already be implemented, saving you from writing lots of unnecessary code. Sometimes you might not be exactly sure what provider your business requires to authenticate against. In this case, Spring Security makes your life easy by allowing you to switch between different providers painlessly.

- **You need to secure your domain model and allow only certain users to access certain objects in your application.** If you need fine-grained security (that is, you need to secure on a per object, per user basis), Spring Security offers the access control list (ACL) module, which help you to do just that in a straightforward way.

- **You want a nonintrusive, declarative way for adding security around your application.** Security is a cross-cutting concern, not a core business functionality of your application (unless you work in a security provider firm). As such, it is better to be treated as a separate and modular add-on that you can declare, configure, and manage independently of your main business concerns. Spring Security is built with this in mind. Using servlet filters, XML configuration, and AOP concepts, the framework tries not to pollute your application with security rules. Even when using annotations, they are still metadata on top of your code. They don't mess with your code logic. As a Java developer, you must try to isolate the Java configuration into a configuration library and decouple it from the rest of the application in a similar way you do with XML.

- **You want to secure your service layer the same way you secure your URLs, and you need to add rules at the method level for**

allowing or disallowing user access. Spring Security allows you to use a consistent security model throughout the layers of your application because it internally enforces this consistent model itself. You configure users, roles, and providers in just one place, and both the service and web layers use this centralized security configuration transparently.

- **You need your application to remember its users on their next visit and allow them access.** Sometimes you don't want or need the users of your application to log in every time they visit your site. Spring supports out-of-the-box, remember-me functionality so that a user can be automatically logged in on subsequent visits to your site, allowing them full or partial access to their profile's functionality.

- **You want to use public/private key certificates to authenticate against your application.** Spring Security allows you to use X.509 certificates to verify the server's identity. The server can also request a valid certificate from the client for establishing mutual authentication.

- **You need to hide elements in your web pages from certain users and show them to others.** View security is the first layer of security in a secured web application. It is normally not enough for guaranteeing security. But it is very important from a usability point of view because it allows the application to show or hide content depending on the user currently logged in to the system.

- **You need more flexibility than simple role-based authentication for your application.** For example, suppose that you want to allow access only to users over 18 years of age using simple script expressions. Spring Security 3.1 uses the Spring Expression Language (SpEL) to allow you to customize access rules for your application.

- **You want your application to automatically handle HTTP status codes related to authorization errors (401, 403, and others).** The built-in exception-handling mechanism of Spring Security for web applications automatically translates the more common exceptions to their corresponding HTTP status codes; for example, `AccessDeniedException` gets translated to the 403 status code.

- **You want to configure your application to be used from other applications (not browsers) and allow these other applications to authenticate themselves against yours.** Another application accessing your application should be forced to use authentication mechanisms to gain access. For example, you can expose your application through REST endpoints that other applications can access with HTTP security.

- **You are running an application outside a Java EE Server.** If you run your application in a simple web container like Apache Tomcat, you probably don't have support for the full Java EE security stack. Spring Security can be easily leveraged in these environments.

- **You are running an application inside a Java EE Server.** Even if you are running a full Java EE container, Spring Security is arguably more complete, flexible, and easy to use than the Java EE counterpart.

- **You are already using Spring in your application and want to leverage your knowledge.** You already know some of the great advantages of Spring. If you are currently using Spring, you probably like it a lot. You will probably like Spring Security as well.

Spring Security Overview

Spring Security 6 includes the following projects.

- Spring Security
- Spring Boot 3.0
- Spring Framework
- Spring Cloud Data Flow
- Spring Cloud
- Spring Data
- Spring Integration
- Spring Authorization Server

- Spring for GraphQL

- Spring Batch

- Spring Hateoas

- Spring REST Docs

- Spring Amqp

- Spring Mobile

- Spring For Android

- Spring Web Flow

- Spring Web Services

- Spring LDAP

- Spring Session

- Spring Shell

- Spring Flo

- Spring Kafka

- Spring Statemachine

- Spring Io Platform

- Spring Roo

- Spring Scala

- Spring Blazeds Integration

- Spring Loaded

- Spring Xd

- Spring Social

For more information, please refer to the Spring project web page at `https://spring.io/projects`.

Each of these projects is built on top of the facilities provided by the Spring Framework itself, which is the original project that started it all. Think of Spring as the hub of all these satellite projects, providing them with a consistent programming model and a set of established practices. The main points you see throughout the different projects is the use of DI, XML namespace-based configuration, and AOP, which, as you see in the next section, are the pillars upon which Spring is built. In the later versions of Spring, annotations have become the most popular way to configure both DI and AOP concerns.

This book introduces Spring Boot, analyzes Spring Framework, and develops Spring Security version 6. Let's start with Spring Boot.

What Is Spring Boot?

Spring Boot is an open source Java-based framework generally used for developing microservice, enterprise-ready applications. Pivotal developed it to help developers create stand-alone and production-ready Spring applications.

Spring Boot is an easy starting point for building all Spring-based applications and running them as quickly as possible, with minimal upfront configuration of Spring.

When this book was written, Spring Boot 3.0 was the latest release (November 2022) using Java 17+ and Jakarta EE 9.

Note   Remember that a Spring Security application can be developed with Maven or Gradle.

Spring Security is one of the Spring projects; it is dedicated exclusively to addressing security concerns in applications.

For more information, please refer to the documentation at `https://spring.io/ projects/spring-security`.

Spring Security began as a non-Spring project. It was originally known as the "Acegi Security System for Spring" and was not the big and powerful framework it is today. Originally, it dealt only with authorization and leveraged container-provided authentication. Because of public demand, the project started gaining traction, as more people started using it and contributing to its continuously growing code base. This eventually led to it becoming a Spring Framework portfolio project, and then later it was rebranded as Spring Security.

The following lists Spring Security's major releases dates.

- 2.0.0 (April 2008)
- 3.0.0 (December 2009)
- 4.0.0 (March 2015)
- 5.0.0 (November 2017)
- 5.1.4 (February 2019)
- 6.1.0 (May 2023)

Java configuration for Spring Security was added to the Spring Framework in Spring 3.1 and extended to Spring Security in Spring 3.2 and is defined in a class annotated @Configuration.

Spring Security 6 requires JDK 17 and uses the Jakarta namespace.

The project for many years now has been under the Pivotal umbrella of projects, powered by the Spring Framework itself. But what exactly is the Spring Framework?

Spring Framework 6: A Quick Overview

We have mentioned the Spring Framework project a lot. It makes sense to give an overview of it at this point, because many of the Spring Security characteristics we cover in the rest of the book rely on the building blocks of Spring.

We admit we're biased. We love Spring and have loved it for many years now. We think Spring has so many advantages and great features that we can't start a new Java project without using it. Additionally, we tend to carry its concepts around when working with other languages and look for a way to apply them because they now feel natural.

Spring Framework 5 was published in September 2017 and can be considered the first major Spring Framework release since version 4 was released in December 2013.

Spring Framework latest release when this manuscipt was written is version 6.0.9 (May 2023).

Next, let's briefly review the most important new features in Spring Framework 6.

JDK 17+ and Jakarta EE 9+ Baseline

- Entire framework based on Java 17 source code level

- Migration from javax to jakarta namespace for Jakarta Servlet, JPA, and so on

- Runtime compatibility with Jakarta EE 9 and Jakarta EE 10 APIs

- Compatible with latest web servers—Tomcat 101, Jetty 11, Undertow 23

- Early compatibility with virtual threads (in preview as of JDK 19)

General Core Revision

- Upgrade to ASM 94 and Kotlin 17

- Complete CGLIB fork with support for capturing CGLIB-generated classes

- Comprehensive foundation for ahead-of-time transformations

- First-class support for GraalVM native images

Core Container

- First-class configuration options for virtual threads on JDK 21

- Lifecycle integration with Project CRaC for JVM checkpoint restore

- Support for resolving SequencedCollection/Set/Map at injection points

- Support for registering a MethodHandle as a SpEL function

- Validator factory methods for programmatic validator implementations

- Basic bean property determination without javabeansIntrospector by default

- AOT processing support in GenericApplicationContext (refreshForAotProcessing)

- Bean definition transformation based on pre-resolved constructors and factory methods

- Support for early proxy class determination for AOP proxies and configuration classes

- PathMatchingResourcePatternResolver uses NIO and module path APIs for scanning, enabling support for classpath scanning within a GraalVM native image and the Java module path, respectively

- DefaultFormattingConversionService supports ISO-based default javatime type parsing

Data Access and Transactions

- Failed CompletableFuture triggers rollback for async transactional method

- Support for predetermining JPA managed types (for inclusion in AOT processing)

- JPA support for Hibernate ORM 61 (retaining compatibility with Hibernate ORM 56)

- Upgrade to R2DBC 10 (including R2DBC transaction definitions)

- Aligned data access exception translation between JDBC, R2DBC, JPA and Hibernate

- Removal of JCA CCI support

Spring Messaging

- RSocket interface client based on @RSocketExchange service interfaces

- Early support for Reactor Netty 2 based on Netty 5 alpha

- Support for Jakarta WebSocket 21 and its standard WebSocket protocol upgrade mechanism

General Web Revision

- HTTP interface client based on @HttpExchange service interfaces

- Support for RFC 7807 problem details

- Unified HTTP status code handling

- Support for Jackson 214

- Alignment with Servlet 60 (while retaining runtime compatibility with Servlet 50)

Spring MVC

- PathPatternParser used by default (with the ability to opt into PathMatcher)

- Removal of outdated Tiles and FreeMarker JSP support

Spring WebFlux

- New PartEvent API to stream multipart form uploads (both on client and server)

- New ResponseEntityExceptionHandler to customize WebFlux exceptions and render RFC 7807 error responses

- Flux return values for non-streaming media types

- Early support for Reactor Netty 2 based on Netty 5 alpha

- JDK HttpClient integrated with WebClient

Observability

Spring 6 introduces Spring Observability , a new initiative that builds on Micrometer and Micrometer Tracing (formerly Spring Cloud Sleuth). The goal is to efficiently record application metrics with Micrometer and implement tracing through providers, such as OpenZipkin or OpenTelemetry.

- Direct observability instrumentation with micrometer observation is in several parts of the Spring Framework. The spring-web module now requires io.micrometer:micrometer-observation:1.10+ as a compile dependency.

- RestTemplate and WebClient are instrumented to produce HTTP client request observations.

- Spring MVC can be instrumented for HTTP server observations using org.springframework.web.filter.ServerHttpObservationFilter.

- Spring WebFlux can be instrumented for HTTP server observations using org.springframework.web.filter.reactive. ServerHttpObservationFilter.

- Integration with micrometer context propagation for flux and mono return values from controller methods.

Pattern Matching

Pattern matching was elaborated in Project Amber.

Testing

- Support for testing AOT-processed application contexts on the JVM or within a GraalVM native image

- Integration with HtmlUnit 264+ request parameter handling

- Servlet mocks (MockHttpServletRequest, MockHttpSession) are based on Servlet API 60 now

Many things attract us to Spring, but the main ones are the two major building blocks of the framework: dependency injection and aspect-oriented programming.

Why are these two concepts so important? They are important because they allow you to develop loosely coupled, single-responsibility, DRY (Don't Repeat Yourself) code practically by default. These two concepts, and Spring itself, are covered extensively in other books and online tutorials; however, we'll give you a brief overview here.

Spring Framework 6 and Spring Boot 3 need the following minimum versions.

- Kotlin 1.7+

- Lombok 1.18.22+ (JDK17 support)

- Gradle 7.3+

Dependency Injection

The basic idea of DI, a type of Inversion of Control (IoC), is that instead of having an object instantiate its needed dependencies, the dependencies are somehow given to the object. In a polymorphic way, the objects given as dependencies to the target object that depends on them are known to this target object just by an abstraction (like an interface in Java) and not by the exact implementation of the dependency.

The major advantages of the IoC architecture are

- Easier switching between different implementations

- Offering a good modularity of a program

- A great feature for testing programs by isolating components dependencies and allowing them to communicate through contracts

- Dividing the execution of a certain task from its implementation

It's easier to look at this in code than explain it; see Listing 2-1.

Listing 2-1. The Object Itself Instantiates Its Dependencies (No Dependency Injection)

```
public class NonDiObject {
private Helper helper ;
public NonDiObject ( ) {
 helper = new HelperImpl ( ) ;
 }
public void doStuffWithHelp( ) {
 helper.help( ) ;
 }
}
```

In this example, every instance of NonDiObject is responsible for instantiating its own Helper in the constructor. It instantiates a HelperImpl, creating a tight, unnecessary coupling to this particular Helper implementation (see Listing 2-2).

Listing 2-2. The Object Receives Its Dependencies from Some External Source (with Dependency Injection)

```
public class DiObject {
private Helper helper ;
public DiObject(Helper helper) {
 this.helper = helper;
 }
public void doStuffWithHelp( ) {
 helper.help( ) ;
 }
}
```

In this version, Helper is passed to DiObject at construction time. DiObject is not required to instantiate any dependency. It doesn't need to know how to do that, what particular implementation type the Helper is, or where it comes from. It just needs a helper and uses it for whatever requirement it has.

The advantage of this approach should be clear. The second version is loosely coupled to the Helper, depending only on the Helper interface, allowing the concrete implementation to be decided at runtime and thus giving lots of flexibility to the design.

Spring dependency injection configuration is normally defined in XML files, although later versions have turned more to annotation-based and Java-based configurations.

Aspect-Oriented Programming

AOP is a technique for extracting cross-cutting concerns from the main application code and transversely applying them across the points where they are needed. Typical examples of AOP concerns are transactions, logging, and security.

The main idea is that you decouple the main business logic of your application from special-purpose concerns that are peripheral to this core logic, and then apply this functionality in a transparent, unobtrusive way through your application. By encapsulating this functionality (which is simply general application logic and not core business logic) in its own modules, they can be used by many parts of the application that need them, avoiding the need to duplicate this code all over the place. The entities encapsulating this cross-cutting logic are referred to as *aspects* in AOP terms.

There are many implementations of AOP in Java. The most popular, perhaps, is AspectJ, which requires a special compilation process. Spring supports AspectJ, but it also includes its own AOP implementation, known simply as Spring AOP, which is a pure Java implementation that requires no special compilation process.

Spring AOP using proxies is available only at the public-method level and only when it is called outside the proxied object. This makes sense because calling a method from inside the object won't call the proxy; instead, it calls the real self object directly (basically a call on the this object). This is very important to be aware of when working with Spring, and sometimes, novice Spring developers overlook it.

Even when using its own AOP implementation, Spring leverages the AspectJ syntax and concepts for defining Aspects.

Spring AOP is a big subject, but the principle behind the way it works is not difficult to understand. Spring AOP works with dynamically created proxy objects that take care of the AOP concerns around invoking your main business objects. You can think of the proxy and Spring AOP in general simply as a decorator pattern implementation, where your business object is the component and the AOP proxy is the decorator. Figure 2-1 shows a simple graphical representation of the concept. Thinking about it this way, you should be able to understand Spring AOP easily. Listing 2-3 shows how the magic happens conceptually.

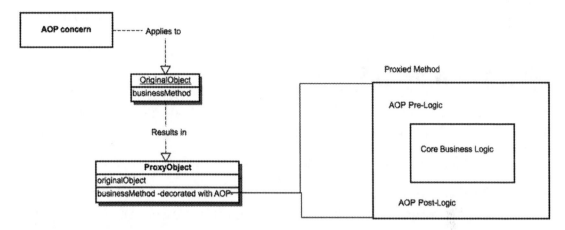

Figure 2-1. *Spring AOP in action*

Listing 2-3. The Business Object, Not Transactional

```
public class Business Object implements BusinessThing {
public void doBusinessThing( ) {
 / / Some business stuff
 }
}
```

Suppose you have an aspect for transactions. Spring creates dynamically at runtime an object that conceptually looks like Listing 2-4.

Listing 2-4. Spring AOP Magic

```
public class BusinessObjectTransactionalDecorator implements
BusinessThing {
private BusinessThing componen t ;
public BusinessObjectTransactionalDecorator(BusinessThing component ) {
 t h i s . co mponent = component ;
 }
public void doBusinessThing( ) {
 / / some start transaction code
  component.doBusinessThing( ) ;
 / / some commit transaction code
 }
}
```

Again, remember this simple idea and Spring AOP should be easier to understand.

What's New in Spring Security 6?

The previous version of this book utilizes Spring Security 5. There are not massive changes from version 5 to 6. The following describes what's new in Spring Security 6.

- The Spring Boot 3 and Spring Security 6 baseline is now Java 17.

- The WebSecurityConfigurerAdapter class has been deprecated and removed in Spring Security 6, so now you must create a bean of type SecurityFilterChain.

- Instead of using authorizeRequests, which has been deprecated, you should now use authorizeHttpRequests, which is part of the HttpSecurity configuration allowing you to configure fine-grained request matching for access control.

- In Spring Security 6, AntMatcher, MvcMatcher, and RegexMatcher have been deprecated and replaced by requestMatchers or securityMatchers for path-based access control, allowing you to match requests based on patterns or other criteria without relying on specific matchers.

Spring Security 5's main features are still valid and in use.

- By default, ContextPath is /. Use /app_name if you need to define a specific contextPath or use the via properties; for instance, `server.servlet.contextPath=/springbootapp`.

- The CSRF token filter has been added to the filter chain and turned on by default since version 3+.

- `j_username`/`j_password` parameters: Starting with version 4, you no longer receive the `username` value in the authentication request. Plus, they were updated to `username` and `password`, removing the `j_` prefix.

- CSRF protection was added in version 5.

- Password encoding is mandatory in version 5.

- `web.xml` files are no longer needed starting with Servlet 3.0.

- Easier Spring Security configurations using Java configuration.

- There is an option to use a combination by setting the debug level to DEBUG in the Log4J2 configuration file.

If you need to migrate from version 5 to version 6, we recommend to follow the official Spring migration documentation at `https://docs.spring.io/spring-security/reference/migration/index.html`.

The following are some of the most important new functionalities included in the Spring Security 6.1.9.RELEASE.

- Compressing simple class name for observation

- Add new DaoAuthenticationProvider constructor

- Add NimbusJwtDecoder#withIssuerLocation

- Clarify documentation code snippet(s)

- Deprecate shouldFilterAllDispatcherTypes

- Document in the reference how to migrate to lambda

- Documentation should mention that an empty SecurityContext should also be saved

- Don't use raw XML SAML authentication request for response validation

- Ensure access token isn't resolved from query for form-encoded requests

- Expression-Based Access Control do not working as explain in Spring Security document for 6.0.2 also tried 6.0.5 the issue persist

- Remove OpenSaml deprecation warnings

- Replace deprecated OpenSaml methods

- Deprecate .and() along with non-lambda DSL methods

Spring Security 6 provides many new features.

The following lists the highlights.

- Core

  - SecuredAuthorizationManager allows customizing underlying AuthorizationManager

  - Add AuthorityCollectionAuthorizationManager

- OAuth 2.0

  - Add Nimbus(Reactive)JwtDecoder#withIssuerLocation

  - Configure principal claim name in ReactiveJwtAuthenticationConverter

- SAML 2.0

  - Support AuthnRequestSigned metadata attribute

  - Metadata supports multiple entities and EntitiesDescriptor

  - Add saml2Metadata to DSL

  - Allow Relying Party to be Deduced from LogoutRequest

  - Allow Relying Party to be Deduced from SAML Response

  - Add RelyingPartyRegistration placeholder resolution component

  - Support issuing LogoutResponse after already logged out

- Observability

  - Customize authentication and authorization observation conventions

- Web

  - Add RequestMatchers factory class

  - Propagate variables through And and OrRequestMatcher

- Docs

  - Revisit Authorization documentation

  - Revisit Session Management documentation

- Revisit Logout documentation

- Revisit CSRF Documentation

Spring Security 5 fundamentals are still in use; they include the following.

- Authentication confirms truth of credentials.

- Authorization defines access policy for principal.

- AuthenticationManager is a controller in the authentication process.

- AuthenticationProvider is an interface that maps to a data store which stores your user data.

- Authentication object is created upon authentication to hold the login credentials.

- GrantedAuthority means application permission is granted to a principal.

- Principal is the user that performs the action.

- SecurityContext holds the authentication and other security information.

- SecurityContextHolder: Provides access to SecurityContext.

- UserDetails is a data object that contains the user credentials and roles.

- UserDetailsService collects the user credentials and authorities (roles), and builds an UserDetails object.

HTTP, LDAP, JAAS API, and CAS are some of the most important technologies Spring Security 6 supports integration with.

Note   The Spring Security 6.0.1.RELEASE can be downloaded at `https://github.com/spring-projects/spring-security/releases`.

Authentication and authorization are some of the fundamental functionalities in Spring Security 6. They are very important functionalities because they allow the Spring Security application to identify and authorize user, prevent unauthorized access, and control the user authorization to access application resources.

This book presents examples demonstrating how to develop an application to authorize and authenticate users.

The Spring Security authentication/authorization flow is shown in Figure 2-2.

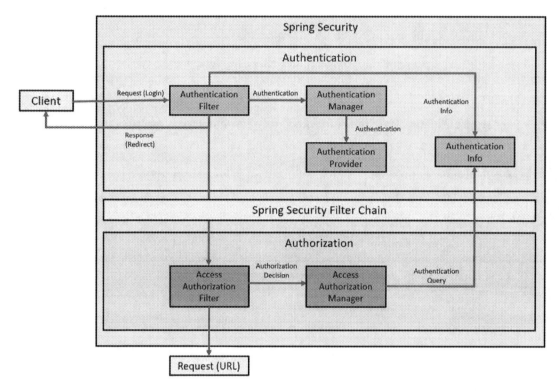

Figure 2-2. *Spring Security authentication/authorization functionalities flow*

Spring Security is utilized via some specific modules as JAR files. The `spring-security-core.jar` file contains the core.

- Authentication and access-control classes and interfaces

- Remoting support and basic provisioning APIs

JAR files are required by any application that uses Spring Security and supports the following.

- Stand-alone applications

- Remote clients

- Method (service layer) security

- JDBC user provisioning

The Spring Security 6 project's most important modules (JAR files) include

- Core: spring-security-core.jar
    - org.springframework.security.core
    - org.springframework.security.access
    - org.springframework.security.authentication
    - org.springframework.security.provisioning

- Remoting: spring-security-remoting.jar
- Web: spring-security-web.jar
- Config: spring-security-config.jar
- LDAP: spring-security-ldap.jar
- OAuth 2.0 Core: spring-security-oauth2-core.jar
- OAuth 2.0 Client: spring-security-oauth2-client.jar
- OAuth 2.0 JOSE: spring-security-oauth2-jose.jar
- OAuth 2.0 Resource Server: spring-security-oauth2-resource-server.jar
- ACL: spring-security-acl.jar
- CAS: spring-security-cas.jar
- Test: spring-security-test.jar
- Taglibs: spring-security-taglibs.jar

Spring Security XML and Java annotations can still be used in version 6 when developing Spring Security applications.

Summary

By now, you should understand what Spring Security is useful for. You also learned what's new in the Spring Security 6. Along the way, we introduced some of the major architectural and design principles behind it and how they are layered on top of the great Spring Framework 6. Dependency injection and AOP were also discussed.

The next chapter sets up the development scene, and you will build your first Spring Security–powered web application.

CHAPTER 3

Setting up the Scene

This chapter guides you through the process of building your first simple Spring Security 6 project using the IntelliJ IDEA Ultimate Edition 2023.1.2. This involves the following steps.

- Setting up the development environment
- Creating a new Java web application project without Spring Security
- Updating the project with Spring Security
- Running the example

Let's start with setting up the development environment.

Setting up the Development Environment

The following lists the software you need to download and install in the given order.

- Java SE Development Kit (JDK) 17+ (version 20 was the latest when writing this book)
- Maven 3.9.2
- IntelliJ IDEA Ultimate Edition 2023.1.2
- Apache Tomcat Server 10 (External)
- Windows OS (This book uses Windows 11.)

Let's go through the steps required to set up everything properly.

Your first step is to set up the JDK. It comes in an installer or package on most operating systems, so there shouldn't be any problems.

© Massimo Nardone, Carlo Scarioni 2024
M. Nardone and C. Scarioni, *Pro Spring Security*, https://doi.org/10.1007/979-8-8688-0035-1_3

Note   Remember that the JDK and Java SE Runtime Environment (JRE) require, at minimum, a Pentium II 266 MHz processor, 128 MB of memory, and 181 MB disk for development tools for 64-bit platforms.

Download the JDK version specific to your Windows operating system from

www.oracle.com/technetwork/java/javase/downloads/jdk11-
downloads-5066655.html.

JDK 20 installed on a Windows 11 machine is used in this book, as shown in Figure 3-1.

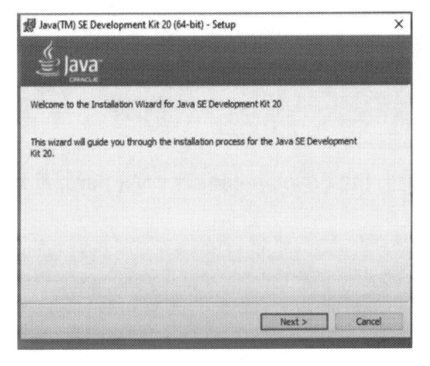

Figure 3-1. *Installing JDK 20*

Let's set a JAVA_HOME system variable by following these steps.

1. Open the Windows Environment Variables.

2. Add the JAVA_HOME variable and point it to the JDK installed folder (e.g., C:\Program Files\Java\ jdk-20).

3.   Append `%JAVA_HOME%\bin` to the system PATH variable so that all
      the Java commands are accessible from everywhere.

The result is shown in Figure 3-2.

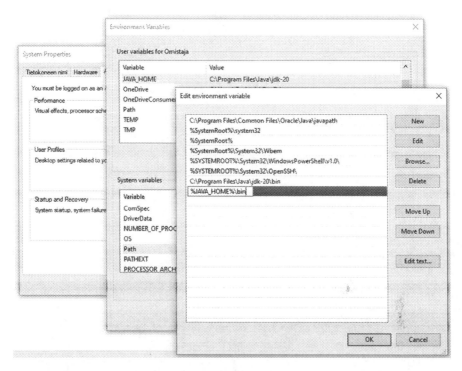

Figure 3-2.   *Setting up the JAVA_HOME system variable*

Let's test if the JDK installation was successful. Open a command prompt and type
the code shown in Figure 3-3.

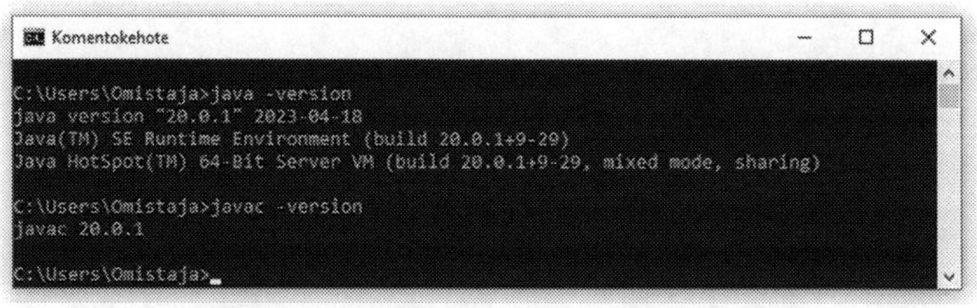

```
C:\Users\Omistaja>java -version
java version "20.0.1" 2023-04-18
Java(TM) SE Runtime Environment (build 20.0.1+9-29)
Java HotSpot(TM) 64-Bit Server VM (build 20.0.1+9-29, mixed mode, sharing)

C:\Users\Omistaja>javac -version
javac 20.0.1

C:\Users\Omistaja>_
```

Figure 3-3.   *Testing the Java installation*

Great! Java is now installed and ready to be used for the examples in the book.

Let's install the IntelliJ IDEA Ultimate Edition 2023.1.2 for web and enterprise development by following these steps.

1. Download the .exe file from https://www.jetbrains.com/idea/ download/?var=1&section=windows#section=windows

2. Install the .exe file, which in our case is named ideaIU-2023.1.2.exe.

Once installed, the directory should look like Figure 3-4.

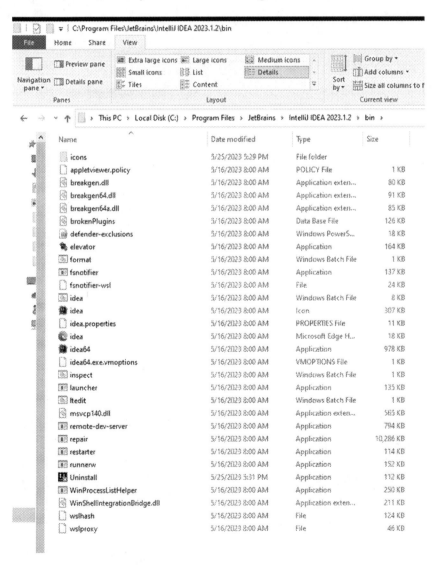

Figure 3-4. *The IntelliJ IDEA 2023.1.2 directory*

Now IntelliJ IDEA Ultimate Edition 2023.1.2 for web and enterprise development tool is ready to be used. Figure 3-5 shows how the dashboard looks when executing it.

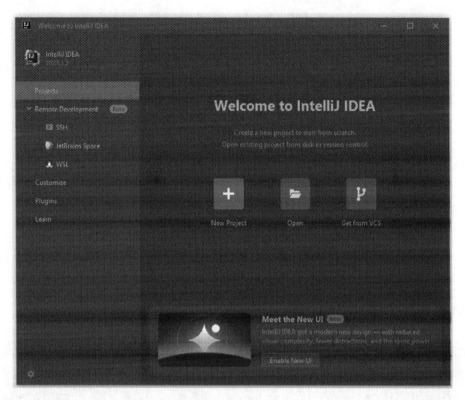

Figure 3-5. *The IntelliJ IDEA Ultimate Edition 2023.1.2 for web and enterprise development dashboard*

The next step is to install Maven 3.9.2 by downloading the .zip file named apache-maven-3.9.2-bin.zip at https://maven.apache.org/download.cgi.

Now run the IntelliJ IDEA 2023.1.2 tool and configure Maven 3.6.1. as shown in Figure 3-6.

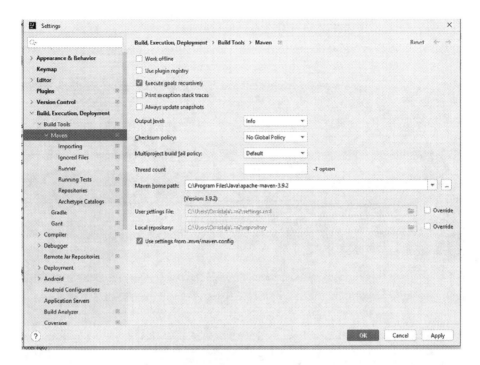

Figure 3-6. *Local Maven 3.9.2 is configured into IntelliJ IDEA 2023.1.2*

Now, Maven 3.9.2 is ready to be used.

The last tool used in this book is the Apache Tomcat Server and plugin 10. The first step is to download and install the Apache Tomcat Server 10 .exe file named apache-tomcat-10.1.9.exe at https://tomcat.apache.org/download-10.cgiInstall the exe file to the default folder, which is C:\Program Files\Apache Software Foundation\Tomcat 10.1. Since you need to allow Spring projects to deploy to Tomcat Servers, you need to define Tomcat users to access Tomcat Manager. This can be done when installing Tomcat 10, as shown in Figure 3-7, or by manually updating the file named tomcat-users.xml in the conf directory and adding the following XML fragment inside the <tomcat-users> element.

```
<role rolename="manager-gui"/>
<role rolename="manager-script"/>
<user username="tomcat" password="tomcat" roles="manager-gui, manager-script"/>
```

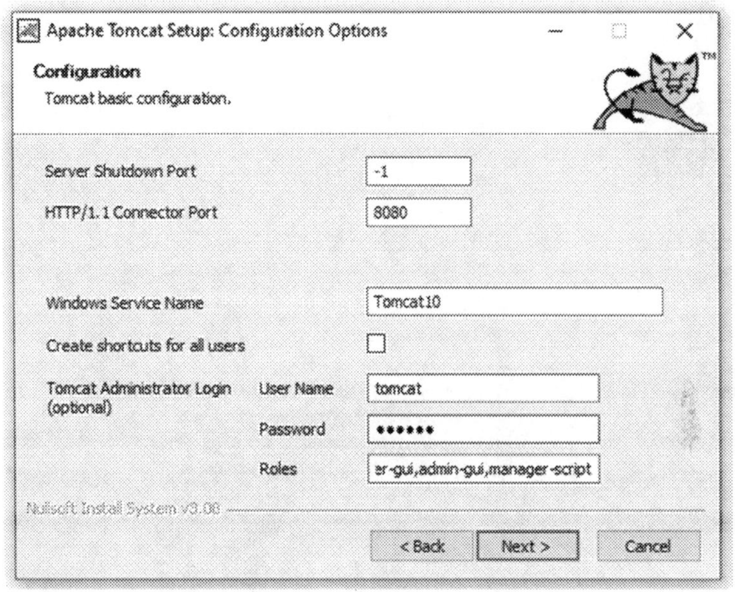

Figure 3-7. *Installation of Tomacat 10 with new roles*

Make sure you add the Tomcat Server to IntelliJ.

Now, the Apache Tomcat Server and plugin 10 are ready to be used.

Before starting a new Spring project, you want to make sure the right JDK package is installed into the IntelliJ IDEA 2023.1.2 IDE tool to compile your examples and avoid the typical compiling issue where the JRE is found instead of JDK. The configuration is shown in Figure 3-8.

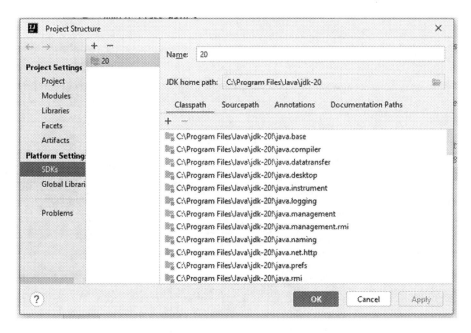

Figure 3-8. *Configuring the JDK to compile your examples*

So now the JDK compiler is set, and you are ready to start writing and running your first Spring web application example.

Creating a New Java Web Application Project

With your development tools set up, you can now create your first Java web application project using IntelliJ IDEA 2023.1.2. The built-in wizard makes creating a new Maven project very easy.

So, let's create your first Java EE web application named Pss01, without security, which produces the following text: Hello Spring Security!

Here are the steps to build a simple Maven web application project.

1. Create a Java EE web application.

2. Create and update the needed .jsp file.

3. Run the Java web application using the external Tomcat Server 10.

First, launch the IntelliJ IDEA tool and select File ➤ New ➤ Project ➤ Jakarta EE ➤ Web Application and fill in all information about the project, as shown in Figures 3-9 and 3-10.

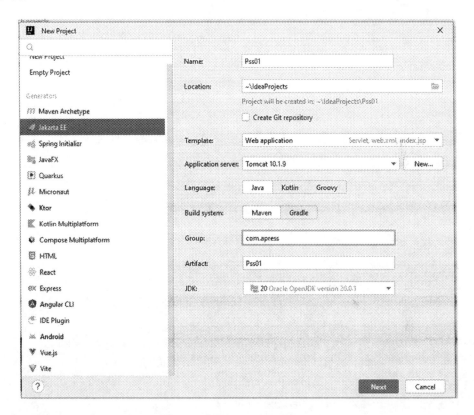

Figure 3-9. *Your first Java web application project*

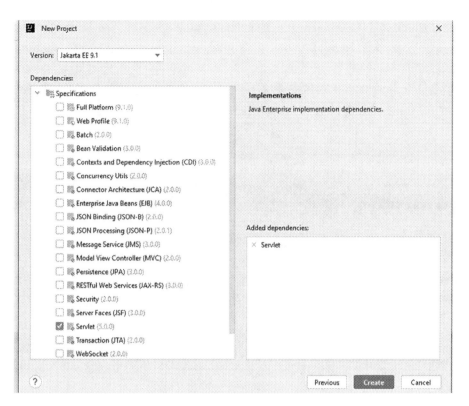

Figure 3-10. *Configuration for your first Java web application project*

In Package Explorer, you should now see your Pss01 project. If you expand it and all its children, you'll see something like Figure 3-11.

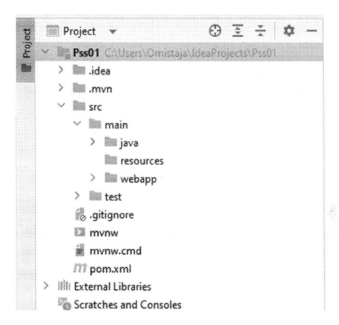

Figure 3-11. *Your first Java web application project structure*

In general, the structure of most Java web application projects contains the following.

- The target directory houses all the output of the build.

- The src directory contains all the source material for building the project, its site, etc.

- src/main/java contains the application/library sources.

- src/main/resources contains the application /library resources

- web contains the web application sources.

- pom.xml is a file that describes the project.

Your next step is to update the Java web application project's files needed for your first simple application. Please note that for this simple Java web application example, you do not need to add any specific dependency to the project file pom.xml, which looks initially like Listing 3-1.

Listing 3-1. The pom.xml File with Servlet Dependencies

```xml
<?xml version="1.0" encoding="UTF-8"?>
<project xmlns="http://maven.apache.org/POM/4.0.0"
         xmlns:xsi="http://www.w3.org/2001/XMLSchema-instance"
         xsi:schemaLocation="http://maven.apache.org/POM/4.0.0
         https://maven.apache.org/xsd/maven-4.0.0.xsd">
  <modelVersion>4.0.0</modelVersion>

  <groupId>com.apress</groupId>
  <artifactId>Pss01</artifactId>
  <version>1.0-SNAPSHOT</version>
  <name>Pss01</name>
  <packaging>war</packaging>
```

The project right now only contains one simple `.jsp` file named `index.jsp`, which you update to show the text you wish, as shown in Listing 3-2.

Listing 3-2. The index.jsp File

```jsp
<%@ page contentType="text/html;charset=UTF-8" language="java" %>
<html>
  <head>
    <title>$Title$</title>
  </head>
  <body>
    <h2>Hello Spring Security!</h2>
  </body>
</html>
```

Next, click the Add Configuration button at the top-right of the IntelliJ tool to configure how to run your first example.

You can run your project using the external Tomcat Server 10, as shown in Figure 3-12.

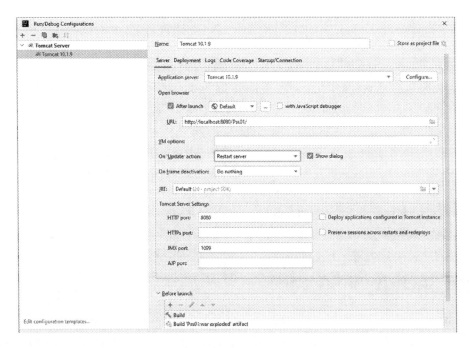

Figure 3-12. *Configure the running steps of your first Maven project*

Now you can open you web browser and type the web address `http://localhost:8080/Pss01`, as shown in Figure 3-13.

Figure 3-13. *The Java web application project running in a web browser*

Your first Java web application project was done now, so let's create a new Spring Security 6 project.

Adding Spring Security 6 to the Java Project

Spring Security builds upon the concepts defined in the previous section and integrates nicely into the general Spring ecosystem. You need to understand those concepts well to take maximum advantage of Spring Security 6. However, you can start using Spring Security without knowing all these details and then learn them as you progress and look to do more advanced things.

There are two ways to create a new Spring project.

You can create a Spring project via Spring Initializr, as discussed in Chapter 5, or via any IDE tool, which is IntelliJ IDEA 2023.1.2.

What kind of Spring Security Maven web application do you want to create?

Let's create a simple Spring Security example where the user must be authenticated as a user or an admin to access a certain secure project resource.

If you are using the stand-alone installation of Spring Security reference release and you decide not to use any IDE tool to build your Maven project, you will find many folders inside the installation directory. Most of the folders in the directory correspond to individual subprojects or modules that split the functionality of Spring Security into more discrete and specialized units.

Spring Security 6 Source

Open source software has an invaluable characteristic for software developers: free access to all source code. With this, you can understand how tools and frameworks work internally. You can also learn a lot about how other (perhaps very good) developers work, including their practices, techniques, and patterns. Free access to source code also enables us, in general, to gather ideas and experience for our development. As a more practical matter, having access to the source code allows you to debug these applications in the context of our application; you can find bugs or simply follow your application's execution through them.

Currently, Spring Security and most Spring projects live on GitHub. You probably know about GitHub (`https://github.com/`). If you don't, you should look at it because it has become a standard public source-code repository for many open source projects in many programming languages.

GitHub is a repository and a hosting service for Git repositories with a very friendly management interface. The Spring Security project is in the SpringSource general GitHub section at `https://github.com/SpringSource/spring-security`. To get the code, just download and install it, as discussed earlier in this chapter.

Spring Security 6.1.0.RELEASE includes several modules and folders, as shown in Figure 3-14.

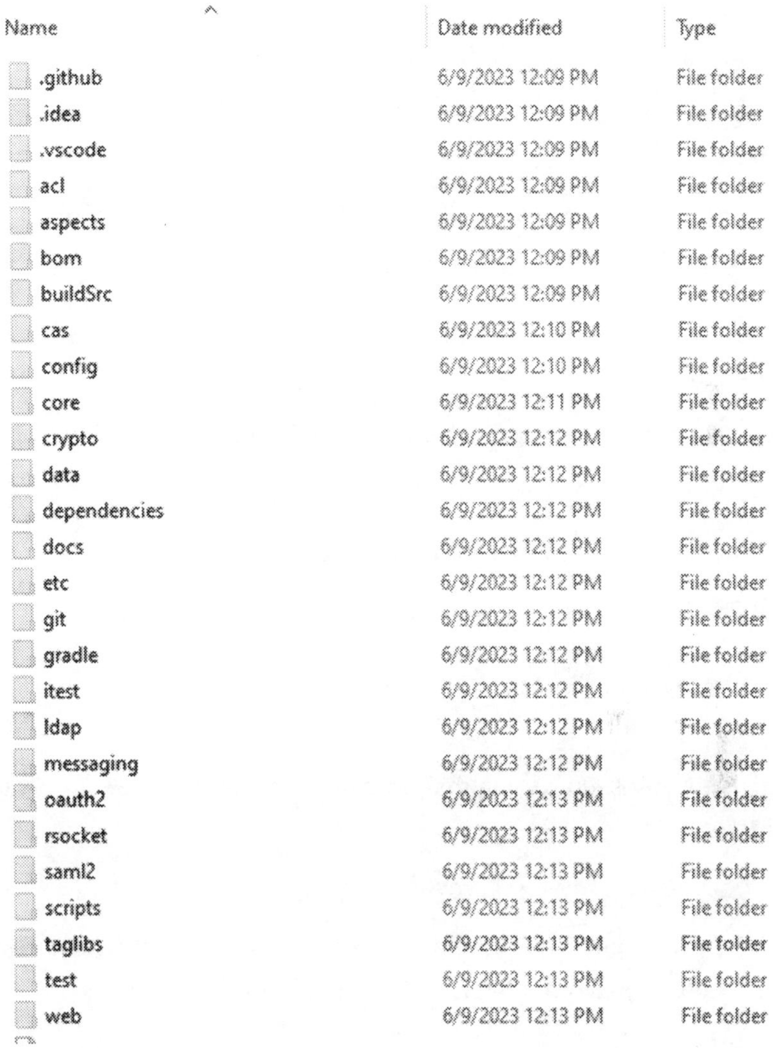

Name	Date modified	Type
.github	6/9/2023 12:09 PM	File folder
.idea	6/9/2023 12:09 PM	File folder
.vscode	6/9/2023 12:09 PM	File folder
acl	6/9/2023 12:09 PM	File folder
aspects	6/9/2023 12:09 PM	File folder
bom	6/9/2023 12:09 PM	File folder
buildSrc	6/9/2023 12:09 PM	File folder
cas	6/9/2023 12:10 PM	File folder
config	6/9/2023 12:10 PM	File folder
core	6/9/2023 12:11 PM	File folder
crypto	6/9/2023 12:12 PM	File folder
data	6/9/2023 12:12 PM	File folder
dependencies	6/9/2023 12:12 PM	File folder
docs	6/9/2023 12:12 PM	File folder
etc	6/9/2023 12:12 PM	File folder
git	6/9/2023 12:12 PM	File folder
gradle	6/9/2023 12:12 PM	File folder
itest	6/9/2023 12:12 PM	File folder
ldap	6/9/2023 12:12 PM	File folder
messaging	6/9/2023 12:12 PM	File folder
oauth2	6/9/2023 12:13 PM	File folder
rsocket	6/9/2023 12:13 PM	File folder
saml2	6/9/2023 12:13 PM	File folder
scripts	6/9/2023 12:13 PM	File folder
taglibs	6/9/2023 12:13 PM	File folder
test	6/9/2023 12:13 PM	File folder
web	6/9/2023 12:13 PM	File folder

Figure 3-14. *The Spring Security 6.1.0.RELEASE folder structure*

The following are short descriptions of some of the most important modules included in Spring Security 6.1.0.RELEASE.

- Core (spring-security-core) is where Spring Security's core classes and interfaces on authentication and access control reside.

- Remoting (spring-security-remoting) is the module with the remoting classes.

- Aspect (spring-security-aspects) provides aspect-oriented programming support within Spring Security.

- Config (spring-security-config) provides XML and Java configuration support.

- Crypto (spring-security-crypto) provides cryptography support.

- Data (spring-security-data) supports integration with Spring Data.

- Messaging (spring-security-messaging) supports Spring Security messaging.

- OAuth 2.x provides support within Spring Security.

  - Core (spring-security-oauth2-core)

  - Client (spring-security-oauth2-client)

  - JOSE (spring-security-oauth2-jose)

- CAS (spring-security-cas) (Central Authentication Service) supports client integration.

- TagLib (spring-security-taglibs) provides various Spring Security tag libraries.

- Test (spring-security-test) provides testing support.

- Web (spring-security-web) contains web security infrastructure code, such as filters and other Servlet API dependencies.

Note   Remember that you are using the IntelliJ IDEA tool, where the Spring Security 6.1.0.RELEASE is integrated and configured in it. Spring Security is used via an XML link at the beginning of the `pom.xml` file.

Let's update our previous project or create a new one named Pss02 and add Spring Security 6.

Here are the steps to build a simple Spring Security Maven web application project.

1. Import the required Spring Framework and Spring Security 6 libraries into the project (into the pom.xml file).

2. Configure the project to be aware of Spring Security.

3. Configure the users and roles that will be part of the system.

4. Configure the URLs that you want to secure.

5. Create all needed Java and web files.

6. Run the Spring Security 6 project using the external Tomcat Server 10.

Note   Implementing the Spring Security in a Spring application using XML- or Java-based configurations is possible. In this chapter, you use the Java configuration for your Spring Security web application since, in general, it is hardly suggested to use XML configuration as minimum as possible.

Since we are using Maven, the first step is to include Spring Security JARs dependencies in pom.xml.

- spring-security-core

- spring-security-config

- spring-security-web

- spring-webmvc

The following are the Maven dependencies you must add to the pom.xml file.

```
<dependency>
    <groupId>org.springframework.security</groupId>
    <artifactId>spring-security-core</artifactId>
    <version>6.1.0</version>
</dependency>
```

```xml
<dependency>
    <groupId>org.springframework.security</groupId>
    <artifactId>spring-security-config</artifactId>
    <version>6.1.0</version>
<dependency>
    <groupId>org.springframework.security</groupId>
    <artifactId>spring-security-web</artifactId>
    <version>6.1.0</version>
</dependency>
<dependency>
    <groupId>org.springframework</groupId>
    <artifactId>spring-webmvc</artifactId>
    <version>6.0.9</version>
</dependency>
```

The new `pom.xml` file is generated when the new Spring Boot 3 and Spring Security 6 project is created, as shown in Listing 3-3.

Listing 3-3. pom.xml

```xml
<?xml version="1.0" encoding="UTF-8"?>
<project xmlns="http://maven.apache.org/POM/4.0.0"
        xmlns:xsi="http://www.w3.org/2001/XMLSchema-instance"
        xsi:schemaLocation="http://maven.apache.org/POM/4.0.0
        https://maven.apache.org/xsd/maven-4.0.0.xsd">
    <modelVersion>4.0.0</modelVersion>

    <groupId>com.apress</groupId>
    <artifactId>Pss02</artifactId>
    <version>1.0-SNAPSHOT</version>
    <name>Pss02</name>
    <packaging>war</packaging>

    <properties>
        <project.build.sourceEncoding>UTF-8</project.build.sourceEncoding>
        <maven.compiler.target>11</maven.compiler.target>
        <maven.compiler.source>11</maven.compiler.source>
```

```xml
    <junit.version>5.9.2</junit.version>
</properties>

<dependencies>
    <dependency>
        <groupId>org.springframework.security</groupId>
        <artifactId>spring-security-core</artifactId>
        <version>6.1.0</version>
    </dependency>
    <dependency>
        <groupId>org.springframework.security</groupId>
        <artifactId>spring-security-config</artifactId>
        <version>6.1.0</version>
    </dependency>
    <dependency>
        <groupId>org.springframework.security</groupId>
        <artifactId>spring-security-web</artifactId>
        <version>6.1.0</version>
    </dependency>
    <dependency>
        <groupId>org.springframework</groupId>
        <artifactId>spring-webmvc</artifactId>
        <version>6.0.9</version>
    </dependency>
    <dependency>
        <groupId>jakarta.servlet</groupId>
        <artifactId>jakarta.servlet-api</artifactId>
        <version>5.0.0</version>
        <scope>provided</scope>
    </dependency>
    <dependency>
        <groupId>org.junit.jupiter</groupId>
        <artifactId>junit-jupiter-api</artifactId>
        <version>${junit.version}</version>
        <scope>test</scope>
    </dependency>
```

```
    <dependency>
        <groupId>org.junit.jupiter</groupId>
        <artifactId>junit-jupiter-engine</artifactId>
        <version>${junit.version}</version>
        <scope>test</scope>
    </dependency>
</dependencies>

<build>
    <plugins>
        <plugin>
            <groupId>org.apache.maven.plugins</groupId>
            <artifactId>maven-war-plugin</artifactId>
            <version>3.3.2</version>
        </plugin>
    </plugins>
</build>
</project>
```

Since Spring Security was added to the project, it secures the entire project by default. It gives a generated security password that is entered with "user" as the username, as shown in Figure 3-15.

Figure 3-15. *Running the new Spring project*

This means that if you type localhost:8080, Spring requires you to provide the newly created username (user) and password (e6fd5a38-b7a8-4d55-b47a-9ece6e3341fa) to log in, as shown in Figure 3-16.

Figure 3-16. *Secure Spring application with login page*

If you enter the correct username and password, you get the "Welcome to Spring Security 6" message, as shown in Figure 3-17.

Welcome to Spring Security 6 authentication example!

You are an authenticated user!

Figure 3-17. *Successful login message*

Configuring the Spring Security 6 Web Project

To activate Spring Security web project configuration in your Maven web application, you need to configure a particular Servlet filter that takes care of preprocessing and postprocessing the requests and managing the required security constraints.

Let's add now some more logic to our code.

First, let's create the Java package where all your Java classes will be located.

- com.apress.pss02.springsecurity.configuration

Then, you must define the Java classes needed for your example under package configuration.

- SecurityConfiguration

- AppInitializer

- SpringSecurityInitializer

In this example, you learn how to enable Spring Security 6 using the @ EnableWebSecurity annotation without using the WebSecurityConfigurerAdapter class; however, this example is built on top of the spring-webmvc Hibernate integration example.

Let's create a new Java Spring Security configuration class named SecurityConfiguration, which utilizes the @EnableWebSecurity annotation to configure Spring Security–related beans such as WebSecurityConfigurer or SecurityFilterChain.

In the new Spring Security 6 SecurityConfiguration Java class (see Listing 3-4), you must do the following.

- Create two demo in-memory users named "user" and "admin", authorized to access a secure project resource.

- Use BCryptPasswordEncoder to encode the user passwords for added security.

- Configure the SecurityFilterChain bean with the HTTP-based method login to the application as basic-auth.

Listing 3-4. SecurityConfiguration Java Class

```
package com.apress.pss02.configuration;
import org.springframework.context.annotation.Bean;
import org.springframework.context.annotation.Configuration;
import org.springframework.security.config.annotation.web.builders.
HttpSecurity;
import org.springframework.security.config.annotation.web.configuration.
EnableWebSecurity;
import org.springframework.security.core.userdetails.User;
import org.springframework.security.core.userdetails.UserDetails;
```

```
import org.springframework.security.core.userdetails.UserDetailsService;
import org.springframework.security.crypto.bcrypt.BCryptPasswordEncoder;
import org.springframework.security.crypto.password.PasswordEncoder;
import org.springframework.security.provisioning.
InMemoryUserDetailsManager;
import org.springframework.security.web.SecurityFilterChain;

import static org.springframework.security.config.Customizer.withDefaults;

@Configuration
@EnableWebSecurity

public class SecurityConfiguration {

    @Bean
    public SecurityFilterChain filterChain1(HttpSecurity http) throws
    Exception {
        http
                .authorizeHttpRequests((authorize) -> authorize
                        .anyRequest().authenticated()
                )
                .formLogin(withDefaults());
        return http.build();
    }

    @Bean
    public UserDetailsService userDetailsService(){
        UserDetails user = User.builder()
                .username("user")
                .password(passwordEncoder().encode("userpassw"))
                .roles("USER")
                .build();
        UserDetails admin = User.builder()
                .username("admin")
                .password(passwordEncoder().encode("adminpassw"))
                .roles("ADMIN")
                .build();
```

```
        return new InMemoryUserDetailsManager(user, admin);
    }

    @Bean
    public static PasswordEncoder passwordEncoder(){
        return new BCryptPasswordEncoder();
    }
}
```

Since Spring Security is implemented using DelegatingFilterProxy, the next step is to create a new Java class named `SpringSecurityInitializer` to initialize Spring Security using the AbstractSecurityWebApplicationInitializer class. This is done so that Spring can do the following.

- Detect the instance of this class during application startup

- Register the DelegatingFilterProxy to use the springSecurityFilterChain before any other registered Filter

- Register a ContextLoaderListener

The `SpringSecurityInitializer` Java class is shown in Listing 3-5.

Listing 3-5. SpringSecurityInitializer Java Class

```
package com.apress.pss02.configuration;

import org.springframework.security.web.context.
AbstractSecurityWebApplicationInitializer;

public class SpringSecurityInitializer extends
AbstractSecurityWebApplicationInitializer {

    //no code needed
}
```

Next, include the SecurityConfiguration class to the new `AppInitializer` Java class, used to initialize the HibernateConfig, SecurityConfiguration, and WebMvcConfig classes, as shown in Listing 3-6.

Listing 3-6. AppInitializer Java Class

```
package com.apress.pss02.configuration;

import jakarta.servlet.ServletContext;
import org.springframework.security.access.SecurityConfig;

import org.springframework.web.WebApplicationInitializer;
import org.springframework.web.context.ContextLoaderListener;
import org.springframework.web.context.support.
AnnotationConfigWebApplicationContext;
import org.springframework.web.filter.DelegatingFilterProxy;

public class AppInitializer implements WebApplicationInitializer {

    @Override
    public void onStartup(ServletContext sc) {

        AnnotationConfigWebApplicationContext root = new
        AnnotationConfigWebApplicationContext();
        root.register(SecurityConfiguration.class);

        sc.addListener(new ContextLoaderListener(root));

        sc.addFilter("securityFilter", new DelegatingFilterProxy(
        "springSecurityFilterChain"))
                .addMappingForUrlPatterns(null, false, "/*");
    }
}
```

Finally, update the index.jsp page, as shown in Listing 3-7.

Listing 3-7. index.jsp

```
<%@ page contentType="text/html; charset=UTF-8" pageEncoding="UTF-8" %>
<!DOCTYPE html>
<html>
<head>
    <title>Welcome to Spring Security 6 authentication example!</title>
</head>
```

```
<body>
<h2>Welcome to Spring Security 6 authentication example!</h2>

<h2>You are an authenticated user!</h2>

</body>
</html>
```

The index.jsp page only displays a welcoming message if the user is authenticated. The structure of your new Spring Security 6 project should look like Figure 3-18.

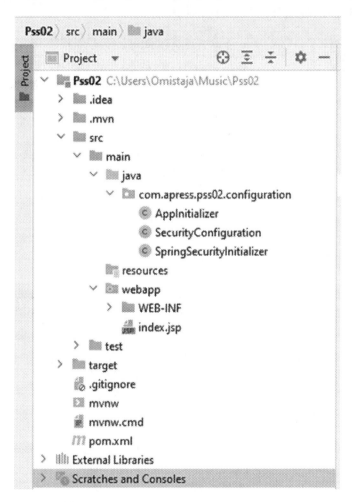

Figure 3-18. *New Spring Security 6 project structure*

Next, build and run the Spring Security 6 project using Tomcat 10, as shown in Figure 3-19.

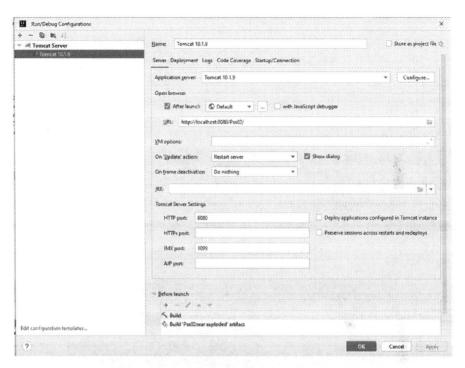

Figure 3-19. *Project running configuration using Tomcat 10*

You can now build the project, deploy the JAR file, start the application running on the stand-alone Tomcat Server 10, and deploy the JAR file automatically.

Your application is deployed successfully. The web browser automatically opens `http://localhost:8080/ /Pss02/login/`. The outcome is shown in Figure 3-20.

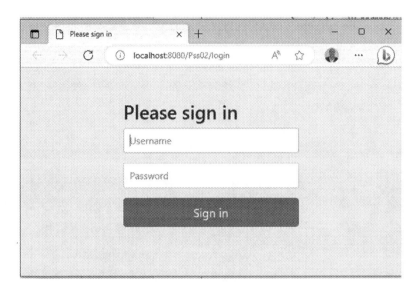

Figure 3-20. *Accessing the Spring Security login web page*

If you try to access using the wrong credentials, you receive an error message like the one shown in Figure 3-21.

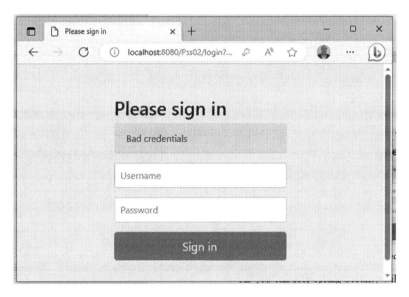

Figure 3-21. *Accessing with the wrong login credentials*

As you can see, Spring Security directly produces a login error and reminds the user that the credentials provided are incorrect.

If you provide the correct user or admin credentials, you receive the content defined in the index.jsp page, which identifies the credentials and displays a welcome message, as shown in Figure 3-22.

Welcome to Spring Security 6 authentication example!

You are an authenticated user!

Figure 3-22. *Accessing with the right admin credentials*

The admin login iteration flow is shown in Figure 3-23.

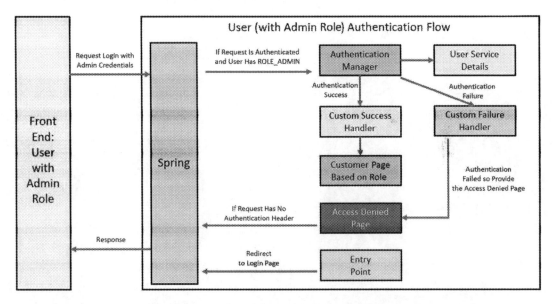

Figure 3-23. *Spring Security user with admin role authentication request flow*

Great! You have built your first Spring Security 6 web application.

The next chapter dives deeply into how this works internally by looking at the Spring Security architecture.

Summary

This chapter introduced all the tools needed to create the environment to develop Spring Security Java web applications. You learned how to install and configure all the tools needed for these examples, and you should have a good idea of what is needed to build a Spring Security 6 project. You learned how to build your first Java web application project without Spring Security, and then you added the security dependencies to update it as a Spring Security 6 application. The next chapter goes deeper into the Spring Framework architecture and design.

## CHAPTER 4

Spring Security Architecture and Design

In Chapter 3, you developed an initial application secured with Spring Security. You got an overview of how this application worked and looked at some of the Spring Security components put into action in common Spring Security–secured applications. This chapter extends those explanations and delve deeply into the framework.

We'll look at the main components of the framework, explain the work of the servlet filters for securing web applications, look at how Spring aspect-oriented programming helps you unobtrusively add security, and, in general, show how the framework is designed internally.

What Components Make up Spring Security?

This section looks at the major components that make Spring Security work. It presents a big-picture framework overview and then delves deeper into each major component.

The 10,000-Foot View

Spring Security is a relatively flexible framework that aims to make it easy for the developer to implement security in an application. At the most general level, it's a framework composed of intercepting rules for granting or not granting access to resources. Figure 4-1 illustrates this.

© Massimo Nardone, Carlo Scarioni 2024
M. Nardone and C. Scarioni, *Pro Spring Security*, https://doi.org/10.1007/979-8-8688-0035-1_4

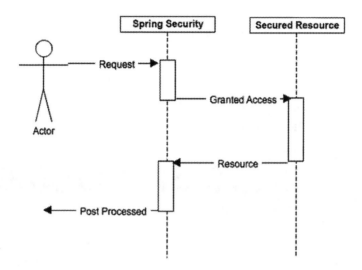

Figure 4-1. *Spring Security 10,000-foot overview*

From this view, you can think of Spring Security as an extra layer built on top of your application, wrapping specific entry points into your logic with determined security rules.

The 1,000-Foot View

Going into more detail, we arrive at AOP and servlet filters.

Spring Security's interception security model applies to two main areas of your application: URLs and method invocations. Spring Security wraps around these two *entry points* of your application and allows access only when the security constraints are satisfied. Both the method call and the filter-based security depend on a central *security interceptor*, where the main logic resides to decide whether access should be granted. Figure 4-2 shows a detailed overview of the framework.

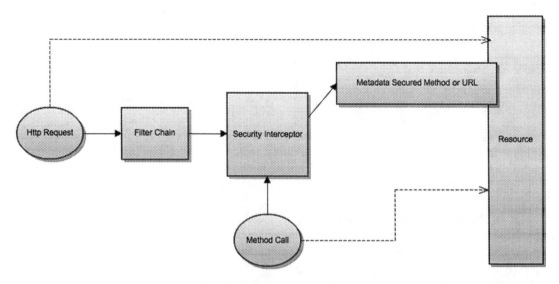

Figure 4-2. *In this view, both method calls and HTTP requests try to access a resource, but first they must go through the Security Interceptor*

The 100-Foot View

Spring Security might seem simple conceptually, but a lot is happening internally in a very well-built software tool. This next overview shows the main collaborating parts that enforce your security constraints. This is particularly achievable with an open source project like Spring Security, which allows you to get into the framework and appreciate its design and architecture by directly accessing the source code. After that, we'll delve deeper into the implementation details.

What follows is the best way to understand Spring Security from the inside. The enumeration of what we consider to be the main components of the framework helps you know where everything belongs and how your application is enforcing the security rules that you specify for it.

The most important Spring Security internal architecture core modules are

- Authentication

- Authorization

The process of the Authentication and Authorization modules were introduced in Chapter 1.

Figure 4-3 illustrates all the concepts/components.

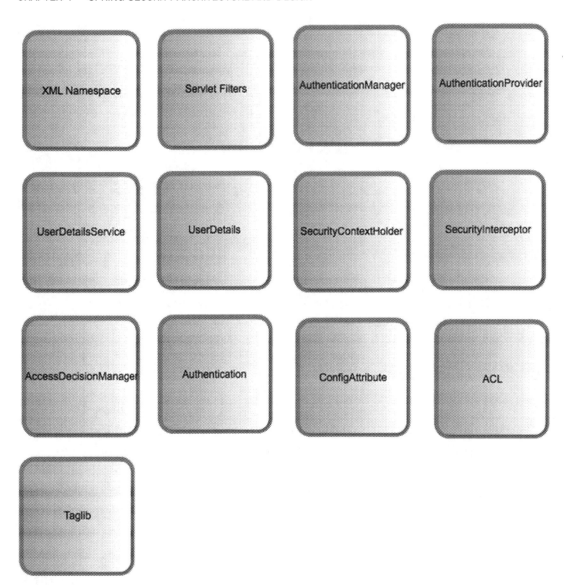

Figure 4-3. *The key components of Spring Security*

The Security Interceptor

One of the most important components of the security interceptor of the framework is the Security Interceptor. With the main logic implemented in AbstractSecurityInterceptor and with two concrete implementations in the form of FilterSecurityInterceptor and MethodSecurityInterceptor (as shown in Figure 4-4), the Security Interceptor is in charge of deciding whether a particular petition should be allowed to go through to a secured resource. `MethodSecurityInterceptor`, as its name should tell you, deals with petitions directed as method calls, while `FilterSecurityInterceptor` deals with petitions directed to web URLs.

The Security Interceptor works with a preprocessing step and a postprocessing step. The preprocessing step looks to see whether the requested resource is secured with some metadata information (or `ConfigAttribute`). If it is not, the request is allowed to continue its way either to the requested URL or method. If the requested resource is secured, the Security Interceptor retrieves the `Authentication` object from the current `SecurityContext`. If necessary, the `Authentication` object is authenticated against the configured `AuthenticationManager` with the following method.

```
public interface AuthenticationManager {
  Authentication authenticate(Authentication authentication)
    throws AuthenticationException;
}
```

An `AuthenticationManager` can do mainly three things with its method.

- Return an Authentication with value `authenticated=true` if the input represents a valid principal and can be verified

- Throw an `AuthenticationException` if the input represents an invalid principal

- Return null if it can't decide

`ProviderManager` (which delegates to a chain of `AuthenticationProvider` instances) is the most commonly used implementation of `AuthenticationManager`.

ProviderManager is the most commonly used implementation of AuthenticationManager. ProviderManager delegates to a List of AuthenticationProvider instances. Each AuthenticationProvider has an opportunity to indicate that authentication should be successful, fail, or indicate it cannot make a decision and allow a downstream AuthenticationProvider to decide. If none of the configured AuthenticationProvider instances can authenticate, authentication fails with a ProviderNotFoundException, which is a special AuthenticationException that indicates that the ProviderManager was not configured to support the type of authentication that was passed into it.

An example of the `AuthenticationManager` hierarchy using `ProviderManager` is shown in Figure 4-4.

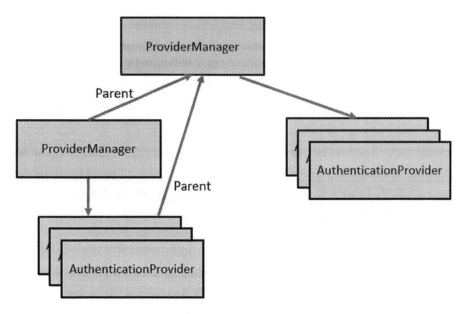

Figure 4-4. *AuthenticationManager hierarchy using ProviderManager*

After the object is authenticated, `AccessDecisionManager` is called to determine whether the authenticated entity can finally access the resource. `AccessDecisionManager` throws an `AccessDeniedException` if the authenticated entity cannot access the resource. If `AccessDecisionManager` decides that the `Authentication` entity is allowed to access the resource, the `Authentication` object is passed to `RunAsManager` if this is configured. If `RunAsManager` is not configured, a no-op implementation is called. `RunAsManager` returns either null (if it's not configured to be used) or a new `Authentication` object containing the same principal, credentials, and granted authorities as the original `Authentication` object, plus a new set of authorities based on the `RUN_AS` that is being used. This new `Authentication` object is put into the current `SecurityContext`.

After this processing, and independently of whether or not a `RUN_AS Authentication` object is used, the Security Interceptor creates a new `InterceptorStatusToken` with information about the `SecurityContext` and the `ConfigAttributes`. This token is used later in the postprocessing step of the Security Interceptor. At this point, the Security Interceptor is ready to allow access to the secured resource, so it passes the invocation through, and the particular secured entity (either a URL or a method) is invoked. After the invocation returns, the second phase of the Security Interceptor comes into play, and the postprocessing begins. The postprocessing step is considerably simpler and involves only calling an AfterInvocationManager's decide method if one is configured. In its current implementation, `AfterInvocationManager` delegates to instances of `PostInvocationAuthorizationAdvice`, which ultimately filters the returned objects or throws an `AccessDeniedException` if necessary. This is the case if you use the post-invocation filters in method-level security, as discussed in Chapter 5. In the case of web security, the `AfterInvocationManager` is null.

That is a lot of work for the security interceptor. However, because the framework is nicely modular at the class level, you can see that the Security Interceptor simply delegates most of the task to a series of well-defined collaborators; under the single-responsibility principle (SRP), it focuses on narrowly scoped responsibilities. This is a good software design and an example you should emulate. As shown in Listing 4-1, you paste the main parts of the code from `AbstractSecurityInterceptor` so that you can see the things we've been talking about. Comments are included in the code so that you can understand better what it does; they start with `//----`.

The AbstractSecurityInterceptor calls AccessDecisionManager, which is responsible for making final access control decisions, and it contains three methods.

```
void decide(Authentication authentication, Object secureObject,
     Collection<ConfigAttribute> attrs) throws AccessDeniedException;

boolean supports(ConfigAttribute attribute);
boolean supports(Class clazz);
```

The Spring Security 6 class is at `https://docs.spring.io/spring-security/site/docs/current/api/org/springframework/security/access/intercept/AbstractSecurityInterceptor.html`.

The entire `AbstractSecurityInterceptor` course code is on GitHub at `https://github.com/spring-projects/spring-security/blob/master/core/src/main/java/org/springframework/security/access/intercept/AbstractSecurityInterceptor.java`.

Listing 4-1. AbstractSecurityInterceptor

```
protected InterceptorStatusToken beforeInvocation(Object object) {
Assert.notNull(object, "Object was null");
final boolean debug = logger.isDebugEnabled();
```

```
// --- Here we are checking if this filter is able to process a particular
type of object. For example FilterSecurityInterceptor is able to process
FilterInvocation objects. MethodSecurityInterceptor is able to process
MethodInvocation objects.
if (!getSecureObjectClass().isAssignableFrom(object.getClass())) {
throw new IllegalArgumentException("Security invocation attempted for object "
                + object.getClass().getName()
                + " but AbstractSecurityInterceptor only configured to
                    support secure objects of type: "
                + getSecureObjectClass());
        }
// ---- Here we are retrieving the security metadata that maps to the
object we are receiving. So if we are receiving a FilterInvocation, the
request is extracted from it and used to find the ConfigAttribute (s) that
match the request path pattern
        Collection<ConfigAttribute> attributes = this.
        obtainSecurityMetadataSource().getAttributes(object);
if (attributes == null || attributes.isEmpty()) {
if (rejectPublicInvocations) {
throw new IllegalArgumentException("Secure object invocation " + object +
" was denied as public invocations are not allowed via this interceptor. "
                        + "This indicates a configuration error
                            because the " + "rejectPublicInvocations
                            property is set to 'true'");
            }
if (debug) {
logger.debug("Public object - authentication not attempted");
            }
publishEvent(new PublicInvocationEvent(object));
return null; // no further work post-invocation
        }
if (debug) {
logger.debug("Secure object: " + object + "; Attributes: " + attributes);
        }
if (SecurityContextHolder.getContext().getAuthentication() == null) {
```

```
credentialsNotFound(messages.getMessage("AbstractSecurityInterceptor.
authenticationNotFound",
                    "An Authentication object was not found in the
                    SecurityContext"), object, attributes);
        }
        Authentication authenticated = authenticateIfRequired();
 // ---- Here we are calling the decision manager to decide if
authorization is granted or not. This will trigger the voting mechanism,
and in case that access is not granted an exception should be thrown.
try {
this.accessDecisionManager.decide(authenticated, object, attributes);
        }
catch (AccessDeniedException accessDeniedException) {
publishEvent(new AuthorizationFailureEvent(object, attributes,
authenticated, accessDeniedException));
throw accessDeniedException;
        }
if (debug) {
logger.debug("Authorization successful");
        }
if (publishAuthorizationSuccess) {
publishEvent(new AuthorizedEvent(object, attributes, authenticated));
        }
   // ---- Here it will try to use the run-as functionality of Spring
   Security that allows a user
// --to impersonate another one acquiring its security roles, or more
precisely, its
//--GrantedAuthority (s)
Authentication runAs = this.runAsManager.buildRunAs(authenticated, object,
attributes);
if (runAs == null) {
if (debug) {
logger.debug("RunAsManager did not change Authentication object");
        }
```

```
                // no further work post-invocation
return new InterceptorStatusToken(SecurityContextHolder.getContext(),
false, attributes, object);
        } else {
if (debug) {
logger.debug("Switching to RunAs Authentication: " + runAs);
            }
SecurityContext origCtx = SecurityContextHolder.getContext();
SecurityContextHolder.setContext(SecurityContextHolder.
createEmptyContext());
SecurityContextHolder.getContext().setAuthentication(runAs);
            // need to revert to token.Authenticated post-invocation
return new InterceptorStatusToken(origCtx, true, attributes, object);
        }
// ---- If the method has not thrown an exception at this point, it is safe
to continue
// ---- the invocation through to the resource. Authorization has been
granted.
    }
protected Object afterInvocation(InterceptorStatusToken token, Object
returnedObject) {
if (token == null) {
            // public object
return returnedObject;
        }
if (token.isContextHolderRefreshRequired()) {
if (logger.isDebugEnabled()) {
logger.debug("Reverting to original Authentication: " + token.
getSecurityContext().getAuthentication());
            }
SecurityContextHolder.setContext(token.getSecurityContext());
        }
// ---- If there is an afterInvocationManager configured, it will
be called.
// ---- It will take care of filtering the return value or actually
throwing an exception
```

```
//----- if it is relevant to do so.
if (afterInvocationManager != null) {
            // Attempt after invocation handling
try {
returnedObject = afterInvocationManager.decide(token.getSecurityContext().
getAuthentication(),
token.getSecureObject(),
token.getAttributes(), returnedObject);
            }
catch (AccessDeniedException accessDeniedException) {
AuthorizationFailureEvent event = new AuthorizationFailureEvent(token.
getSecureObject(), token .getAttributes(), token.getSecurityContext().
getAuthentication(), accessDeniedException);
publishEvent(event);
throw accessDeniedException;
            }
        }
// ---- Here is the full authorization cycled finished. The response is
returned to the caller.
return returnedObject;
    }
```

The Security Interceptor lies at the core of the Spring Security framework. Every call to a secured resource in Spring Security passes through this interceptor. The AbstractSecurityInterceptor shows its versatility when you realize that two not-very-related kinds of resources (URL endpoints and methods) leverage most of the functionality of this abstract interceptor. Once again, this shows the effort put into the design and implementation of the framework.

Figure 4-5 shows the interceptor in an unified modeling language (UML) class diagram. Figure 4-6 shows a simplified sequence diagram.

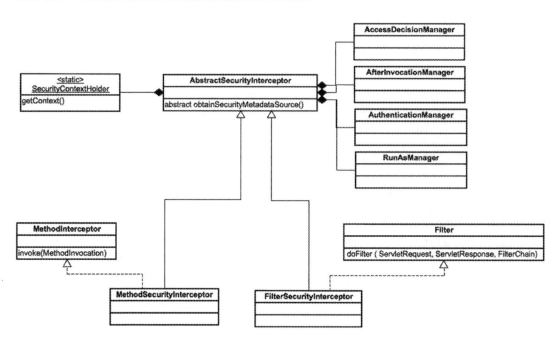

Figure 4-5. *SecurityInterceptor UML class diagram, simplified*

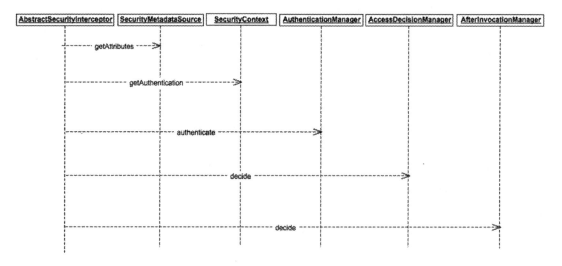

Figure 4-6. *AbstractSecurityInterceptor sequence diagram, simplified*

You know how security interceptors work, but how do they come to be? How do they know what to intercept? The answer lies in the next few components, so keep reading.

The XML Namespace

The XML namespace is of extreme importance to the general appeal and usability of the framework namespace, yet it is, in theory, not strictly necessary. If you know how the Spring Framework's namespaces work, you probably have a good idea of what is going on when you define your security-specific XML configuration in your application context definition files. If you don't know how they work, maybe you think Spring is somehow made aware of how to treat these specific elements and how to load them in the general Spring application context. Either way, here we explain the process behind defining a custom namespace in Spring, particularly the elements in the Spring Security namespace.

Originally, Spring did not support custom XML. All that Spring understood was its own classes defined in the standard Spring Core namespace, where you can define `<bean>`s on a bean-to-bean basis and can't define anything conceptually more complex without adding that complexity yourself to the configuration.

This `<bean>`-based configuration was, and still is, very good for configuring general-purpose bean instances, but it can get messy fast for defining more domain-specific utilities. Beyond being messy, it is also very poor at expressing the business domain of the beans you define.

We'll explore this manual configuration later in the book, but it is not needed for standard cases, and you should simply use the namespace. However, remember that under the hood, the namespace is nothing more than syntactic sugar. You still end up with standard Spring beans and objects.

Spring 2.0 introduced support for defining custom XML namespaces. Since then, many projects have used this facility, making them more attractive to work with.

An XML custom namespace is simply an XML-based domain-specific language (DSL), guided by the rules of an XML schema (`.xsd`) file that allows developers to create Spring beans using concepts and syntax more in synch with the programming concerns they are trying to model.

Note   A DSL is a language customized to represent the concepts of a particular application domain. Sometimes, a whole new language is created to support the new domain, which is referred to as an *external DSL*. An existing language is sometimes tweaked to allow for new expressions that represent the domain's concepts, which is an *internal DSL*. In the case presented in this chapter, you are using a general-purpose language (XML); however, you are defining certain constraints about the elements (using XSD) and thus are creating an internal DSL to represent security concepts.

Making Spring aware of a new namespace is simple. (That's not to say it is simple to parse the XML's information and convert it to beans—this depends on the complexity of your DSL.) All you need is the following.

- An `.xsd` file defining your particular XML structure

- A `spring.schemas` file where you specify the mapping between a URL-based schema location and the location of your `.xsd` file in your classpath

- A `spring.handlers` file where you specify which class is in charge of handling everything related to your namespace

- Several parser classes that parse each of the top elements are defined in your XML file.

Chapter 8 provides some examples of how to create a new namespace element and integrate it with Spring Security.

All the namespace configuration-related information resides in the config module for Spring Security. In Figure 4-7, you can see the expanded structure of the `config` module as seen in the IntelliJ IDEA 2023.1.2 integrated development environment (IDE) used in this book.

Figure 4-7. *Spring Security's file structure*

The files `spring.handlers` and `spring.schemas` should reside in the `META-INF` directory in the classpath so that Spring can find them there.

OK, so enough of the general namespace information. More specifically, how does the Spring Security namespace work?

Let's suppose you create and run a Spring-based application using XML-defined application context configuration with some Spring Security namespace definitions. When it starts to load, it looks in the application context's namespace definitions at the top of the XML configuration file. It finds the reference to the Spring Security namespace (normally a reference like xmlns:security="http://www.springframework.org/ schema/security"). Using the information from the spring.handlers mapping file, it sees that the file to handle the security elements is the final class, org.springframework. security.config.SecurityNamespaceHandler. Spring calls the parse method of this class for every top element in the configuration file that uses the security namespace. Figure 4-8 shows the load-up sequence for this process.

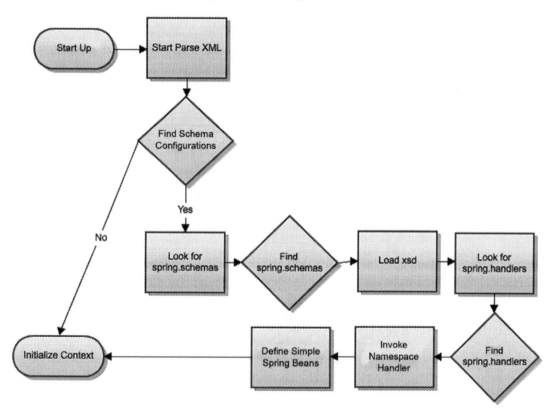

Figure 4-8. *Sequence of loading up a Spring namespace*

SecurityNamespaceHandler delegates to a series of BeanDefinitionParser objects for the individual parsing of each top-level element. The whole list of elements supported in the Spring Security namespace configuration is defined in the class org.springframework. security.config.Elements as constants. This class is shown in Listing 4-2.

Listing 4-2. Constants for All the Spring Security Namespace Elements

```
package org.springframework.security.config;
public abstract class Elements {
public static final String ACCESS_DENIED_HANDLER = "access-denied-handler";
public static final String AUTHENTICATION_MANAGER = "authentication-
manager";
public static final String AFTER_INVOCATION_PROVIDER = "after-invocation-
provider";
public static final String USER_SERVICE = "user-service";
public static final String JDBC_USER_SERVICE = "jdbc-user-service";
public static final String FILTER_CHAIN_MAP = "filter-chain-map";
public static final String INTERCEPT_METHODS = "intercept-methods";
public static final String INTERCEPT_URL = "intercept-url";
public static final String AUTHENTICATION_PROVIDER = "authentication-
provider";
public static final String HTTP = "http";
public static final String LDAP_PROVIDER = "ldap-authentication-provider";
public static final String LDAP_SERVER = "ldap-server";
public static final String LDAP_USER_SERVICE = "ldap-user-service";
public static final String PROTECT_POINTCUT = "protect-pointcut";
public static final String EXPRESSION_HANDLER = "expression-handler";
public static final String INVOCATION_HANDLING = "pre-post-annotation-
handling";
public static final String INVOCATION_ATTRIBUTE_FACTORY = "invocation-
attribute-factory";
public static final String PRE_INVOCATION_ADVICE = "pre-invocation-advice";
public static final String POST_INVOCATION_ADVICE = "post-
invocation-advice";
public static final String PROTECT = "protect";
public static final String SESSION_MANAGEMENT = "session-management";
public static final String CONCURRENT_SESSIONS = "concurrency-control";
public static final String LOGOUT = "logout";
public static final String FORM_LOGIN = "form-login";
public static final String BASIC_AUTH = "http-basic";
```

```
public static final String REMEMBER_ME = "remember-me";
public static final String ANONYMOUS = "anonymous";
public static final String FILTER_CHAIN = "filter-chain";
public static final String GLOBAL_METHOD_SECURITY = "global-method-
security";
public static final String PASSWORD_ENCODER = "password-encoder";
public static final String SALT_SOURCE = "salt-source";
public static final String PORT_MAPPINGS = "port-mappings";
public static final String PORT_MAPPING = "port-mapping";
public static final String CUSTOM_FILTER = "custom-filter";
public static final String REQUEST_CACHE = "request-cache";
public static final String X509 = "x509";
public static final String JEE = "jee";
public static final String FILTER_SECURITY_METADATA_SOURCE = "filter-
security-
metadata-source";
public static final String METHOD_SECURITY_METADATA_SOURCE = "method-
security-metadata-source";
    @Deprecated
public static final String FILTER_INVOCATION_DEFINITION_SOURCE = "filter-
invocation-definition-source";
public static final String LDAP_PASSWORD_COMPARE = "password-compare";
public static final String DEBUG = "debug";
public static final String HTTP_FIREWALL = "http-firewall";
}
```

From the list of elements presented in the previous class, the top-level ones used in the XML configuration files are as follows. (Listing 4-2 refers to them by the constant name, not the XML element name).

- LDAP_PROVIDER configures your application's Lightweight Directory Access Protocol (LDAP) authentication provider in case you require one.

- LDAP_SERVER configures an LDAP server in your application.

- LDAP_USER_SERVICE configures the service for retrieving user details from an LDAP server and populating that user's authorities (Spring Security uses the term "authorities" to refer to the permission names that are granted to a particular user. For example, ROLE_USER is an authority).

- USER_SERVICE defines the in-memory user service where you can store user names, credentials, and authorities directly in the application context definition file. This type of configuration is specific for test environments and academic purposes because it is easy to set up and fast.

- JDBC_USER_SERVICE allows you to set up a database-driven user service, where you specify a DataSource and the queries to retrieve the user information from a database.

- AUTHENTICATION_PROVIDER defines DaoAuthenticationProvider, which is an authentication provider that delegates to an instance of UserDetailsService, which can be any of the ones defined in the previous three elements or a reference to a customized one.

- GLOBAL_METHOD_SECURITY sets up the global support in your application to the annotations @Secured, @javax.annotation. security.RolesAllowed, @PreAuthorize, and @PostAuthorize. This element is the one that handles the registration of a method interceptor that is aware of all the metadata of the bean's methods to apply the corresponding security advice.

- AUTHENTICATION_MANAGER registers a global ProviderManager in the application and sets up the configured AuthenticationProviders on it.

- METHOD_SECURITY_METADATA_SOURCE registers MapBasedMethodSecurityMetadataSource in the application context. It holds Map<RegisteredMethod, List<ConfigAttribute>>. It does this so that when a request is made to a method, the method can be retrieved, and its security constraints can be checked.

- DEBUG registers a DebugFilter in the security filter chain.

- HTTP is the main element for a web-based secure application. The HTTP element is really powerful. It allows for the definition of URL-based security-mapping strategies, the configuration of the filters, the Secure Sockets Layer (SSL) support, and other HTTP-related security configurations.

- HTTP_FIREWALL uses a firewall element and adds it to the filter chain if it is configured. The firewall referenced should be an implementation of Spring's own HttpFirewall interface.

- FILTER_INVOCATION_DEFINITION_SOURCE has been deprecated. See the following one.

- FILTER_SECURITY_METADATA_SOURCE wraps a list of <intercept-url> elements. These elements map the relationship between URLs and the ConfigAttributes required for accessing those URLs.

- FILTER_CHAIN allows you to configure the Spring Security filter chain used in the application, which filters you want to add to the chain, and a request matcher to customize how the chain matches requests. The most important request matches are ant-based and regexp-based.

The Spring Security namespace is used throughout the book, so many of the elements described here are revisited in later chapters.

The Filters and Filter Chain

The filter chain model is what Spring Security uses to secure web application filters and filter chains. This model is built on top of the standard *servlet filter* functionality. Working as an intercepting filter pattern, the filter chain in Spring Security is built of a few single-responsibility filters that cover all the different security constraints required by the application.

The filter chain in Spring Security preprocesses and postprocesses all the HTTP requests sent to the application and then applies security to URLs that require it.

A typical filter for a single HTTP request is shown in Figure 4-9.

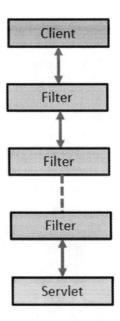

Figure 4-9. *Spring Security filter example for a single HTTP request*

The Spring Security filter chain is made up of Spring beans; however, standard servlet-based web applications don't know about Spring beans.

From the container's point of view, Spring Security is a single filter, which internally contains a lot of filters with different purposes.

Spring Security is installed as a single filter in the FilterChainProxy chain, which contains all the security needed, as shown in Figure 4-10.

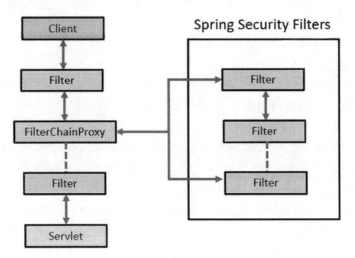

Figure 4-10. *Spring Security filters overview*

In the security filter, a special layer of indirection is installed in the DelegatingFilterProxy container, which does not need to be a Spring bean.

The flow works so that the DelegatingFilterProxy filter delegates to a FilterChainProxy, which instead is always a bean with a fixed name of springSecurityFilterChain, which at the end is responsible, within your application, for the following.

- Protecting the application URLs

- Validating the submitted username and passwords

- Redirecting to the login form

The DelegatingFilterProxy process containing the FilterChainProxy is shown in Figure 4-11.

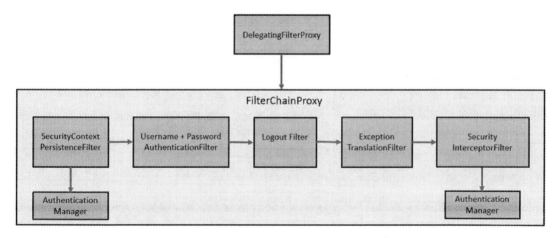

Figure 4-11. *Spring Security filter chain overview*

The Spring Security filter configuration is achieved via a special servlet and two main XML files, web.xml and applicationContext.xml. Starting with Servlet 3.0, web.xml is no longer necessary.

This special servlet filter is needed to cross the boundaries between the standard servlet API and life cycle and the Spring application where the bean filters reside. This is the job of the org.springframework.web.filter.DelegatingFilterProxy. It is defined in web.xml, which uses the WebApplicationContextUtils.getWebApplicationContext utility method to retrieve the root application context of the application. These two classes are from Spring Framework, not Spring Security.

Figure 4-12 shows the configuration of the filter chain.

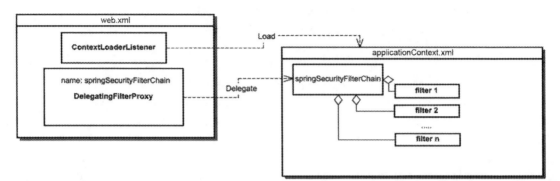

Figure 4-12. *Understanding the Spring Security filter configuration. The filter in the web.xml file has the same name as the bean in the Spring application context so that the listener can find it*

More information about migrating from Spring Security 6 filters is at `https://docs.spring.io/spring-security/reference/servlet/architecture.html#servlet-securityfilterchain`.

The filter chain is explained in Chapter 5. However, here we'll provide an overview of the available filters and what they do. The available filters in version 6 are defined as enums in the `org.springframework.security.web.SecurityFilterChain` file.

The enums are then referenced later in the startup process when instantiating the bean definitions for each filter. The following describes the defined filters.

- `CHANNEL_FILTER` ensures that the request is handled by the correct channel—meaning, in most cases, it determines whether HTTPS handles the request.

- `CONCURRENT_SESSION_FILTER` is part of the concurrent session-handling mechanism. Its main function is to query the session to see if it has expired (which happens mainly when the maximum number of concurrent sessions per user are reached) and to log out the user if that is the case.

- `SECURITY_CONTEXT_FILTER` populates `SecurityContextHolder` with a new or existing security context to be used by the rest of the framework.

- LOGOUT_FILTER is based, by default, on a particular URL invocation (/logout). It handles the logout process, including clearing the cookies, removing the "remember me" information, and clearing the security context.

- X509_FILTER extracts the principal and credentials from an X509 certificate using the class java.security.cert.X509Certificate and attempts to authenticate with these preauthenticated values.

- PRE_AUTH_FILTER is used with the J2EE authentication mechanism. The J2EE authenticated principal is the preauthenticated principal in the framework.

- FORM_LOGIN_FILTER is used when a username and password are required on a login form. This filter takes care of authenticating with the requested username and password. It handles (since Spring 4) requests to a particular URL (/login) with a particular set of username and password parameters (username, password).

- LOGIN_PAGE_FILTER generates a default login page when the user doesn't provide a custom one. It is activated when /spring_security_login is requested.

- DIGEST_AUTH_FILTER processes HTTP Digest authentication headers. It looks for the presence of both Digest and Authorization HTTP request headers. It can provide Digest authentication to standard user agents, like browsers, or application clients like SOAP. On successful authentication, the SecurityContext is populated with the valid Authentication object.

- BASIC_AUTH_FILTER processes the BASIC authentication headers in an HTTP request. It looks for the header Authorization and tries to authenticate with these credentials.

- REQUEST_CACHE_FILTER retrieves a request from the request cache that matches the current request, and it sends the cached one through the rest of the filter chain.

- SERVLET_API_SUPPORT_FILTER. wraps the request in a request wrapper that implements the Servlet API security methods, like isUserInRole, and delegates it to SecurityContextHolder. This allows for the convenient use of the request object to get the security information. For example, you can use request.getAuthentication to retrieve the Authentication object.

- JAAS_API_SUPPORT_FILTER tries to obtain and use javax.security. auth.Subject, which is a final class, and continue the filter chain execution with this subject.

- REMEMBER_ME_FILTER checks whether any "remember me" functionality is active and any "remember me" authentication is available if no user is logged in. If there is, this filter tries to log in automatically and authenticate with this "remember me" information.

- ANONYMOUS_FILTER checks to see whether there is already an Authentication in the context. If not, it creates a new Anonymous one and sets it in the security context.

- SESSION_MANAGEMENT_FILTER passes the Authentication object corresponding to the authenticated user who is logged in to the system to some configured session management processors to do session-related handling of the Authentication. Mainly, these processors do some kind of validation and throw SessionAuthenticationException if appropriate. Currently, these processors (or strategies) include only one main class, org. springframework.security.web.authentication.session. ConcurrentSessionControlStrategy, dealing with both session fixation and concurrent sessions.

- EXCEPTION_TRANSLATION_FILTER handles the translation between Spring Security exceptions (like AccessDeniedException) and the corresponding HTTP status code. It also redirects to the application entry point if the exception is thrown because there is not yet an authenticated user in the system.

- `FILTER_SECURITY_INTERCEPTOR` handles the authorization mechanism for defined URLs. It delegates to its parent class (`AbstractSecurityInterceptor`) functionality (covered later in the chapter) the actual workflow logic of granting or not granting access to the specific resource.

- `SWITCH_USER_FILTER` allows a user to impersonate another one by visiting a URL that has been updated from `/j_spring_security_switch_user` to `/login/impersonate` since Spring 4. This URL should be secured to allow certain users access to this functionality. Also, the method `attemptSwitchUser` in the implementing class `SwitchUserFilter` can be overridden to add constraints so that you can use more finely-grained information to decide whether certain users are allowed or not allowed to impersonate other users.

Many interfaces (e.g., Open ID and ConfigAttribute) have been deprecated since API version 5.6.2. The entire list is at `https://docs.spring.io/spring-security/site/docs/5.6.2/api/deprecated-list.html`.

The Authentication Object

In Spring Security 6, the Authentication interface serves two main purposes within Spring Security.

- An input to AuthenticationManager to provide the credentials a user has provided to authenticate. When used in this scenario, isAuthenticated() returns false.

- Represent the currently authenticated user. You can obtain the current authentication from SecurityContext.

The Authentication interface contains the following.

- **principal** identifies the user. Authenticating with a username/password is often an instance of UserDetails.

- **credentials** is usually the password. It is often cleared after the user is authenticated to ensure it is not leaked.

- **authorities** means the GrantedAuthority instances, which are high-level permissions the user is granted. Two examples are roles and scopes.

The Authentication object is an abstraction representing the entity that logs in to the system—most likely a user. Because it is normally a user authenticating, we'll assume so and use the term "user" in the rest of the book. There are a few implementations of the Authentication object in the framework, as shown in Figure 4-13.

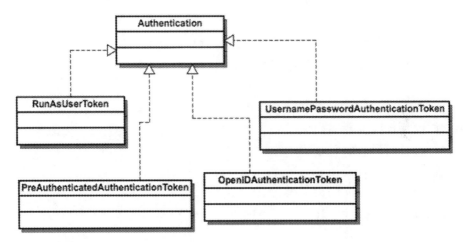

Figure 4-13. Authentication hierarchy

An Authentication object is used when an authentication request is created (when a user logs in) to carry around the different layers and classes of the framework the requesting data and when it is validated, containing the authenticated entity and storing it in SecurityContext.

The most common behavior is that when you log in to the application, a new Authentication object is created, storing your username, password, and permissions, which are technically known as principal, credentials, and authorities, respectively.

Authentication is a simple interface, as Listing 4-3 shows.

Note   There are many implementations of the Authentication interface. In this book, we typically refer to the general Authentication interface when we are not interested in the implementation type. Of course, we refer to the concrete classes when discussing the specifics of an implementation detail.

Listing 4-3. The Authentication Interface

```
package org.springframework.security.core;
import java.io.Serializable;
import java.security.Principal;
import java.util.Collection;
import org.springframework.security.authentication.AuthenticationManager;
import org.springframework.security.core.context.SecurityContextHolder;
public interface Authentication extends Principal, Serializable {
Collection<? extends GrantedAuthority> getAuthorities();
    Object getCredentials();
    Object getDetails();
    Object getPrincipal();
Boolean isAuthenticated();
Void setAuthenticated(boolean isAuthenticated) throws
IllegalArgumentException;
}
```

As Figure 4-13 shows, currently, there are a few implementations of `Authentication` in the framework.

- `UsernamePasswordAuthenticationToken`: This simple implementation contains the username and password information of the authenticated (or pending authentication) user. It is the most common `Authentication` implementation used throughout the system, as many `AuthenticationProvider` objects depend directly on this class.

- `PreAuthenticatedAuthenticationToken`: This implementation exists for handling preauthenticated `Authentication` objects. Preauthenticated authentications are those where an external system handles the actual authentication process. Spring Security only extracts the principal (or user) information from the external system's messages.

- RunAsUserToken: This implementation is used by the RunAsManager, which the Security Interceptor calls when the accessed resource contains a ConfigAttribute that starts with the prefix RUN_AS_. If there is a ConfigAttribute with this value, RunAsManager adds new GrantedAuthorities to the authenticated user corresponding to the RUN_AS value.

SecurityContext and SecurityContextHolder

At the heart of Spring Security's authentication model is the SecurityContextHolder. It contains the SecurityContext.

The SecurityContextHolder is where Spring Security stores the details of who is authenticated. Spring Security does not care how the SecurityContextHolder is populated. It is used as the currently authenticated user if it contains a value.

Here is an example of SecurityContextHolder usage.

```
SecurityContext context = SecurityContextHolder.createEmptyContext();
Authentication authentication =
    new TestingAuthenticationToken("username", "password", "ROLE_USER");
context.setAuthentication(authentication);

SecurityContextHolder.setContext(context);
```

The interface org.springframework.security.core.context.SecurityContext (its implementation is SecurityContextImpl) is where Spring Security stores the valid Authentication object, associating it with the current thread. The org.springframework.security.core.context.SecurityContextHolder is the class used to access SecurityContext from many parts of the framework. It is built mainly of static methods to store and access SecurityContext, delegating to configurable strategies to handle this SecurityContext—for example, one SecurityContext per thread (default), one global SecurityContext, or a custom strategy. The class diagram for these classes can be seen in Figure 4-14, and Listings 4-4 and 4-5 show the two classes.

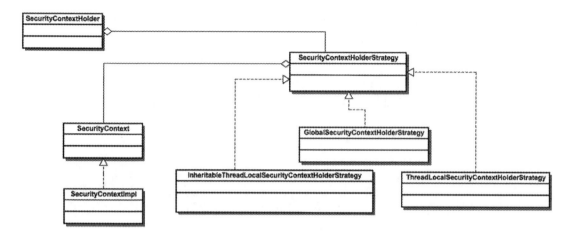

Figure 4-14. *SecurityContext and SecurityContextHolder*

Listing 4-4. SecurityContext Interface

```
package org.springframework.security.core.context;
import org.springframework.security.core.Authentication;
import java.io.Serializable;
public interface SecurityContext extends Serializable {
    Authentication getAuthentication();
void setAuthentication(Authentication authentication);
}
```

The entire SecurityContextHolder reference is on GitHub at https://github. com/spring-projects/spring-security/blob/master/core/src/main/java/org/ springframework/security/core/context/SecurityContext.java.

Listing 4-5. SecurityContextHolder Class

```
package org.springframework.security.core.context;
import org.springframework.util.ReflectionUtils;
import java.lang.reflect.Constructor;
public class SecurityContextHolder {
public static final String MODE_THREADLOCAL = "MODE_THREADLOCAL";
public static final String
  MODE_INHERITABLETHREADLOCAL = "MODE_INHERITABLETHREADLOCAL";
public static final String MODE_GLOBAL = "MODE_GLOBAL";
```

```java
public static final String SYSTEM_PROPERTY = "spring.security.strategy";
private static String strategyName = System.getProperty(SYSTEM_PROPERTY);
private static SecurityContextHolderStrategy strategy;
private static int initializeCount = 0;
static {
initialize();
    }
public static void clearContext() {
strategy.clearContext();
    }
public static SecurityContext getContext() {
return strategy.getContext();
    }
public static int getInitializeCount() {
return initializeCount;
    }
private static void initialize() {
if ((strategyName == null) || "".equals(strategyName)) {
strategyName = MODE_THREADLOCAL;
        }
if (strategyName.equals(MODE_THREADLOCAL)) {
strategy = new ThreadLocalSecurityContextHolderStrategy();
        } else if (strategyName.equals(MODE_INHERITABLETHREADLOCAL)) {
strategy = new InheritableThreadLocalSecurityContextHolderStrategy();
        } else if (strategyName.equals(MODE_GLOBAL)) {
strategy = new GlobalSecurityContextHolderStrategy();
        } else {
try {
            Class<?> clazz = Class.forName(strategyName);
            Constructor<?> customStrategy = clazz.getConstructor();
strategy = (SecurityContextHolderStrategy) customStrategy.newInstance();
            } catch (Exception ex) {
ReflectionUtils.handleReflectionException(ex);
            }
        }
```

```
initializeCount++;
    }
public static void setContext(SecurityContext context) {
strategy.setContext(context);
    }
public static void setStrategyName(String strategyName) {
SecurityContextHolder.strategyName = strategyName;
initialize();
    }
public static SecurityContextHolderStrategy getContextHolderStrategy() {
return strategy;
    }
public static SecurityContext createEmptyContext() {
return strategy.createEmptyContext();
    }
public String toString() {
        return "SecurityContextHolder[strategy='" + strategyName + "';
        initializeCount=" + initializeCount + "]";
    }
}
```

AuthenticationProvider

AuthenticationProvider is the main entry point for authenticating an Authentication object. This interface has only two methods, as Listing 4-6 shows. This is one of the major extension points of the framework, as you can tell by the many classes that currently extend this interface. Each implementing class deals with a particular external provider to authenticate against. So, if you come across a particular provider that is not supported and need to authenticate against it, you probably need to implement this interface with the required functionality. You see examples of this later in the book.

AuthenticationProvider (see Figure 4-15) is very similar to AuthenticationManager, but it has an extra method that can be used to call a query if it supports a given Authentication type, as shown here.

```java
public interface AuthenticationProvider {
        Authentication authenticate(Authentication authentication)
                        throws AuthenticationException;
        boolean supports(Class<?> authentication);
}
```

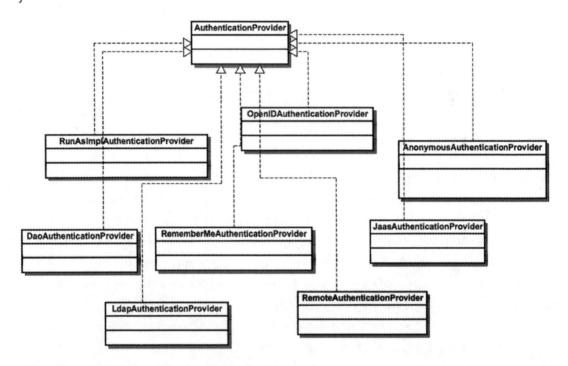

Figure 4-15. *AuthenticationProvider hierarchy*

Here are some of the existing providers that come with the framework.

CasAuthenticationProvider

JaasAuthenticationProvider

DaoAuthenticationProvider

RememberMeAuthenticationProvider

LdapAuthenticationProvider

The entire AuthenticationProvider reference is on GitHub at https://github.
com/spring-projects/spring-security/blob/master/core/src/main/java/org/
springframework/security/authentication/AuthenticationProvider.java.

Listing 4-6. AuthenticationProvider Interface

```
package org.springframework.security.authentication;
import org.springframework.security.core.Authentication;
import org.springframework.security.core.AuthenticationException;
public interface AuthenticationProvider {
    Authentication authenticate(Authentication authentication) throws
    AuthenticationException;
boolean supports(Class<?> authentication);
}
```

AccessDecisionManager

AccessDecisionManager is the class in charge of deciding whether a particular Authentication object is allowed or not allowed to access a particular resource. In its main implementations, it delegates to AccessDecisionVoter objects, which compare the GrantedAuthorities in the Authentication object against the ConfigAttribute(s) required by the resource accessed, deciding whether or not access should be granted. They emit their vote to allow access or not. The AccessDecisionManager implementations consider the voters' output and apply a determined strategy on whether or not to grant access. Voters, however, also can abstain from voting.

The AccessDecisionManager interface can be seen in Listing 4-7. Its UML class diagram is shown in Figure 4-16.

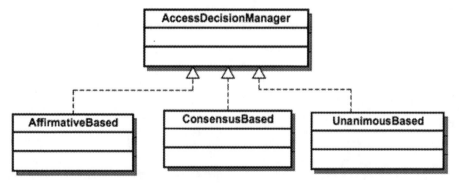

Figure 4-16. *AccessDecisionManager hierarchy*

The entire AccessDecisionManager reference is on GitHub at https://github.
com/spring-projects/spring-security/blob/master/core/src/main/java/org/
springframework/security/access/AccessDecisionManager.java.

Listing 4-7. AccessDecisionManager

```
package org.springframework.security.access;
import java.util.Collection;
import org.springframework.security.authentication.
InsufficientAuthenticationException;
import org.springframework.security.core.Authentication;
public interface AccessDecisionManager {
void decide(Authentication authentication, Object object,
Collection<ConfigAttribute> configAttributes)
throws AccessDeniedException, InsufficientAuthenticationException;
boolean supports(ConfigAttribute attribute);
boolean supports(Class<?> clazz);
}
```

The current AccessDecisionManager implementations delegate to voters, but they
work slightly differently. The current voters, described in the following sections, are
defined in the package org.springframework.security.access.vote.

More information about AccessDecisionManager is at https://docs.spring.io/
spring-security/reference/servlet/authorization/architecture.html#authz-
access-decision-manager.

AffirmativeBased

This access decision manager calls all its configured voters, and if any of them vote that
access should be granted, this is enough for the access decision manager to allow access
to the secured resource. If no voters grant access or at least one votes not to grant it, the
access decision manager throws an AccessDeniedException denying access. If there
are only abstaining voters, a decision is made based on the AccessDecisionManager's
instance variable allowIfAllAbstainDecisions, which is a Boolean that defaults to
false, determining whether access should be granted or not when all voters abstain.

ConsensusBased

This access decision manager implementation calls all its configured voters to decide
to either grant or deny access to a resource. The difference with the AffirmativeBased
decision manager is that the ConsensusBased decision manager decides to grant access
only if more voters grant access than voters deny it. So the majority wins in this case. If
there are the same number of granting voters as denying voters, the value of the instance
variable allowIfEqualGrantedDeniedDecisions is used to decide. This variable's value
is true by default, and access is granted. When all voters abstain, the access decision is
decided the same way as it is for the AffirmativeBased manager.

UnanimousBased

As you probably guessed, this access decision manager grants access to the resource
only if all the configured voters vote to allow access to the resource. If any voter votes to
deny the access, the AccessDeniedException is thrown. The "all abstain" case is handled
the same way as with the other implementations of AccessDecisionManager.

AccessDecisionVoter

This discussion of the AccessDecisionManager and its current implementations should
have clarified the importance of the Access Decision Voters, because they are the ones,
working as a team, who ultimately determine if a particular Authentication object has
enough privileges to access a particular resource.

The org.springframework.security.access.AccessDecisionVoter interface is
very simple as shown in Listing 4-8.

The main method is vote, and as can be deduced from the interface, it return one of
three possible responses (ACCESS_GRANTED, ACCES_ABSTAIN, ACCESS_DENIED), depending
on whether the required conditions are satisfied.

The satisfaction or not of the conditions is given by analyzing the Authentication
object's rights against the required resource. In practice, this means that the
Authentication's authorities are compared against the resource's security attributes
looking for matches.

The following are the current `AccessDecisionVoter` implementations.

- `org.springframework.security.access.annotation.Jsr250Voter` votes on resources secured with JSR 250 annotations—namely, `DenyAll`, `PermitAll,` and `RolesAllowed`. Their names are very descriptive. `DenyAll` won't allow access to the resource, independent of the security information carried by the `Authentication` object trying to access it. `PermitAll` allow access to everyone, regardless of what roles they have. The `RolesAllowed` annotation can be configured with a series of roles. If an `Authentication` object tries to access the resource, it must have one of the roles configured in the `RolesAllowed` annotation to get access granted by this voter.

- `org.springframework.security.access.prepost.` `PreInvocationAuthorizationAdviceVoter` votes on resources with expression configurations based on `@PreFilter` and `@` `PreAuthorize` annotations. `@PreFilter` and `@PreAuthorize` annotations support a `value` attribute with a SpEL expression. The `PreInvocationAuthorizationAdviceVoter` is in charge of evaluating the SpEL expressions (of course with the help of Spring's SpEL evaluation mechanism) provided in these annotations. SpEL expressions are discussed throughout this book so this concept becomes clearer as the book advances.

- `org.springframework.security.access.vote.AbstractAclVoter`: This is the abstract class with the skeleton to write voters dealing with domain ACL rules so that other implementing class builds on its functionality to add voting behavior. Currently, it is implemented in `AclEntryVoter`, which votes on users' permissions on domain objects. This voter is covered in Chapter 7.

- `org.springframework.security.access.vote.AuthenticatedVoter` votes whenever a `ConfigAttribute referencing` any of the three possible levels of authentication is present on the secured resource. The three levels are `IS_AUTHENTICATED_FULLY`, `IS_AUTHENTICATED_ REMEMBERED`, and `IS_AUTHENTICATED_ANONYMOUSLY`. The voter emits a positive vote if the `Authentication` object's authentication level

matches (or is a stronger level in the hierarchy IS_AUTHENTICATED_
FULLY > IS_AUTHENTICATED_REMEMBERED > IS_AUTHENTICATED_
ANONYMOUSLY) the authentication level configured in the resource.

- org.springframework.security.access.vote.RoleVoter is
perhaps the most commonly used voter of them all. This voter,
by default, can vote on resources that have ConfigAttribute(s)
containing security metadata starting with the prefix ROLE_ (which
can be overridden). When an Authentication object tries to access
the resource, its GrantedAuthorities are matched against the
relevant ConfigAttributes. If there is a match, access is granted. If
there isn't, access is denied.

- org.springframework.security.access.expression.
WebExpressionVoter: This is the voter in charge of evaluating SpEL
expressions in the context of web requests in the filter chain—
expressions like 'hasRole' in the <intercept-url> element. To use
this voter and support SpEL expressions in web security, the use-
expressions="true" attribute must be added to the <http> element.

The voters model is yet another one in the framework open for extension and
customization. You can easily create your own implementation and add it to the
framework. You see how to do this in Chapter 8.

The entire AccessDecisionVoter reference is on GitHub at https://github.
com/spring-projects/spring-security/blob/master/core/src/main/java/org/
springframework/security/access/AccessDecisionVoter.java.

Listing 4-8. AccessDecisionVoter Interface

```
package org.springframework.security.access;
import java.util.Collection;
import org.springframework.security.core.Authentication;
public interface AccessDecisionVoter<S> {
int ACCESS_GRANTED = 1;
int ACCESS_ABSTAIN = 0;
int ACCESS_DENIED = -1;
boolean supports(ConfigAttribute attribute);
boolean supports(Class<?> clazz);
```

```
int vote(Authentication authentication, S object,
Collection<ConfigAttribute> attributes);
}
```

UserDetailsService and AuthenticationUserDetailsService

The interface org.springframework.security.core.userdetails.
UserDetailsService is in charge of loading the user information from the underlying
user store (in-memory, database, and so on) when an authentication request arrives in
the application. UserDetailsService uses the provided user name to look up the rest of
the required user data from the datastore. It defines just one method, as shown in
Listing 4-9. The hierarchy is shown in Figure 4-17.

Listing 4-9. UserDetailsServicepackage org.springframework.security.core.
userdetails

```
public interface UserDetailsService {
  UserDetails loadUserByUsername(String username)
throws  UsernameNotFoundException;
}
```

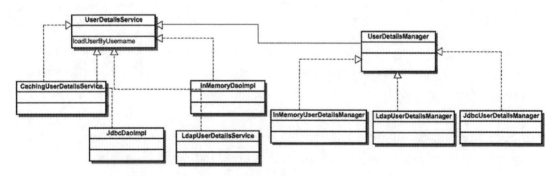

Figure 4-17. *UserDetailsService hierarchy*

The interface org.springframework.security.core.userdetails.
AuthenticationUserDetailsService is more generic. It allows you to retrieve a
UserDetails using an Authentication object instead of a user name String, making
it more flexible to implement. An implementation of AuthenticationUserDetailsService
(UserDetailsByNameServiceWrapper) simply delegates to a UserDetailsService
extracting the user name from the Authentication object.

113

Listing 4-10 shows the `AuthenticationUserDetailsService` interface. The two main strategies (AuthenticationUserDetailsService and UserDetailsService) are used to retrieve user information when attempting authentication. They are usually called from the particular `AuthenticationProvider` used in the application. For example, the `CasAuthenticationProvider` delegate to an `AuthenticationUserDetailsService` to obtain the user details, while the `DaoAuthenticationProvider` delegates directly to a `UserDetailsService`. Some other providers don't use a user details service of any kind (for example, `JaasAuthenticationProvider` uses its own mechanism to retrieve the principal from a `javax.security.auth.login.LoginContext`), and some others use a completely custom one (for example, `LdapAuthenticationProvider` uses a `UserDetailsContextMapper`).

Listing 4-10. AuthenticationUserDetailsService

```
package org.springframework.security.core.userdetails;
  public interface AuthenticationUserDetailsService<T extends
  Authentication> {
  UserDetails loadUserDetails(T token) throws UsernameNotFoundException;
}
```

UserDetails

The interface `org.springframework.security.core.userdetails.UserDetails` object is the main abstraction in the system, and it's used to represent a full user in the context of Spring Security. It can also be accessed later in the system from any point with access to `SecurityContext`. Normally, developers implement this interface to store user details they need or want (like email, telephone, address, and so on). Later, they can access this information, which is encapsulated in the `Authentication` object, and they can be obtained by calling the `getPrincipal` method on it.

Some of the current `UserDetailsService` (for example, `InMemoryUserDetailsManager`) implementations use the `org.springframework.security.core.userdetails.User` class, available in the framework's core, as the `UserDetails` implementation returned by the method `loadUserByUsername`. However, this is another of those configurable points of the framework, and you can easily create your own `UserDetails implementation` and use that in your application. Listing 4-11 shows the `UserDetails` interface.

Listing 4-11. UserDetails Interface

```
package org.springframework.security.core.userdetails;
import org.springframework.security.core.Authentication;
import org.springframework.security.core.GrantedAuthority;
import java.io.Serializable;
import java.util.Collection;
public interface UserDetails extends Serializable {
Collection<? extends GrantedAuthority> getAuthorities();
String getPassword();
String getUsername();
boolean isAccountNonExpired();
boolean isAccountNonLocked();
boolean isCredentialsNonExpired();
boolean isEnabled();
}
```

ACL

The ACL is the module in charge of securing your application at the individual domain object level with a fine level of granularity. This means assigning an ID to each domain object in your application and creating a relationship between these objects and the different users of the application. These relationships determine whether or not a determined user is allowed access to a particular domain. The ACL model offers a fine-grained, access-level configuration to define different rules for accessing the objects depending on who is trying to access it. (For example, a user might be allowed read access while another user have write/read access over the same domain object.)

The current support for ACLs is configured to get the configuration rules from a relational database. The data definition language (DDL) for configuring the database comes with the framework and is in the ACL module.

ACL security is covered in Chapter 7.

JSP Taglib

If you are working to secure a Java web application, the `taglib` component of the framework is the one you use to hide or show certain elements in your pages according to your users' permissions.

The tags are simple to use and, at the same time, very convenient for making a more usable web site. They help you adapt the UI of your application on a per-user (or more commonly, per-role) basis.

Good Design and Patterns in Spring Security

We said it before but repeat it here: One of the great aspects of working with open source software is that you can (and *should*) look at the source code and understand the software at a new, deeper level. Also, you can look at how the software is built, what is good, and what is bad (at least by your own subjective standards) and learn how other developers work. This can greatly impact the way you work, because you might discover a way of doing things that you couldn't have learned on your own.

The code for Spring Security is publicly available on GitHub at `https://github.com/spring-projects/spring-security`.

Sometimes, you find things you don't like, but that is also good. You can learn from other people's mistakes as much as from their successes.

Spring in general and Spring Security in particular have achieved something invaluable in the Java development space—that is, they can make us better developers even without our noticing it. For instance, we often ask ourselves, "How many people would be using a template pattern for accessing databases if they weren't using Spring, instead of a more awkward DB access layer?" or "How many people would be just programming against implementation classes all the time, creating unnecessary coupling if it wasn't for Spring's DI support?" or "How many people would have cross-cutting concerns, like transactions, all over their code base if it wasn't for how easily Spring brings AOP into the development process?"

We think helping good practices almost without noticing is a great Spring achievement. It won't create great developers by itself, but it helps the average developer not make mistakes they might make if they didn't have the support of the framework and its principles to adhere to.

As you might see from the description of the main components of the framework, Spring Security itself is built with good design principles and patterns in mind. Let's briefly look at some of the things we find interesting in the framework, and from which you can learn.

This section won't help you do more with Spring Security, but it serves as a way to appreciate the good work done in constructing this fantastic framework.

Strategy Pattern

A big part of the pluggability and modularity of the framework is achieved thanks
to the wide use of the Strategy pattern. You can find it, for example, in the type
of `SecurityContext` to be used, the `AuthenticationProvider` hierarchy, the
`AccessDecisionVoters`, and many other elements. Covering design patterns is outside
the scope of this book. But as a reminder of the strategy pattern's power, we leave you
with this definition from Wikipedia: "The strategy pattern defines a family of algorithms,
encapsulates each one, and makes them interchangeable. Strategy lets the algorithm
vary independently from clients that use it."

That definition shows a great deal of the power of working with interfaces. You
can have different implementations of the same interface and pass any of them to a
client class for doing different kinds of work. The client classes don't need to know or
care about the implementation details they are working with. Knowing the interface or
contract is enough to leverage its job.

Decorator Pattern

Built into Spring's core AOP framework, you can find the Decorator pattern—mostly
in the way that your annotated business classes and methods get security constraints
applied to them. Basically, your objects have only certain meta information related
to the security constraints that should be applied to them, and then by some "Spring
magic" they get wrapped with security handling. Listing 4-12 shows the invoke method
of `MethodSecurityInterceptor`. You can see how the objects are decorated with
prefunctionality and postfunctionality surrounding the actual method's invocation.

Listing 4-12. MethodSecurityInterceptor's Invoke Method

```
public Object invoke(MethodInvocation mi) throws Throwable {
InterceptorStatusToken token = super.beforeInvocation(mi);
        Object result = mi.proceed();
returnsuper.afterInvocation(token, result);
    }
```

SRP

Spring Security's code seems to take very seriously the single-responsibility principle. There are many examples of it around the framework, because any object you choose seems to have one and only one responsibility. For example, the `AuthenticationProvider` deals only with the general concern of authenticating a principal with its credentials in the system. The `SecurityInterceptor` is simply in charge of intercepting the requests and delegates all security-checking logic to collaborating objects. A lot more examples like this can be extracted from the framework.

DI

Again, this is built into the Spring Framework itself, and of course as everything in the Spring architecture, it is also inherited by the rest of the Spring projects, including Spring Security. Dependency injection (DI) is one of Spring's most important features. Almost every component in Spring Security is configured through dependency injection. The `AccessDecisionManager` is injected into the `AbstractSecurityInterceptor`, and `AccessDecisionVoter` implementations are injected into the `AccessDecisionManager`. And like this, most of the framework is built by composing components together through dependency injection.

Summary

This was a complex chapter, but going through the inner workings of a software tool is the best way to understand it and take advantage of it. And that is what you did. You got an in-depth explanation of Spring Security's architecture, major components, and how it works from the inside.

You should now understand how the XML namespace works, how AOP fits into the framework, and how, in general, the servlet filter functionality is used to enforce web-level security.

We demystified the "Spring magic" by going through all the components that help you add security to your applications in a seemingly simple way.

You looked at some code snippets from the framework itself to better appreciate its work and better understand why things work the way they do.

You also studied the modularity inherent in the framework and saw how it helps to create flexible and extensible software.

Even with all that is covered in this chapter, this was an introduction and a reference to have in hand when you read the upcoming chapters and you start looking at the options to secure your applications. From now on, you will understand where everything fits in the framework and how the different components link.

In the next chapter, you start developing an example application. You begin with a simple web application and see how to secure it. You will use your knowledge of the framework to tweak the configuration and test different ways of implementing security at the web level.

CHAPTER 5

Web Security

This chapter shows how to build a Java web application using Spring Security 6 in Spring Boot 3. You see the inner workings of the security filter chain and the different metadata options at your disposal to define security constraints in your application.

Let's build your Java web application using Spring Security 6 in Spring Boot 3, and please make sure you're using Java 17+, as the baseline for Spring Boot 3 and Spring Security 6 is now Java 17. Java 20 is used in this demo.

The following steps build the simple Spring Security Maven web application project.

1. Create a new Spring Security Spring Boot 3 project, including Spring Security and Spring Web dependencies, using the start. spring.io Spring Initializr website.

2. Configure the users and roles that will be part of the system.

3. Configure the URLs that you want to secure.

4. Create all needed Java and web files.

5. Run the Spring Security 6 project using the external Tomcat Server 10.

First, you create a new Spring project named pss01_Security using the Spring Initializr web tool at https://start.spring.io/, as shown in Figure 5-1.

Java 20, Maven, and JAR, with Spring Security and Web, are dependencies in this example.

Once the project is generated, unzip the file and open the project with your IDE tool.

© Massimo Nardone, Carlo Scarioni 2024
M. Nardone and C. Scarioni, *Pro Spring Security*, https://doi.org/10.1007/979-8-8688-0035-1_5

Figure 5-1. *New Spring project using Spring Initializr*

The new project files and the pss01_Security project structure are shown in Figure 5-2.

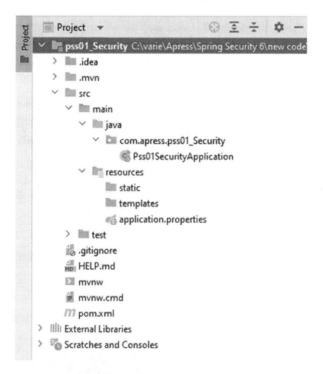

Figure 5-2. *New Spring project structure*

Note   Implementing the Spring Security in a Spring application using XML- or Java-based configurations is possible. This chapter uses Java configuration for your Spring Security web application since it is hardly suggested to use XML configuration as minimum as possible.

If Spring Security is in the classpath, Spring Boot automatically secures all HTTP endpoints with Basic authentication, generating a security password to be used as a credential with "user" as the username, as shown in Figure 5-3.

Figure 5-3. Running the new Spring project

This means that if you type **localhost:8080**, Spring requires that you enter **user** as the username and **e6fd5a38-b7a8-4d55-b47a-9ece6e3341fa** as the password to log in, as shown in Figure 5-4.

Figure 5-4. Secure Spring application with login page

Since this web application is based on Spring MVC, you need to configure Spring MVC and set up view controllers to expose the HTML templates that you will create later.

Let's create a simple controller to get a simple "Welcome to Spring Security 6" message when entering the right login information, as shown in Listing 5-1.

Listing 5-1. A Simple UserController Java Class

```
package com.apress.pss01_Security;

import org.springframework.web.bind.annotation.GetMapping;
import org.springframework.web.bind.annotation.RestController;

@RestController

public class UserController {
    @GetMapping ("/welcome")

    public String welcome() {
        return "Welcome to Spring Security 6";
    }
}
```

If you enter the right username and password, you get the "Welcome to Spring Security 6" message, as shown in Figure 5-5.

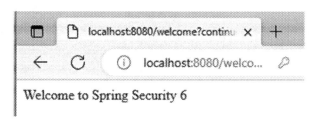

Figure 5-5. *Successful login message*

Let's add some more logic to our code.

First, let's look at the new pom.xml file generated when creating the new Spring Boot 3 and Spring Security 6 projects, as shown in Listing 5-2.

Listing 5-2. pom.xml

```xml
<?xml version="1.0" encoding="UTF-8"?>
<project xmlns="http://maven.apache.org/POM/4.0.0"
xmlns:xsi="http://www.w3.org/2001/XMLSchema-instance"
    xsi:schemaLocation="http://maven.apache.org/POM/4.0.0
    https://maven.apache.org/xsd/maven-4.0.0.xsd">
    <modelVersion>4.0.0</modelVersion>
    <parent>
        <groupId>org.springframework.boot</groupId>
        <artifactId>spring-boot-starter-parent</artifactId>
        <version>3.1.0</version>
        <relativePath/> <!-- lookup parent from repository -->
    </parent>
    <groupId>com.apress</groupId>
    <artifactId>pss01_security</artifactId>
    <version>0.0.1-SNAPSHOT</version>
    <name>pss01_security</name>
    <description>Spring Security demo</description>
    <properties>
        <java.version>20</java.version>
    </properties>
    <dependencies>
        <dependency>
            <groupId>org.springframework.boot</groupId>
            <artifactId>spring-boot-starter-security</artifactId>
        </dependency>
        <dependency>
            <groupId>org.springframework.boot</groupId>
            <artifactId>spring-boot-starter-web</artifactId>
        </dependency>
        <dependency>
            <groupId>org.springframework.boot</groupId>
            <artifactId>spring-boot-starter-test</artifactId>
            <scope>test</scope>
        </dependency>
```

```
<dependency>
    <groupId>org.springframework.security</groupId>
    <artifactId>spring-security-test</artifactId>
    <scope>test</scope>
</dependency>
<dependency>
<groupId>org.thymeleaf.extras</groupId>
<artifactId>thymeleaf-extras-springsecurity6</artifactId>
<version>3.1.1.RELEASE</version>
</dependency>
  </dependencies>
```

```
</project>
```

We used Thymeleaf, a Java template engine for processing and creating HTML, XML, CSS, JavaScript, and plain text.

Configuring the new Spring Security 6 Project

To activate Spring Security web project configuration in your Maven web application, you need to configure a particular servlet filter that takes care of preprocessing and postprocessing the requests and managing the required security constraints.

The next example defines two users, but only the "Admin" role is authorized to access the secured resource called authenticated.html.

Let's start building the Spring Security Maven web application.

First, make sure that all the tools and directories are created as described previously.

Next, create simple HTML files under a new project directory called `src/main/resources/templates/`.

Your project utilizes two HTML pages.

- `welcome.html`, which is the starting welcome web page of the project

- `authenticated.html`, which is the admin web page to access when the user successfully logs in

The `welcome.html` page is shown in Listing 5-3.

Listing 5-3. welcome.html

```
<!DOCTYPE html>
<html xmlns="http://www.w3.org/1999/xhtml"
xmlns:th="https://www.thymeleaf.org">
<html lang="en">
<head>
    <meta http-equiv="Content-Type" content="text/html;
    charset=ISO-8859-1">
    <title>Spring Security 6 authentication example!</title>
</head>
<body>

<div th:if="${param.error}">
    Invalid username and password.
</div>
<div th:if="${param.logout}">
    You have been logged out.
</div>

<h2>Welcome to Spring Security 6 authentication example!</h2>

<p>Click <a th:href="@{/authenticated}">here</a> to get authenticated!</p>
</body>
</html>
```

The welcome.html page only displays a welcoming message and provide the link to the authenticated page, /authenticated.

Let's now create the authenticated.html page; see Listing 5-4.

Listing 5-4. authenticated.html

```
<!DOCTYPE html>
<html xmlns="http://www.w3.org/1999/xhtml" xmlns:th="https://www.
thymeleaf.org"
    xmlns:sec="https://www.thymeleaf.org/thymeleaf-extras-
    springsecurity6">
```

```
<head>
    <title>Spring Security 6 authentication example</title>
</head>
<body>
<h2>Welcome to Spring Security 6 authentication example!</h2>
<h2 th:inline="text">You are an authenticated user: <span th:remove="tag"
sec:authentication="name">thymeleaf</span>!</h2>

<p>click <a th:href="@{/logout}">here</a> to logout!!</p>

</body>
</html>
```

Next, you need to define the Java classes needed for your example.

- Under package controller: `UserController`

- Under package configuration: `SecurityConfiguration`

Let's create the two Java packages where your Java classes are located.

- package `com.apress.pss01_security.configuration`

- package `com.apress.pss01_security.controller;`

Create the `UserController` Java class under the `com.apress.pss01_security.controller` package, as shown in Listing 5-5.

Listing 5-5. UserController Java Class

```
package com.apress.pss01_security.controller;

import org.springframework.stereotype.Controller;
import org.springframework.ui.ModelMap;
import org.springframework.web.bind.annotation.GetMapping;

@Controller
public class UserController {

    @GetMapping("/")
    public String homePage() {
        return "welcome";
    }
```

```
    @GetMapping("/welcome")
    public String welcomePage() {
        return "welcome";
    }

    @GetMapping ("/authenticated")
    public String AuthenticatedPage() {
        return "authenticated";
    }

    @GetMapping ("/logout")
    public String logoutPage() {
    return "redirect:/welcome";
    }
}
```

Note that, for web security, it doesn't matter if you use a Spring MVC controller as you do here, if you use simple servlets as you did in Chapter 3, or if you use any other servlet-based framework for developing your application. Remember that, at the core, the web part of Spring Security attaches itself to the standard Java servlet filter architecture. So, if your application uses servlets and filters, you can leverage Spring Security's web support.

Since Spring Framework 4.3, there are new HTTP mapping annotations based on @RequestMapping.

- @GetMapping

- @PostMapping

- @PutMapping

- @DeleteMapping

- @PatchMapping

For instance, @GetMapping is a specialized version of the @RequestMapping annotation, which acts as a shortcut for @RequestMapping(method = RequestMethod. GET). @GetMapping annotated methods to handle the HTTP GET requests matched with a certain given URI expression.

As all developers know, MVC applications aren't service-oriented, which means a view resolver will render the final views based on data received from the controller.

RESTful applications are designed to be service-oriented and return raw data, generally JSON/XML. Since these applications don't do any view rendering, there are no view resolvers. The controller is typically expected to send data directly via the HTTP response.

The UserController Java class, via Spring MVC, does the following.

- Intercepts any incoming request

- Converts the payload of the request to the internal structure of the data

- Sends the data to model for any needed further processing

- Gets processed data from the model, and advances it to the view for rendering

In our example, the UserController Java class returns a "welcome" view. The view resolver tries to resolve the welcome.html page in the templates folder.

Let's analyze our next Java class, `SecurityConfiguration`.

Chapter 2 explained how to enable Spring Security 6 using the annotation named @EnableWebSecurity without using the WebSecurityConfigurerAdapter class, and introduced in that chapter the Java Spring Security configuration class named `SecurityConfiguration`, which utilizes the @EnableWebSecurity annotation to help configure Spring Security–related beans, such as WebSecurityConfigurer or SecurityFilterChain.

The following describes what `SecurityConfiguration` does in this example.

- It creates two demo in-memory users via `UserDetailsService` named "user" and "admin," which are authorized to access a secure resource of the project so that only the admin can access the secured "Authenticated" web resource.

- It uses BCryptPasswordEncoder to encode the user passwords for added security.

- It configures the SecurityFilterChain bean with the username/password Basic authentication mechanism to authenticate the users.

Listing 5-6 shows the SecurityConfiguration Java class.

Listing 5-6. SecurityConfiguration.java

```java
package com.apress.pss01_security.configuration;

import org.springframework.context.annotation.Bean;
import org.springframework.context.annotation.Configuration;
import org.springframework.security.config.Customizer;
import org.springframework.security.config.annotation.web.builders.
HttpSecurity;
import org.springframework.security.config.annotation.web.configuration.
EnableWebSecurity;
import org.springframework.security.core.userdetails.User;
import org.springframework.security.core.userdetails.UserDetails;
import org.springframework.security.core.userdetails.UserDetailsService;
import org.springframework.security.crypto.bcrypt.BCryptPasswordEncoder;
import org.springframework.security.crypto.password.PasswordEncoder;
import org.springframework.security.provisioning.
InMemoryUserDetailsManager;
import org.springframework.security.web.SecurityFilterChain;

@Configuration
@EnableWebSecurity

public class SecurityConfiguration {

    @Bean
    public SecurityFilterChain filterChain1(HttpSecurity http) throws
    Exception {
        http
                .authorizeHttpRequests((authorize) -> authorize
                        .requestMatchers("/", "/welcome").permitAll()
                        .requestMatchers("/authenticated").hasRole("ADMIN")
                        .anyRequest().denyAll()
                )
                .csrf(Customizer.withDefaults())
                .formLogin(withDefaults())
```

```
            .logout((logout) -> logout
                    .logoutSuccessUrl("/welcome")
                    .deleteCookies("JSESSIONID")
                    .invalidateHttpSession(true)
                    .permitAll()
            );

        return http.build();
    }

    @Bean
    public UserDetailsService userDetailsService(){

        UserDetails user = User.builder()
                .username("user")
                .password(passwordEncoder().encode("userpassw"))
                .roles("USER")
                .build();

        UserDetails admin = User.builder()
                .username("admin")
                .password(passwordEncoder().encode("adminpassw"))
                .roles("ADMIN")
                .build();

        return new InMemoryUserDetailsManager(user, admin);
    }

    @Bean
    public static PasswordEncoder passwordEncoder(){
        return new BCryptPasswordEncoder();
    }
}
```

Spring Security allows you to model your authorization at the request level. In the example, the /welcome page is permitted to all pages under /admin, requiring one authority, while all other pages require authentication.

By default, Spring Security requires that every request be authenticated. That said, whenever you use an HttpSecurity instance, you must declare your authorization rules.

Whenever you have an HttpSecurity instance, you should at least do the following.

```
http
    .authorizeHttpRequests((authorize) -> authorize
        .anyRequest().authenticated()
    )
```

In our example, the following applies.

- "/" and "/welcome" are permitted to all.

- "/authenticated" can only be accessed when presenting a user with the "Admin" role via the .hasRole("ADMIN") declaration.

- .logout((logout) -> logout is permitted to all and, if utilized, requests the welcome.html page.

More information is at `https://docs.spring.io/spring-security/reference/servlet/authorization/authorize-http-requests.html`.

In an application where end users can log in, it is important to consider how to protect against cross-site request forgery (CSRF). Spring Security protects against CSRF attacks by default for unsafe HTTP methods, such as a POST request, so no additional code is necessary.

In a CSRF attack, a hacker can modify the state of any HTTP method (GET or POST), redirecting the client, for instance, by clicking a modified link to a non-secure web page with the result of stealing a user's sensitive information.

Let's look at CSRF and how to prevent CSRF attacks using Spring Security. The following are common CSRF attacks.

- An HTTP GET request convinces the victim to click a fake GET link to get sensitive information (username/password, etc.)

- An HTTP POST request is the same as GET but uses the POST method.

To use the Spring Security CSRF protection, you must ensure the right HTTP methods (PATCH, POST, PUT, DELETE, etc.) can modify the state.

As of Spring Security 6.0.1 and Spring Boot 3.0.2, the method CookieCsrfTokenRepository.saveToken only gets called when the CsrfFilter calls deferredCsrfToken.get(), which only gets called on POST, PUT, PATCH, and DELETE methods. Unfortunately, the client must expect a failure on the first request under the current implementation. Under previous versions of Spring Security, you could count on the token's cookie being included in the response to GET, HEAD, or OPTIONS requests.

For more information, refer to

`https://docs.spring.io/spring-security/reference/6.1-SNAPSHOT/servlet/exploits/csrf.html`

In the example, the default configuration is specified explicitly using `.csrf(Customizer.withDefaults())`. The default form login is used by adding line `.formLogin(withDefaults());`.

The structure of your new Spring Security 6 project should look like Figure 5-6.

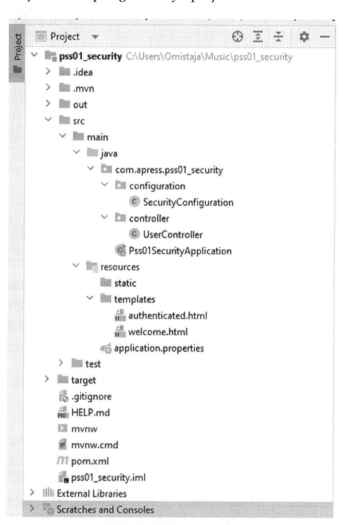

Figure 5-6. *New Spring Security 6 in Boot 3 project structure*

Next, build and run the Spring Security 6 project.

You can now build the project, deploy the JAR file, start the application running on the stand-alone Tomcat Server 10, and deploy the JAR file automatically.

Your application is deployed successfully. Open the web browser and type the following link: `http://localhost:8080/welcome/`. The outcome is shown in Figure 5-7.

Figure 5-7. *Browsing the new Spring Security project*

You can now access the security `authenticated.html` by clicking the Login link. The outcome is shown in Figure 5-8.

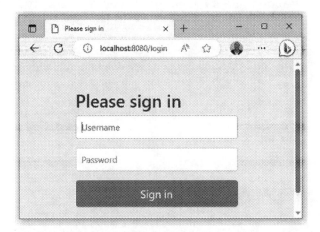

Figure 5-8. *Accessing the Spring Security login web page*

Now, if you access with bad credentials, such as without having the "ADMIN" role, you receive an error message like the one in Figure 5-9.

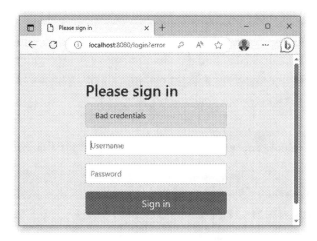

Figure 5-9. *Accessing with wrong login credentials*

As you can see, Spring Security directly produces the login error and reminds the user that the credentials provided are incorrect.

If you next provide the right user admin/adminpassw credentials for the "Admin" role, you will receive the content defined in the `authenticated.html` page, as shown in Figure 5-10.

Figure 5-10. *Accessing with the right admin credentials*

If you log out, you see the result shown in Figure 5-11 and are redirected to the Welcome page.

Figure 5-11. *Logout page*

When you make the HTTP request to the configured URL, and after your servlet container deals with it, the request lands in the DelegatingFilterProxy, which delegates the processing to the security FilterChainProxy.

In general, Spring Security utilizes a lot of filters. The HTTP request filter is used to do the following.

- Intercept the request.

- Detect authentication (or absence of).

- Redirect to the authentication entry point.

- Pass the request to the authorization service.

- Send the request to the servlet or throw a security exception.

In Spring Security 6, the most important filters are the following.

- ForceEagerSessionCreationFilter

- ChannelProcessingFilter

- WebAsyncManagerIntegrationFilter

- SecurityContextPersistenceFilter

- HeaderWriterFilter

- CorsFilter

- CsrfFilter

- LogoutFilter

- OAuth2AuthorizationRequestRedirectFilter

- Saml2WebSsoAuthenticationRequestFilter

- X509AuthenticationFilter

- AbstractPreAuthenticatedProcessingFilter

- CasAuthenticationFilter

- OAuth2LoginAuthenticationFilter

- Saml2WebSsoAuthenticationFilter

- UsernamePasswordAuthenticationFilter

- DefaultLoginPageGeneratingFilter

- DefaultLogoutPageGeneratingFilter

- ConcurrentSessionFilter

- DigestAuthenticationFilter

- BearerTokenAuthenticationFilter

- BasicAuthenticationFilter

- RequestCacheAwareFilter

- SecurityContextHolderAwareRequestFilter

- JaasApiIntegrationFilter

- RememberMeAuthenticationFilter

- AnonymousAuthenticationFilter

- OAuth2AuthorizationCodeGrantFilter

- SessionManagementFilter

- ExceptionTranslationFilter

- AuthorizationFilter

- SwitchUserFilter

The following are the most important Spring Security 6 filters.

- BasicAuthenticationFilter tries to authenticate the user with the header's username and password if it finds a Basic Auth HTTP header on the request.

- UsernamePasswordAuthenticationFilter tries to authenticate the user with those values if it finds a username/password request parameter/POST body.

- DefaultLoginPageGeneratingFilter generates a default login page when enabling Spring Security unless you don't explicitly disable that feature.

- DefaultLogoutPageGeneratingFilter generates a logout page unless you explicitly disable that feature.

- FilterSecurityInterceptor does the authorization.

Let's learn more about our example's Spring Security 6 filters.

The HTTP request and authentication processes and filters are explained in Chapter 4.

Let's see what happens when incorrect or correct credentials are provided when logging in. When the browser is redirecting and asks for /login, the following occurs, the process is the same as the first request until it reaches the DefaultLoginPageGeneratingFilter. At this point, the filter detects the request for /login and writes the login form's HTML data directly in the response object. Then, the response is rendered.

Now, try to log in with incorrect credentials. Let's follow the request through the framework to see what happens.

1. In the login form, type **admin** as the username and **adminpassw** as the password.

2. When the form is submitted, the filters are activated again in the same order. This time, however, when the request arrives at the UsernamePasswordAuthenticationFilter, the filter checks whether the request is for /login and sees that this is indeed the case. The filter extracts the username and password

authentication information from the HTTP request parameters username and password, respectively. With this information, it creates the UsernamePasswordAuthenticationToken Authentication object, which then sends it to the AuthenticationManager (or, more exactly, its default implementation, ProviderManager) for authentication.

3. DaoAuthenticationProvider is called from the ProviderManager with the Authentication object. The DaoAuthentication provider implements AuthenticationProvider, which uses a strategy of UserDetailsService to retrieve the users from whichever storage they live in. With your current configuration, it tries to find the username of the configured InMemoryUserDetailsManager (the implementation of UserDetailsService that maintains an in-memory user storage in a java.util.Map). Because no user has this username, the provider throws a UsernameNotFoundException exception.

4. The provider catches this exception and converts it into a BadCredentialsException to hide the fact that there is no such user in the application; instead, it treats the error as a common username-password combination error.

5. UsernamePasswordAuthenticationFilter catches the exception. This filter delegates to an instance of an implementation of AuthenticationFailureHandler, which in turn decides to redirect the response to /login?error. This way, the login form is displayed again in the browser with an error message.

Documentation on filters is at https://docs.spring.io/spring-security/ reference/6.1-SNAPSHOT/servlet/architecture.html#servlet-filters-review.

Restart the application and go to http:/localhost:8080/welcome, which triggers the login page. Type **admin** as the username and **adminpassw** as the password in the form. Then click the Login button.

*   The request follows the same filter journey as before. This time, InMemoryUserDetailsManager finds a user with the requested username and returns that to DaoAuthenticationProvider, which creates a successful Authentication object.

- After successful authentication,
  UsernamePasswordAuthenticationFilter delegates to an instance
  of SavedRequestAwareAuthenticationSuccessHandler, which looks
  for the original requested URL (/authenticated) in the session and
  redirects the response to that URL.

When http://localhost:8080/authenticated is requested, the request
works through the filter chain as in the previous cases. This time, though, you
already have a fully authenticated entity in the system. The request arrives in
FilterSecurityInterceptor.

- FilterSecurityInterceptor receives an access request to
  / authenticated. Then, it recovers the necessary credentials to
  access that URL (ROLE_ADMIN).

- The AffirmativeBased access-decision manager gets called and calls
  the RoleVoter voter. The voter evaluates the authenticated entity's
  authorities and compares them with the required credentials to
  access the resource. Because the voter finds a match (ROLE_ADMIN is
  in both the Authentication authorities and the resource's config
  attributes), it votes with an ACCESS_GRANTED vote.

- FilterSecurityInterceptor forwards the request to the next
  element in the request-handling chain, which, in this case, is Spring's
  DispatcherServlet.

- The request gets to the AdminController, which simply returns the
  authenticated page.

- This is the complete flow of the authentication and authorization
  process. Figure 5-12 shows this full interaction in a pseudo
  flow chart.

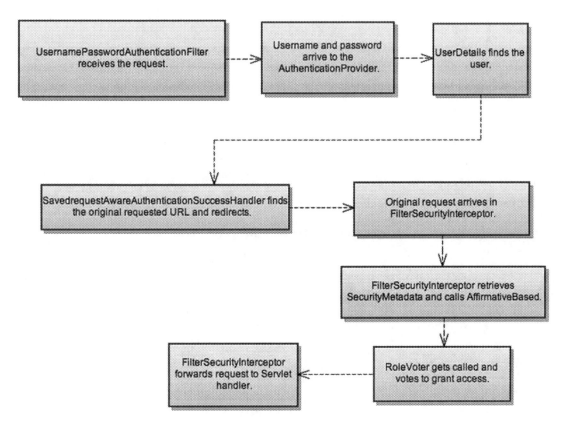

Figure 5-12. *Overall flow of a successful authentication and authorization process*

The Special URLs

From the preceding explanation, you can see that Spring Security's support for web security defines a few preconfigured URLs for you to use in your application. These URLs get special treatment in the framework. The following are the main ones.

- /login: This is the URL that Spring Security uses to show the login form for the application. The framework redirects to this URL when an authentication is needed, but it doesn't exist yet.

- /logout: The framework uses this URL to log out the currently logged-in user, invalidating the corresponding session and SecurityContext.

In the previous URLs, the first thing that comes to mind is how to configure your own login form in the application and, in general, how to customize the login process instead of using the default one. That is what we'll do next.

Note   /login replaced /j_spring_security_check in Spring Security 5.

Custom Login Form

The user authentication request to your application has been made via the http.authorizeRequests() method since Spring Security 5.

When you configure the http element via the http.authorizeHttpRequests () method, as you did before, Spring Security sets up a default login and logout process for you, including a login URL, login form, default URL after login, and other options. Basically, when Spring Security's context starts to load up, it finds that there is no custom login page URL configured, so it assumes the default one and creates a new instance of DefaultLoginPageGeneratingFilter that is added to the filter chain. This filter is the one that generates the login form for you.

If you want to configure your own form, you must do a few tasks. First, tell the framework to replace the default handling with your own. You define the following element as a child of the http.authorizeRequests() method in the SecurityConfiguration Java file.

formLogin((form) -> form

This element tells Spring Security to change its default login-handling mechanism on startup. DefaultLoginPageGeneratingFilter is no longer instantiated. Let's try the first configuration. With the new configuration in place, restart the application and try to access http://localhost:8080/ /authenticated.

You are redirected to /login and get a 404 HTTP error because you haven't defined any handler for this URL yet, as shown in Figure 5-13.

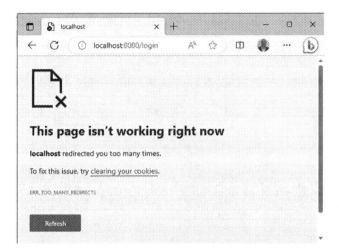

Figure 5-13. *Error 404 that appears when defining a new login handler page*

Let's add a login controller in the `UserController`, as shown in Listing 5-7.

Listing 5-7. Login Controller Added to the UserController

```
@GetMapping("/login")
  public String loginPage() {
     return "login";
}
```

Next, add the following line to the SecurityConfiguration file.

```
formLogin((form) -> form
        .loginPage("/login")
        .permitAll()
)
```

Create the `login.html` page from Listing 5-8 in the `templates` folder in your application.

Listing 5-8. Custom login.html

```
<!DOCTYPE html>
<html xmlns="http://www.w3.org/1999/xhtml" xmlns:th="https://www.
thymeleaf.org">
```

```
<head>
  <title>Spring Security Example </title>
</head>
<body>
<div th:if="${param.error}">
  Invalid username and password.
</div>
<div th:if="${param.logout}">
  You have been logged out.
</div>
<h1>Spring Security v6 Custom Login Form</h1>
<h2>Login with Username and Password:</h2>
<form th:action="@{/login}" method="post">
  <div><label> Username : <input type="text" name="username"/>
  </label></div>
  <div><label> Password: <input type="password" name="password"/>
  </label></div>
  <div><label>Remember Me:<input type="checkbox" name="remember-me"/>
  </label></div>
  <div><input type="submit" value="Login"/></div>
</form>
</body>
</html>
```

In the authenticated.html file, replace the following line

```
<p>Click <a th:href="@{/logout}">here</a> to logout!!</p>
```

with this

```
<form th:action="@{/logout}" method="post">
    <input type="submit" value="Logout"/>
</form>
```

If you restart the application and again go to `http://localhost:8080/` `authenticated`, you should see your new login form when you get redirected to the `/login` URL. The form is shown in Figures 5-14 and 5-15. If you type **admin** as the username and **adminpassw** as the password, you can access the `authenticated` page, as you did with the default login form.

Figure 5-14. *Custom login form*

Figure 5-15. *Successful custom login form*

Click the Logout button to sign out the current user.

If you look at the login.html, you can see certain names for the username field, password field, the remember me checkbox, and the form element's action attribute. These are not random names. Spring Security expects using these particular names to treat the authentication process correctly. Also, the form should use POST to send the information to the server because the framework requires this.

The Remember Me checkbox shown in Figure 5-16 is explained later.

The element `<form-login>` supports many more configuration options, including changing the authentication request parameters' default username and password names.

The `<form-login>` attributes might include

- `always-use-default-target`
- `authentication-details-source-ref`
- `authentication-failure-handler-ref`
- `authentication-failure-url`
- `authentication-success-handler-ref`
- `default-target-url`
- `login-page`
- `login-processing-url`
- `password-parameter`
- `username-parameter`
- `authentication-success-forward-url`
- `authentication-failure-forward-url`

Give this attribute the value `/login`. Then, in your `login.html`, add the content from Listing 5-9 just after the `<body>` tag.

Listing 5-9. Snippet Showing an Error in login.jsp

```
<div th:if="${param.error}">
  Invalid username and password.
</div>
```

If you restart the application and try to access `http://localhost:8080/` `/authenticated` and use an incorrect username and password, you are sent to the login page again, but with an "Invalid username and password." error message shown at the top, as shown in Figure 5-16.

Figure 5-16. *A custom error shown in the custom form*

Note that this URL could be a different one, unrelated to the login URL. But the common pattern is to allow the user another attempt at logging in, showing her any errors.

- `authentication-success-handler-ref`: Reference to an `AuthenticationSuccessHandler` bean in the Spring application context. This bean is called upon successful authentication and should handle the next step after authentication, usually deciding the redirect destination in the application. A current implementation in the form of `SavedRequestAwareAuthenticationSuccessHandler` takes care of redirecting the logged-in user to the original requested URL after successful authentication.

- `authentication-failure-handler-ref`: Reference to an `AuthenticationFailureHandler` bean in the Spring application context. It is used to handle failed authentication requests. When an authentication fails, this handler gets called. A standard behavior for this handler is to present the login screen again or return a 401 HTTP status error. This behavior is provided by the concrete class `SimpleUrlAuthenticationFailureHandler`.

When authenticating a Spring Security application, there are three different interfaces to consider: AuthenticationSuccessHandler, AuthenticationFailureHandler, and AccessDeniedHandler.

Let's develop a simple example implementation of the
AuthenticationFailureHandler interface. It returns a 500 status code when failing to
authenticate. Create the class CustomAuthenticationFailureHandler from Listing 5-10.

Listing 5-10. AuthenticationFailureHandler Implementation for
ServerErrorFailureHandler

```
package com.apress.pss01_security.configuration;

import jakarta.servlet.http.HttpServletRequest;
import jakarta.servlet.http.HttpServletResponse;
import org.springframework.security.core.AuthenticationException;
import org.springframework.security.web.authentication.
AuthenticationFailureHandler;

import java.io.IOException;

public class CustomAuthenticationFailureHandler implements
AuthenticationFailureHandler {

    @Override
    public void onAuthenticationFailure(HttpServletRequest request,
    HttpServletResponse response, AuthenticationException exception)
            throws IOException {
        response.sendError(500);
    }
}
```

Add the following to the SecurityConfiguration class file.

```
.formLogin((form) -> form
        .loginPage("/login")
        .defaultSuccessUrl("/authenticated")
        .permitAll()
        .failureHandler(authenticationFailureHandler())
```

Add the following to the new bean.

```
@Bean
public AuthenticationFailureHandler authenticationFailureHandler() {
    return new CustomAuthenticationFailureHandler();
}
```

Restart the application, go to `http://localhost:8080/authenticated`, use a random username and password, and click the Submit button. You should get a 500 error in the browser.

Basic HTTP Authentication

Sometimes, you can't use a login form for authenticating users. For instance, if your application is meant to be called by other systems instead of a human user, showing a login form to the other application doesn't make sense. This is a pretty common use case. Web services talk to each other without user interaction, ESB systems integrate with one another, and JMS clients produce and consume messages from other systems.

In the context of HTTP-exposed interfaces that require no human user to access them, a common approach is to use HTTP Basic authentication headers. HTTP authentication headers allow you to embed the security information (username and password) in the header of the request that you send to the server instead of sending it in the body of the request, as is the case for the login form authentication.

HTTP uses a standard header for carrying this information. The header is appropriately named `Authorization`. When using this header, the client that is sending the request (for example, a browser) concatenates the username and the password with a colon between them. Then, Base64 encodes the resulting string, sending the result in the header. For example, if you use **neve** as the username and **nardone** as the password, the client creates a `neve:nardone` string and encodes it prior to sending it in the header.

Let's use basic HTTP authentication in your application. The first and only thing you need to do is remove any authentication method in your `SecurityConfiguration` file and instead add the following.

```
.httpBasic(withDefaults())
```

After replacing it, restart the application and go to `http://localhost:8080/` `authenticated` in the browser. A standard HTTP authentication pop-up box asks for your authentication details, as Figure 5-17 shows. Type **admin** and **admin123** as the username and password, and send the request. You will successfully arrive on the movies page (see Figure 5-5).

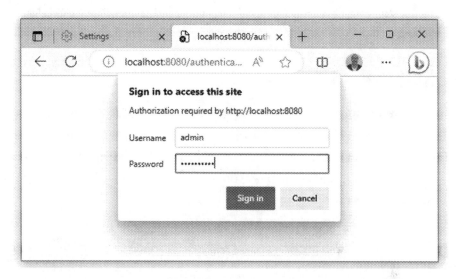

Figure 5-17. *Standard HTTP authentication form, Basic authentication configuration*

When you use the `httpBasic` configuration element, Spring Security's `BasicAuthenticationFilter` appears. A `BasicAuthenticationEntryPoint` strategy is configured into the `ExceptionTranslationFilter` on startup. When you make the first request to `/movies`, the framework behaves as before, throwing an access-denied exception that the `ExceptionTranslationFilter` handles. This filter delegates to a particular implementation strategy of `AuthenticationEntryPoint`—in this case, `BasicAuthenticationEntryPoint`. `BasicAuthenticationEntryPoint` adds the header `WWW-Authenticate: Basic realm="Spring Security Application"` to the response and then sends the client an HTTP status of 401 (Unauthorized). The client should know how to handle this code and work accordingly. (In the case of a browser, it simply shows the authentication pop-up.)

When you introduce the username and password and submit the request, the request again follows the filter chain until it reaches the `BasicAuthenticationFilter`. This filter checks the request headers, looking for the `Authorization` header starting with `Basic`. The filter extracts the content of the header and uses `Base64.decode` to decode the string, then extracts the username and password. The filter creates a `UsernamePasswordAuthenticationToken` object and sends it to the authentication manager for authentication in the standard way. The authentication manager asks the authentication provider to retrieve the user and create an `Authentication` object. This process is standard and independent of using Basic authentication or form authentication.

Digest Authentication

Digest authentication helps to solve many of the weaknesses of Basic authentication, specifically by ensuring credentials are never sent in clear text across the wire.

Digest authentication is a very close sibling of basic HTTP authentication. Its main purpose is to avoid sending clear text passwords on the wire, as Basic authentication does, by hashing the password before sending it to the server. This makes Digest authentication more complex than Basic authentication.

Digest authentication works with HTTP headers in the same way that Basic authentication does.

Digest authentication is based on using a nonce for hashing the passwords. A *nonce* is an arbitrary server-generated number that is used in the authentication process and is used only once. It is passed through the digest computation with the username, password, nonce, URI being requested, and so on.

In the authentication process, the server and client do the digest computation, which should match.

A *nonce* is central to Digest authentication. It is a value the server generates. The following shows Spring Security's nonce format.

```
Digest Syntax
base64(expirationTime + ":" + md5Hex(expirationTime + ":" + key))
expirationTime:   The date and time when the nonce expires, expressed in
milliseconds
key:              A private key to prevent modification of the nonce token
```

The main processing lies in two classes: `DigestAuthenticationFilter` and `DigestAuthenticationEntryPoint`.

DigestAuthenticationFilter queries the request's headers, looking for the Authorization header, and then it checks that the header's value starts with Digest. If this is the case, the request carries the security credentials used for authentication.

DigestAuthenticationEntryPoint is the class invoked to generate a response that demands a digest security authentication process begin. This class sets the header WWW-Authenticate with the correct values (including the nonce) so that the client agent (the browser) knows it has to start the Digest authentication process.

To configure the Digest authentication, update the SecurityConfiguration file with the following lines.

```
.exceptionHandling(e -> e.authenticationEntryPoint(authentication
EntryPoint()))
.addFilterBefore(digestFilter());
```

You must ensure that you configure insecure plain text Password Storage using NoOpPasswordEncoder.

Next, add the following bean to configure the Digest authentication.

```
@Autowired
UserDetailsService userDetailsService;

DigestAuthenticationEntryPoint entryPoint() {
    DigestAuthenticationEntryPoint result = new
    DigestAuthenticationEntryPoint();
    result.setRealmName("My Security App Realm");
    result.setKey("3028472b-da34-4501-bfd8-a355c42bdf92");
}

DigestAuthenticationFilter digestAuthenticationFilter() {
    DigestAuthenticationFilter result = new DigestAuthenticationFilter();
    result.setUserDetailsService(userDetailsService);
    result.setAuthenticationEntryPoint(entryPoint());
}
```

Then, define the username and password using inMemoryUserDetailsManager.

```
@Override
@Bean
public UserDetailsService userDetailsServiceBean() {
    InMemoryUserDetailsManager inMemoryUserDetailsManager = new
    InMemoryUserDetailsManager();
    inMemoryUserDetailsManager.createUser(User.withUsername("admin").
    password(passwordEncoder.encode("adminpassw")).roles( "ADMIN").
    build());
    return inMemoryUserDetailsManager;
}
```

If you restart the application and go to http://localhost:8080/authenticated, you are presented with a browser dialog box asking for a username and password exactly like the one shown for Basic authentication. This is the DigestAuthenticationEntryPoint's work. As explained, the entry point fills the response object with the required headers so that the browser knows it needs to show the login form. Log in with the **admin** username and **adminpassw** as the password, and you should be able to access the requested URL.

The browser creates its own digested message with the password input included and puts it in the header. It also puts the rest of the information—namely, nonce, cnonce, realm, and so on—in the Digest header. The following is a Digest header sent to the server with your current request.

```
'Digest username="admin", realm=" Security Digest Authentication",
nonce="MTM1NTY3NDc3NDIy....==", uri=" /authenticated",
response="225ea6fbad618cfdf1da7d4f7efe53b8", qop=auth,
nc=00000002, cnonce="376a9b27621880bd"'
```

When the request reaches DigestAuthenticationFilter, the request headers contain the required Digest authentication header. The information in this header arrives as a CSV string containing all the required information shown in the last paragraph, including the nonce and the client nonce (cnonce). (A nonce is an arbitrary number used only once in a cryptographic communication. See http://en.wikipedia.org/wiki/Cryptographic_nonce.). The filter extracts the information from the header, retrieves the user from the UserDetailsService, and then computes the digest with the password from the retrieved user to see if it matches the one sent in the header by the client. If they match, access is granted.

Remember-Me Authentication

The remember-me authentication functionality allows returning application users to use it without logging in every time. The application remembers certain visitors, allowing them to just open the application and be greeted with their personalized version of the application as if they were logged in.

Remember-me functionality is very convenient for users but is also very dangerous and recommended for private (from home) use only.

The problem should be obvious. If you use an application from a public computer and this application remembers your profile information, the next person who accesses that application from that computer can impersonate you with minimum effort.

It is also common practice to offer limited functionality in the remember-me session. This means that even if you are logged in automatically, thanks to the remember-me functionality, you won't have access to the whole functionality of the application. More sensitive parts of the application might require you to formally log in to use them.

This is the case, for example, with Amazon.com. When you visit Amazon.com and log in, the next time you visit Amazon, the site remembers you, your recommendations, your name, and other information about you. But to buy something, you must log in fully to access that functionality.

Remember-me authentication is typically supported by sending a cookie to the browser, which then, on subsequent sessions in the application, is sent back to the server for auto login.

How does the remember-me functionality work in Spring Security?

Remember-me functionality in Spring Security is mainly supported by the `RememberMeServices` interface and the `RememberMeAuthenticationFilter` class. Let's see how they work in the context of a request.

When the application starts, the `RememberMeAuthenticationFilter` is in the server's filter chain. Also, a `TokenBasedRememberMeServices` is instantiated and injected into the `AbstractAuthenticationProcessingFilter`, replacing the no-op `NullRememberMeServices`.

Go to `http://localhost:8080/authenticated`, and log in with **admin** as the username and **adminpassw** as the password.

When the request gets into the application, `UsernamePasswordAuthenticationFilter` (a subclass of `AbstractAuthenticationProcessingFilter`) handles the authentication process in the standard way already explained.

155

After successful authentication, UsernamePasswordAuthenticationFilter invokes the configured TokenBasedRememberMeServices's loginSuccess method. This method looks to see if the request contains the parameter remember-me to apply the remember-me functionality. (If the property alwaysRemember is set to true in the service, it also applies the remember-me functionality.) Because you didn't send this request, nothing happened.

So let's add the parameter to the login form you have. Open the login.html file, and paste the following element somewhere inside <form>.

```
<div><label>Remember Me:<input type="checkbox" name="remember-me"/>
</label></div>
```

In the SecurityConfiguration configuration file, add the following.

```
.rememberMe((remember) -> remember
        .rememberMeParameter("remember-me")
        .key("uniqueAndSecretKey")
        .tokenValiditySeconds(1000)
        .rememberMeCookieName("rememberloginnardone")
        .rememberMeParameter("remember-me")
)
```

These lines define the key name, the parameter name, the cookie name, and the validity time in seconds.

Restart the application and visit http://localhost:8080/authenticated. You should now see a check box with username and password fields. Select the check box, and log in with **admin/adminpassw**.

This time, the request carries the required parameter, and TokenBasedRememberMeServices works. It extracts the username and password from the Authentication object and creates a token with this information and an expiration time. And it creates an MD5 encoding out of the resulting string. This value is then Base65-encoded with the username again and added to the response as a cookie named rememberloginnardone that is returned to the browser. You can see this cookie in Figure 5-18.

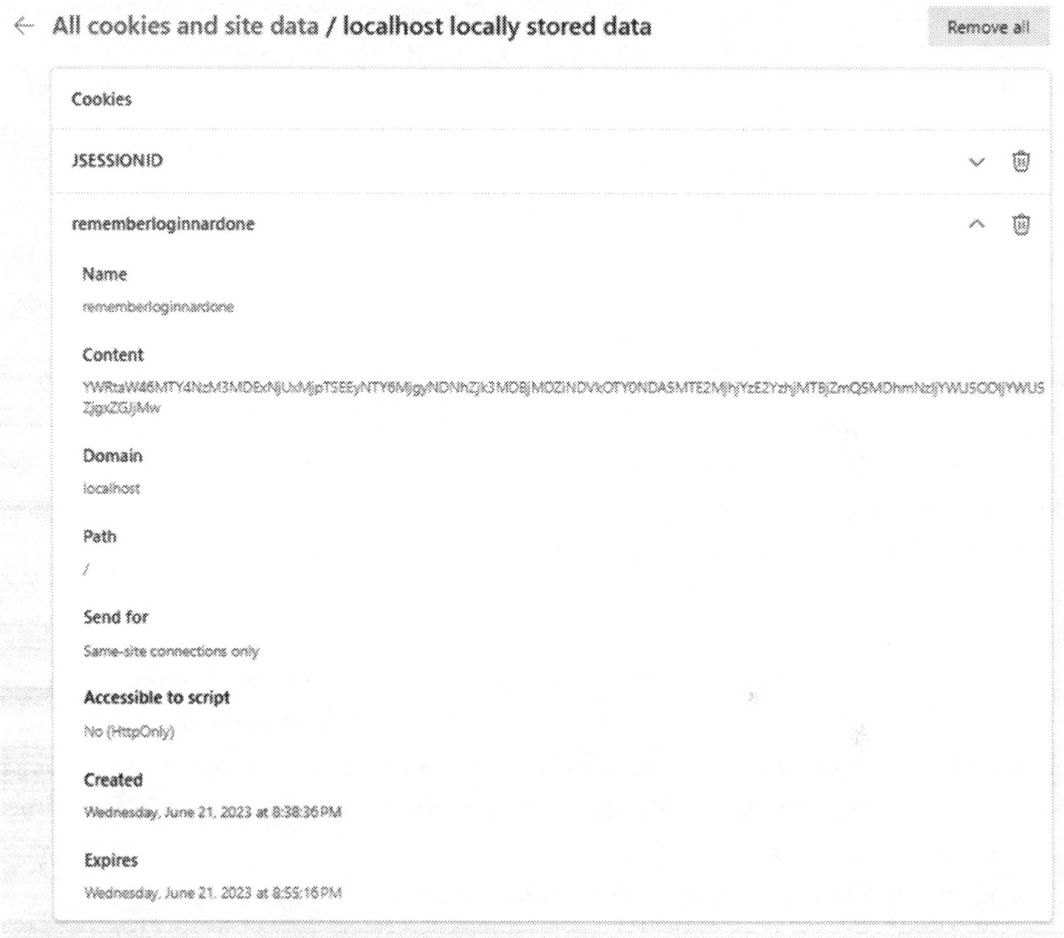

Figure 5-18. *Remember-me cookie example*

Restart the application. Visit `http://localhost:8080/authenticated`. You should be able to access the page without logging in.

When this request gets into the system, it is intercepted by `RememberMeAuthenticationFilter`, which goes into action. The first thing the filter does is check that there is no current `Authentication` in `SecurityContext`. Because this means there is no user logged in, the filter calls `RememberMeServices`'s `autoLogin` method.

In the standard configuration, `TokenBasedRememberMeServices` is the concrete class that implements `RememberMeServices`. This implementation's `autoLogin` method tries to parse the incoming cookie into its composing elements, which are the username, the hashed value of the combined elements (

base64(username + ":" + expirationTime + ":" + algorithmName + ":"

algorithmHex(username + ":" + expirationTime + ":" password + ":" + key))),

and the expiry time of the token. Then, it retrieves the `UserDetails` from the `UserDetailsService` with the username, recomputes the hashed value with the retrieved user, and compares it with the arriving one. If they don't match, an `InvalidCookieException` is thrown. If they do match, `UserDetails` is checked, and an `Authentication` object is created and returned to the caller.

The `autoLogin` method extracts the remember-me cookie from the request, decodes it, does some validation, and then calls the configured `UserDetailsService`'s `loadUserByUsername` method with the username extracted from the cookie. It then creates a `RememberMeAuthenticationToken` object (an implementation of `Authentication`).

The `RememberMeAuthenticationFilter` then tries to authenticate this new `Authentication` object against the `AuthenticationProvider`'s implementation of `RememberMeAuthenticationProvider`, which simply returns the same `Authentication` object after making sure that the hash from the incoming request matches the stored one for the remember-me key.

The security interceptor uses this `Authentication` object to allow access to the requested URL.

Logging Out

Logging out is pretty simple. When you log out of an application, you want the application to end your current session and remove any information it might have stored on the client for you.

`/logout` has replaced `/j_spring_security_logout` since Spring Security 5.

In Spring Security, logging out is very easy. The only thing you need to do by default is to visit `/logout`. Let's try that.

Add the following lines to the `UserController` file.

```
@GetMapping ("/logout")
public String logoutPage() {
    return "redirect:/welcome";
}
```

Update the `SecurityConfiguration` file with the following lines.

```
.logout((logout) -> logout
        .logoutSuccessUrl("/welcome")
        .deleteCookies("JSESSIONID")
        .invalidateHttpSession(true)
        .permitAll()
);
.logout((logout) -> logout
        .logoutSuccessUrl("/welcome")
        .deleteCookies("JSESSIONID")
        .invalidateHttpSession(true)
        .permitAll()
);
```

These lines tell the application to delete the JSESSIONID cookie, invalidate the HTTP session, and redirect to the index web page once logged out.

Now go to `http://localhost:8080/aithenticated` and log in with **admin**/**adminpassw** again. Select the check box for activating `remember-me` functionality. You should be able to log in without problems.

If you look at the cookies stored in your browser, you should see two cookies for the localhost domain: `JSESSIONID` and `rememberloginnardone`. Figure 5-18 shows the two cookies. If you log out, you would expect these two cookies to disappear from the browser, basically removing any trace of the application from your browser. Let's do it.

Click the logout link on the `movies.jsp` page. You should be logged out of the application. If you open your browser's cookies, you see that the cookie `rememberloginnardone` is gone. The `JSESSIONID` cookie exists, but the framework already invalidated the session. Figure 5-19 shows remember-me and session cookies.

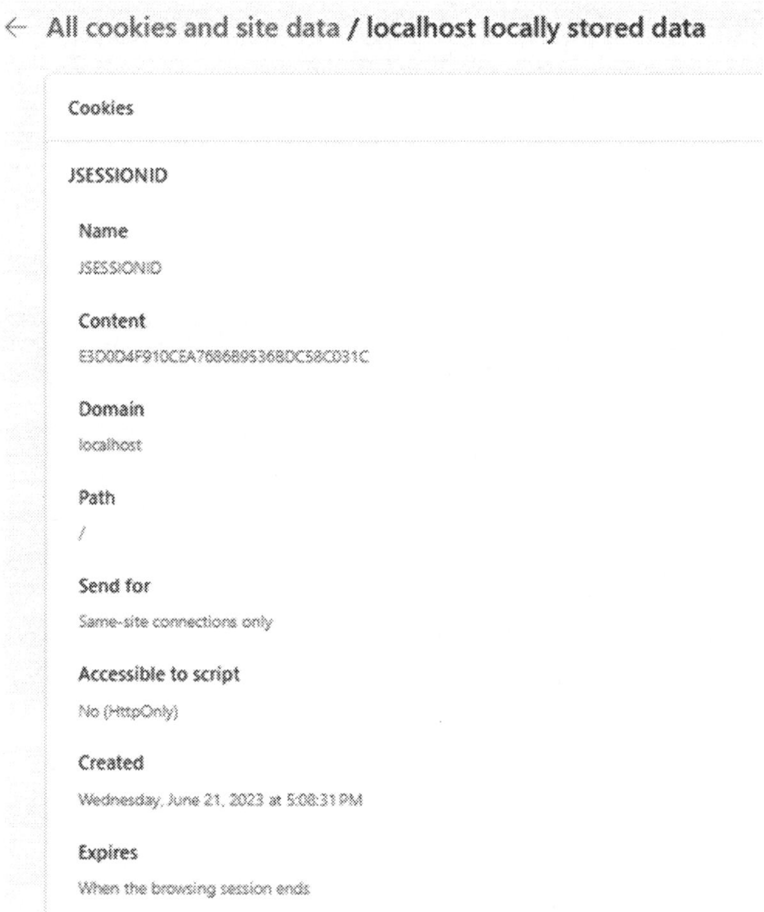

← All cookies and site data / localhost locally stored data

Cookies

JSESSIONID

Name
JSESSIONID

Content
E3O0D4F910CEA76868953680C58C031C

Domain
localhost

Path
/

Send for
Same-site connections only

Accessible to script
No (HttpOnly)

Created
Wednesday, June 21, 2023 at 5:08:31 PM

Expires
When the browsing session ends

Figure 5-19. *Remember-me and session cookies*

The flow of the logout request is as follows: When the request arrives, it follows the filter chain until it arrives at LogoutFilter. This filter notices that the URL that is being requested is for logout. The filter calls the configured LogoutHandler(s), which in the running application are SecurityContextLogoutHandler and TokenBasedRememberMeServices. (They implement the LogoutHandler interface.)

SecurityContextLogoutHandler invalidates the servlet session in the standard servlet way, calling the invalidate method on the HttpSession object and clearing the SecurityContext from Spring Security as shown using

```
.logout()
.invalidateHttpSession(true).
```

`TokenBasedRememberMeServices` simply removes the remember-me cookie by setting its age to 0.

Finally, the JSESSIONID cookie was deleted by adding the `.logout()` line.

```
.deleteCookies("JSESSIONID")
```

Session Management

Another area of Spring Security's web support is the management of user sessions. One very important thing to do regarding sessions is to create a new session ID when a user authenticates successfully. Doing this reduces the likelihood of session fixation attacks, in which one user sets another user's session identifier to impersonate him in the application. Spring Security also offers a feature to specify the number of concurrent sessions the same user can have open at any given time.

These two features are controlled by the `SessionFixationProtectionStrategy` class, which implements `SessionAuthenticationStrategy`. This strategy is invoked from `AbstractAuthenticationProcessingFilter` and `SessionManagementFilter`. Let's look at how they work.

`SessionFixationProtectionStrategy` is already configured by default in `UsernamePasswordAuthenticationFilter`, which is configured in the application. When you log in, this strategy is invoked. When the strategy is invoked, it retrieves the current session (normally anonymous) and invalidates it. It immediately creates a new one. It also tries to migrate certain attributes—normally, those used by Spring Security, but a list can also be specified.

To summarize this strategy, when you log in, it invalidates the current session, creates a new one, and copies certain attributes from the old one to the new one.

Since Spring Session 2.0 contains the Spring Session Core module and several other modules like Spring Session Data MongoDB module, Spring Session Data Geode modules, etc.

In Spring Security, you can control exactly when our session is created and how to interact with it by defining the following line to the `SecurityConfiguration` class.

```
.sessionCreationPolicy(SessionCreationPolicy."ADD A VALUE")
```

The value can be one of the following.

- always: A session is always created if one doesn't already exist.

- ifRequired: A session is created if required (default).

- never: The framework will never create a session itself, but it will use one if it already exists.

- stateless: No session will be created or used by Spring Security.

The first step in enabling this feature is adding the HttpSessionEventPublisher listener to your application to limit multiple logins for the same user through session management.

```
@Bean
public HttpSessionEventPublisher httpSessionEventPublisher() {
    return new HttpSessionEventPublisher();
}
```

Let's go over how to configure it in your application.

1. Add the following line to the SecurityConfiguration file.

    ```
    .sessionCreationPolicy(SessionCreationPolicy.ALWAYS)
    .maximumSessions(1))
    ```

    .maximumSessions(1)) means that no multiple concurrent sessions are possible.

2. Restart the application.

3. Open Chrome and go to http://127.0.0.1:8080/authenticated. Log in with username **admin** and password **adminpassw**. You should be able to access the page without a problem.

4. Open another browser, for instance, Firefox, and visit http://127.0.0.1:8080/authenticated. Log in with the **admin** username and the **adminpassw** password. You should be able to access the page without a problem.

5. Go to Chrome and refresh the page. You get the message: "This session has expired (possibly due to multiple concurrent logins being attempted as the same user)."

Now let's allow two sessions at the same time by adding the following line to the `SecurityConfiguration` file.

```
.sessionManagement().maximumSessions(2)
```

Restart the application and follow the same flow as before. This time, you should have both sessions active at the same time.

Finally, in Listing 5-11, you see the entire `SecurityConfiguration` Java class.

Listing 5-11. SecurityConfiguration.java

```java
package com.apress.pss01_security.configuration;

import org.springframework.context.annotation.Bean;
import org.springframework.context.annotation.Configuration;
import org.springframework.security.config.Customizer;
import org.springframework.security.config.annotation.web.builders.
HttpSecurity;
import org.springframework.security.config.annotation.web.configuration.
EnableWebSecurity;
import org.springframework.security.config.http.SessionCreationPolicy;
import org.springframework.security.core.userdetails.User;
import org.springframework.security.core.userdetails.UserDetails;
import org.springframework.security.core.userdetails.UserDetailsService;
import org.springframework.security.crypto.bcrypt.BCryptPasswordEncoder;
import org.springframework.security.crypto.password.PasswordEncoder;
import org.springframework.security.provisioning.
InMemoryUserDetailsManager;
import org.springframework.security.web.SecurityFilterChain;
import org.springframework.security.web.access.AccessDeniedHandler;
import org.springframework.security.web.authentication.
AuthenticationFailureHandler;
import org.springframework.security.web.authentication.
AuthenticationSuccessHandler;
import org.springframework.security.web.authentication.www.
DigestAuthenticationEntryPoint;
import org.springframework.security.web.authentication.www.
DigestAuthenticationFilter;
```

```java
import org.springframework.security.web.session.HttpSessionEventPublisher;

@Configuration
@EnableWebSecurity

public class SecurityConfiguration {

    @Bean
    public SecurityFilterChain filterChain1(HttpSecurity http) throws
    Exception {
        http
                .authorizeHttpRequests((authorize) -> authorize
                        .requestMatchers("/", "/welcome").permitAll()
                        .requestMatchers("/authenticated").hasRole("ADMIN")
                        .requestMatchers("/customError").permitAll()
                        .anyRequest().denyAll()
                )

                .csrf(Customizer.withDefaults())

                // .httpBasic(withDefaults())     using Basic Authentication
                //.formLogin(withDefaults())      using Form Authentication
                not customized

                .rememberMe((remember) -> remember
                        .rememberMeParameter("remember-me")
                        .key("uniqueAndSecretKey")
                        .tokenValiditySeconds(1000)
                        .rememberMeCookieName("rememberloginnardone")
                        .rememberMeParameter("remember-me")
                )

                .sessionManagement(session -> session
                        .sessionCreationPolicy(SessionCreationPolic
                        y.ALWAYS)
                        .maximumSessions(1))

                // using customized login html page
                .formLogin((form) -> form
                        .loginPage("/login")
```

```
                    .defaultSuccessUrl("/authenticated")
                    .failureUrl("/login?error=true")
                    .failureHandler(authenticationFailureHandler())
                    .permitAll()
            )

            .logout((logout) -> logout
                    .logoutSuccessUrl("/welcome")
                    .deleteCookies("JSESSIONID")
                    .invalidateHttpSession(true)
                    .permitAll()
            );

    return http.build();
}

@Bean
public AuthenticationFailureHandler authenticationFailureHandler() {
    return new CustomAuthenticationFailureHandler();
}

@Bean
public HttpSessionEventPublisher httpSessionEventPublisher() {
    return new HttpSessionEventPublisher();
}

@Bean
public UserDetailsService userDetailsService(){
    UserDetails user = User.builder()
            .username("user")
            .password(passwordEncoder().encode("userpassw"))
            .roles("USER")
            .build();

    UserDetails admin = User.builder()
            .username("admin")
            .password(passwordEncoder().encode("adminpassw"))
            .roles("ADMIN")
```

```
                .build();
        return new InMemoryUserDetailsManager(user, admin);
    }

    @Bean
    public static PasswordEncoder passwordEncoder(){
        return new BCryptPasswordEncoder();
    }

    /*  to use Digest Authentication

        DigestAuthenticationEntryPoint entryPoint() {
        DigestAuthenticationEntryPoint result = new
        DigestAuthenticationEntryPoint();
        result.setRealmName("My Security App Realm");
        result.setKey("3028472b-da34-4501-bfd8-a355c42bdf92");
    }

    @Autowired
    UserDetailsService userDetailsService;

    DigestAuthenticationFilter digestAuthenticationFilter() {
        DigestAuthenticationFilter result = new
        DigestAuthenticationFilter();
        result.setUserDetailsService(userDetailsService);
        result.setAuthenticationEntryPoint(entryPoint());
    }

    @Bean
    public SecurityFilterChain filterChain(HttpSecurity http) throws
    Exception {
        http
                // ...
                .exceptionHandling(e -> e.authenticationEntryPoint(
                authenticationEntryPoint()))
                .addFilterBefore(digestFilter());
        return http.build();
    } */
}
```

Summary

This chapter covered one of the biggest concerns of the framework: web support in Spring Security. You saw that the main functionality comes in the form of servlet filters. This is a good thing from a standards point of view because it means you can leverage Spring Security web support in other frameworks that use the standard Java servlet model.

You should now know a lot of details about the main filters that build the framework, how they work internally, and how they fit within each other and with the rest of the framework. We explained it using practical, real-life scenarios.

The next chapter covers the second major concern of Spring Security—namely, method-level security. We show how it compares to web-level security. You can leverage a lot of your current knowledge to apply it to the method-level security layer.

CHAPTER 6

Configuring Alternative Authentication Providers

One of Spring Security's strongest points is that you can plug different authentication mechanisms into the framework. Spring Security was built to create, as much as possible, a pluggable architecture model where different things can be plugged into the framework easily and unobtrusively. In the authentication layer, an abstraction exists that takes care of this part of the security process. This abstraction comes mainly in the form of the AuthenticationProvider interface, but specific security servlet filters and user details services also support it.

Spring Security 6 supports many different authentication mechanisms, including the following.

- Databases

- LDAP

- X.509

- OAuth 2/OpenID Connect 1.0

- WebSocket

- JSON Web Token (JWT)

- JAAS

- CAS

Most of this chapter explains how these authentication systems work independently of Spring Security. Although it gives you certain key details, it won't be an in-depth explanation. Of course, you see how Spring Security implements each of these

© Massimo Nardone, Carlo Scarioni 2024
M. Nardone and C. Scarioni, *Pro Spring Security*, https://doi.org/10.1007/979-8-8688-0035-1_6

authentication mechanisms, and you see that they have many things in common when it comes to the parts of Spring Security they use. This chapter focuses on how to add an H2 database to Spring Boot with Spring Security and JDBC authentication.

Let's look at how to create a new Spring Boot project with Spring Security, Spring Data JDBC, and H2.

Let's go to start.spring.io and create a new project, shown in Figure 6-1, with the following settings.

- Build tool: Maven

- Language: Java

- Packaging: JAR

- Java version: 20

Next, add the following dependencies.

- Web

- Spring Security

- Spring Data JDBC

- H2 Database

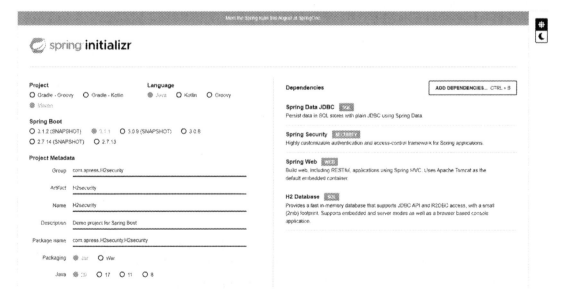

Figure 6-1. *Creating a new JDBS and H2 DB project*

Generate the project and unzip it on your machine.

You must enable and configure the H2 in-memory database console in the application.properties file as follows.

```
spring.h2.console.enabled=true
spring.datasource.name=securitydb
spring.datasource.url=jdbc:h2:mem:securitydb
spring.jpa.database-platform=org.hibernate.dialect.H2Dialect
spring.datasource.driverClassName=org.h2.Driver
```

These lines tell the web application to enable the console, the name of the DB you wish to use, the datasource URL and driver class, and the Spring JOA DB platform.

Let's use the same Java classes and HTML files used in the Chapter 5, as shown in Figure 6-2.

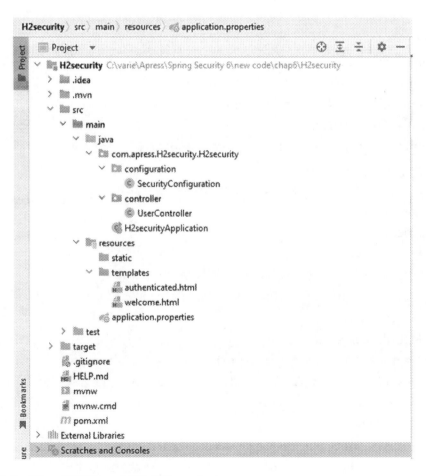

Figure 6-2. *New JDBS and H2 DB project*

Listing 6-1 shows the new pom.xml file after generating this new project.

Listing 6-1. Updated pom.xml File

```xml
<?xml version="1.0" encoding="UTF-8"?>
<project xmlns="http://maven.apache.org/POM/4.0.0" xmlns:xsi="http://www.
w3.org/2001/XMLSchema-instance"
    xsi:schemaLocation="http://maven.apache.org/POM/4.0.0
    https://maven.apache.org/xsd/maven-4.0.0.xsd">
    <modelVersion>4.0.0</modelVersion>
    <parent>
        <groupId>org.springframework.boot</groupId>
        <artifactId>spring-boot-starter-parent</artifactId>
        <version>3.1.0</version>
        <relativePath/> <!-- lookup parent from repository -->
    </parent>
    <groupId>com.apress.H2security</groupId>
    <artifactId>H2security</artifactId>
    <version>0.0.1-SNAPSHOT</version>
    <name>H2security</name>
    <description>Demo project for Spring Boot</description>
    <properties>
        <java.version>20</java.version>
    </properties>
    <dependencies>
        <dependency>
            <groupId>org.springframework.boot</groupId>
            <artifactId>spring-boot-starter-data-jdbc</artifactId>
        </dependency>
        <dependency>
            <groupId>org.springframework.boot</groupId>
            <artifactId>spring-boot-starter-security</artifactId>
        </dependency>
        <dependency>
            <groupId>org.springframework.boot</groupId>
            <artifactId>spring-boot-starter-web</artifactId>
```

```xml
        </dependency>
        <dependency>
            <groupId>com.h2database</groupId>
            <artifactId>h2</artifactId>
            <scope>runtime</scope>
        </dependency>
        <dependency>
            <groupId>org.springframework.boot</groupId>
            <artifactId>spring-boot-starter-test</artifactId>
            <scope>test</scope>
        </dependency>
        <dependency>
            <groupId>org.springframework.security</groupId>
            <artifactId>spring-security-test</artifactId>
            <scope>test</scope>
        </dependency>
        <dependency>
            <groupId>org.thymeleaf.extras</groupId>
            <artifactId>thymeleaf-extras-springsecurity6</artifactId>
            <version>3.1.1.RELEASE</version>
        </dependency>
    </dependencies>

    <build>
        <plugins>
            <plugin>
                <groupId>org.springframework.boot</groupId>
                <artifactId>spring-boot-maven-plugin</artifactId>
            </plugin>
        </plugins>
    </build>

</project>
```

The new Maven dependencies are JDBC and H2.

```
<dependency>
    <groupId>org.springframework.boot</groupId>
    <artifactId>spring-boot-starter-data-jdbc</artifactId>
</dependency>
<dependency>
    <groupId>com.h2database</groupId>
    <artifactId>h2</artifactId>
    <scope>runtime</scope>
</dependency>
```

Let's update our files now.

The welcome.html file remains as it is in Chapter 5.

Let's update the authenticated.html file by adding the following lines.

```
<form th:action="@{/h2-console}" method="post">
    <input type="submit" value="check the h2-console"/>
</form>
```

Once the user is authenticated, this creates a new button to open the H2 console and check the updated databases using our example.

The Java class named UserController remains the same as in Chapter 5.

Let's update the SecurityConfiguration Java class to use the H2 embedded database, as shown in Listing 6-2.

Listing 6-2. Updated SecurityConfiguration Java Class

```
package com.apress.H2security.H2security.configuration;

import org.springframework.context.annotation.Bean;
import org.springframework.context.annotation.Configuration;
import org.springframework.jdbc.datasource.embedded.EmbeddedDatabase;
import org.springframework.jdbc.datasource.embedded.
EmbeddedDatabaseBuilder;
import org.springframework.jdbc.datasource.embedded.EmbeddedDatabaseType;
import org.springframework.security.config.Customizer;
import org.springframework.security.config.annotation.web.builders.
HttpSecurity;
```

```java
import org.springframework.security.config.annotation.web.configuration.
EnableWebSecurity;
import org.springframework.security.core.userdetails.User;
import org.springframework.security.core.userdetails.UserDetails;
import org.springframework.security.core.userdetails.jdbc.JdbcDaoImpl;
import org.springframework.security.crypto.bcrypt.BCryptPasswordEncoder;
import org.springframework.security.crypto.password.PasswordEncoder;
import org.springframework.security.provisioning.JdbcUserDetailsManager;
import org.springframework.security.web.SecurityFilterChain;
import org.springframework.security.web.util.matcher.AntPathRequestMatcher;

import javax.sql.DataSource;

@Configuration
@EnableWebSecurity

public class SecurityConfiguration {

    @Bean
    public SecurityFilterChain filterChain1(HttpSecurity http) throws
    Exception {
        http
                .csrf(csrf -> csrf.ignoringRequestMatchers("/h2-console/**"))

                    .authorizeHttpRequests((authorize) -> authorize
                            .requestMatchers("/", "/welcome").permitAll()
                            //.requestMatchers("/authenticated").
                            hasRole("ADMIN")
                            .requestMatchers("/authenticated").
                            hasAnyRole("USER", "ADMIN")
                            .requestMatchers(AntPathRequestMatcher.antMatch
                            er("/h2-console/**")).permitAll()
                    )

                    .csrf(csrf -> csrf
                            .ignoringRequestMatchers(AntPathRequestMatcher.antM
                            atcher("/h2-console/**")))

                    .formLogin(Customizer.withDefaults())
```

```
                .headers(headers -> headers.disable())

                .logout((logout) -> logout
                        .logoutSuccessUrl("/welcome")
                        .deleteCookies("JSESSIONID")
                        .invalidateHttpSession(true)
                        .permitAll()
                );

        return http.build();
    }

    @Bean
    EmbeddedDatabase datasource() {
        return new EmbeddedDatabaseBuilder()
                .setName("securitydb")
                .setType(EmbeddedDatabaseType.H2)
                .addScript(JdbcDaoImpl.DEFAULT_USER_SCHEMA_DDL_LOCATION)
                .build();
    }

    @Bean
    JdbcUserDetailsManager users(DataSource dataSource, PasswordEncoder
    encoder) {
        UserDetails user = User.builder()
                .username("user")
                .password(encoder.encode("userpassw"))
                .roles("USER")
                .build();
        UserDetails admin = User.builder()
                .username("admin")
                .password(encoder.encode("adminpassw"))
                .roles("ADMIN")
                .build();
        JdbcUserDetailsManager jdbcUserDetailsManager = new JdbcUserDetails
        Manager(dataSource);
        jdbcUserDetailsManager.createUser(user);
```

```
        jdbcUserDetailsManager.createUser(admin);
        return jdbcUserDetailsManager;
    }

    @Bean
    public static PasswordEncoder passwordEncoder(){
        return new BCryptPasswordEncoder();

    }
}
```

Let's analyze this new Java class.

The PasswordEncoder bean stays the same as in previous examples.

Spring Security's JdbcDaoImpl implements UserDetailsService to support username-and-password-based authentication that is retrieved using JDBC. JdbcUserDetailsManager extends JdbcDaoImpl to provide management of UserDetails through the UserDetailsManager interface. UserDetails-based authentication is used by Spring Security when configuring to accept a username/password for authentication.

Spring Security provides default queries for JDBC-based authentication, for which you can adjust the schema to match any customizations to the queries and the database dialect you use.

JdbcDaoImpl requires tables to load the password, account status (enabled or disabled), and a list of authorities (roles) for the user. The default schema is also exposed as a classpath resource named org/springframework/security/core/userdetails/jdbc/users.ddl, which is provided in the following listing.

```
create table users(
      username varchar_ignorecase(50) not null primary key,
      password varchar_ignorecase(500) not null,
      enabled boolean not null
);

create table authorities (
      username varchar_ignorecase(50) not null,
      authority varchar_ignorecase(50) not null,
      constraint fk_authorities_users foreign key(username) references
      users(username)
);
```

Before configuring JdbcUserDetailsManager, you must create a DataSource. In this example, we set up an embedded DataSource initialized with the default user schema via the EmbeddedDatabase datasource bean created to build a new H2 database (in our case named securitydb) using the preconfigured JdbcDaoImpl default user DDL via DJdbcDaoImpl.DEFAULT_USER_SCHEMA_DDL_LOCATION.

```
@Bean
EmbeddedDatabase datasource() {
    return new EmbeddedDatabaseBuilder()
            .setName("securitydb")
            .setType(EmbeddedDatabaseType.H2)
            .addScript(JdbcDaoImpl.DEFAULT_USER_SCHEMA_DDL_LOCATION)
            .build();
```

The next step is to create the JdbcUserDetailsManager bean, as described in Listing 6-3.

Listing 6-3. JdbcUserDetailsManager Java Bean

```
@Bean
JdbcUserDetailsManager users(DataSource dataSource, PasswordEncoder
encoder) {
    UserDetails user = User.builder()
            .username("user")
            .password(encoder.encode("userpassw"))
            .roles("USER")
            .build();
    UserDetails admin = User.builder()
            .username("admin")
            .password(encoder.encode("adminpassw"))
            .roles("ADMIN")
            .build();
    JdbcUserDetailsManager jdbcUserDetailsManager = new JdbcUserDetails
    Manager(dataSource);
    jdbcUserDetailsManager.createUser(user);
    jdbcUserDetailsManager.createUser(admin);
    return jdbcUserDetailsManager;
}
```

In this example, let's create two users to access the authenticated resource: user/userpassw and admin/adminpassw.

The last bean is SecurityFilterChain, as shown in Listing 6-4.

Listing 6-4. SecurityFilterChain Java Bean

```
@Bean
public SecurityFilterChain filterChain1(HttpSecurity http) throws
Exception {
    http

            .authorizeHttpRequests((authorize) -> authorize
                    .requestMatchers("/", "/welcome").permitAll()
                    .requestMatchers("/authenticated").hasAnyRole("USER",
                    "ADMIN")
                    .requestMatchers(AntPathRequestMatcher.antMatcher("/h2-
                    console/**")).permitAll()
            )

            .csrf(csrf -> csrf
                    .ignoringRequestMatchers(AntPathRequestMatcher.antMatch
                    er("/h2-console/**")))

            .formLogin(Customizer.withDefaults())

            .headers(headers -> headers.disable())

            .logout((logout) -> logout
                    .logoutSuccessUrl("/welcome")
                    .deleteCookies("JSESSIONID")
                    .invalidateHttpSession(true)
                    .permitAll()
            );

    return http.build();
}
```

First, create `requestMatchers` in this bean.

- `.requestMatchers("/", "/welcome").permitAll()` permits all to access "/" and "welcome " pages.

- `.requestMatchers("/authenticated").hasAnyRole("USER", "ADMIN")` permits the user and admin to access the authenticated page.

- `.requestMatchers(AntPathRequestMatcher.antMatcher("/h2-console/**")).permitAll()` permits access to the H2 console.

Since our Spring Boot project uses Spring Security and the class is annotated with the @EnableWebSecurity annotation, you must disable the HTTP header frame options and add the following to that class's configure() method.

The frame options are necessary to prevent a browser from loading your HTML page in an <iframe> or <frame> tag. To enable the H2 console page to load, you need to disable this option with this line.

```
.headers(headers -> headers.disable())
```
The line `.csrf(csrf -> csrf`
```
        .ignoringRequestMatchers(AntPathRequestMatcher.antMatch
    er("/h2-console/**")))
```

allows ignoring RequestMatchers for the H2 "/h2-console/**" console path.

Build and run the Spring Boot application and open http://localhost:8080/welcome in the browser window. Authenticate with "user/userpassw" or "admin/adminpassw", as shown in Figures 6-3 and 6-4.

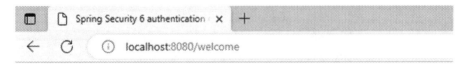

Welcome to Spring Security 6 authentication example!

Click here to get authenticated!

Figure 6-3. *welcome.html page*

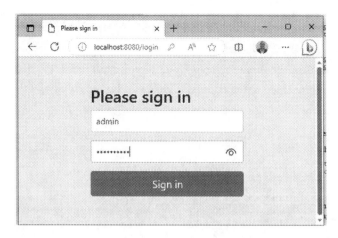

Figure 6-4. *Login page*

If authenticated, you can access the autnenticated.html page, which informs that the admin is an authenticated user and provides a "check the h2-console" button, as shown in Figure 6-5.

Figure 6-5. *authenticated.html page*

Click the "check the h2-console" button to log in to the H2 console, as shown in Figure 6-6.

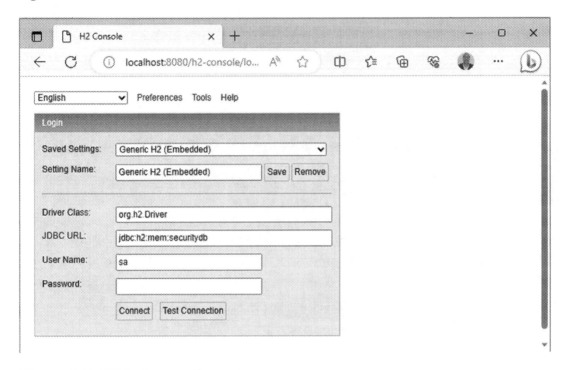

Figure 6-6. *H2 login console page*

Let's connect now to the H2 and discover the content, as shown in Figure 6-7.

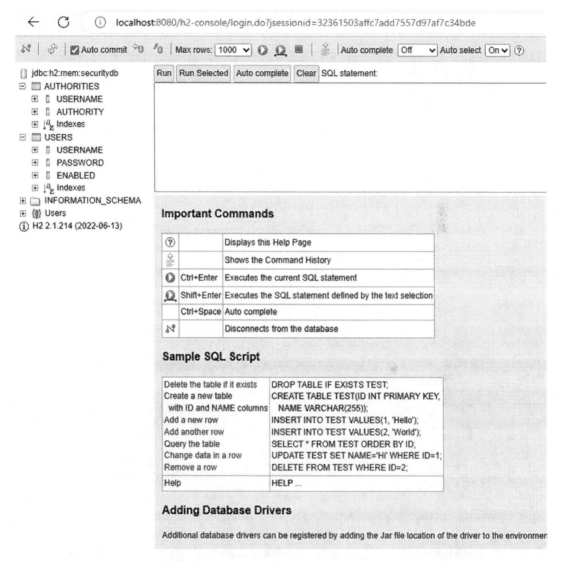

Figure 6-7. *H2 console page with securitydb tables*

The H2 console includes the two tables used for this example via JDBC authentication, such as Authorities and Users.

Let's run the following SQL scripts against the securitydb database to see the content of the tables.

The result of running the SELECT * FROM AUTHORITIES SQL script is shown in Figure 6-8.

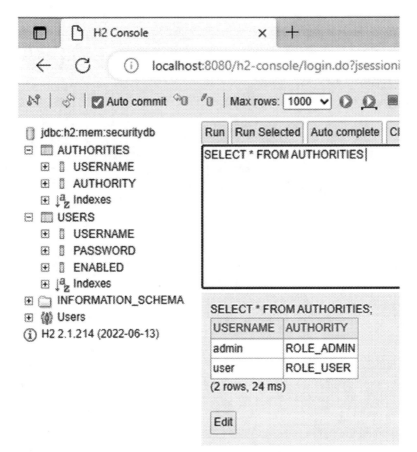

Figure 6-8. *H2 authorities table script outcome*

There are two new authorities in the database: admin/ROLE_ADMIN and user/ROLE_USER.

The result of running the SELECT * FROM USERS SQL script is shown in Figure 6-9.

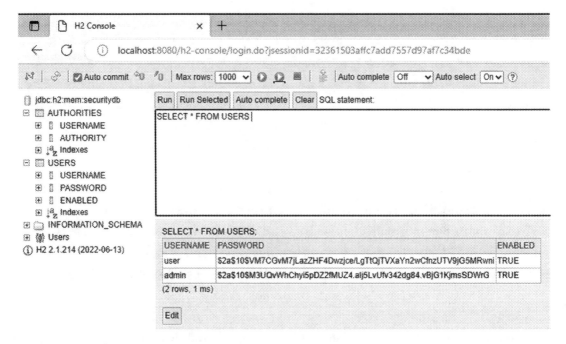

Figure 6-9. *H2 users table script outcome*

There are two new enabled users: "user/userpassw" and "admin/adminpassw".
These are the users who authenticate the example.

LDAP Authentication

The Lightweight Directory Access Protocol (LDAP) is an application-level, message-oriented protocol for storing and accessing information through an accessible tree-like directory. A directory, in general, is simply an organized data store that allows for easy queries in its particular domain. For example, a TV Guide is a directory that allows you to find TV shows easily, and a phone book is a directory that provides easy access to phone numbers.

LDAP allows the storage of very different kinds of information in a directory. Probably the most widely known use of LDAP-like structures is the Microsoft Windows Active Directory system. Other LDAP systems are widely used to store the corporate user databases of many companies that serve as the centralized user store.

LDAP is not easy to understand, and we try to explain it using the example in this section. Let's use the same code as in the previous section but modify it to work with LDAP instead of database authentication. Remember that the previous section offered a bootstrap application to start working on all the examples in this chapter, including this one.

The first thing to do is configure your users in the LDAP directory. To do this, you need to understand the LDAP information model, which defines the type of data you can store in your directory.

Entries, attributes, and values define the data in LDAP. An *entry* is the basic unit of information in the directory and commonly represents an entity from the real world, like a user. Entries are normally defined by a particular object class. Each entry in the directory has an identification known as a *distinguished name* (or, more commonly, DN). Each entry in the directory also has a set of *attributes* that describe different things about the entry. Each attribute has a type and one or more *values*.

You must define the data you need. You use users, groups, and credentials, as you have done so far. In LDAP, the user entry definition is commonly known as *people*, so use that name to define the user entries. Your user also uses the standard LDAP object class person to define its attributes.

Using an Embedded LDAP

For simplicity, an embedded LDAP server is used in this example since Spring Security uses ApacheDS 1.x, which is no longer maintained, and unfortunately, ApacheDS 2.x has only released milestone versions with no stable release. Consider updating once a stable release of ApacheDS 2.x is available.

If you wish to use Apache DS, specify the following Maven dependencies.

```
<dependency>
      <groupId>org.apache.directory.server</groupId>
      <artifactId>apacheds-core</artifactId>
      <version>1.5.5</version>
      <scope>runtime</scope>
</dependency>
<dependency>
      <groupId>org.apache.directory.server</groupId>
```

```
<artifactId>apacheds-server-jndi</artifactId>
<version>1.5.5</version>
<scope>runtime</scope>
</dependency>
```

Let's create a new Spring Boot project with Spring Security, Spring Web, and LDAP.

Go to start.spring.io to create a new project (as shown in Figure 6-10) with the following settings.

- Build Tool: Maven

- Language: Java

- Packaging: Jar

- Java Version: 17

Next, add the following dependencies.

- Web

- Spring Security

- Spring LDAP

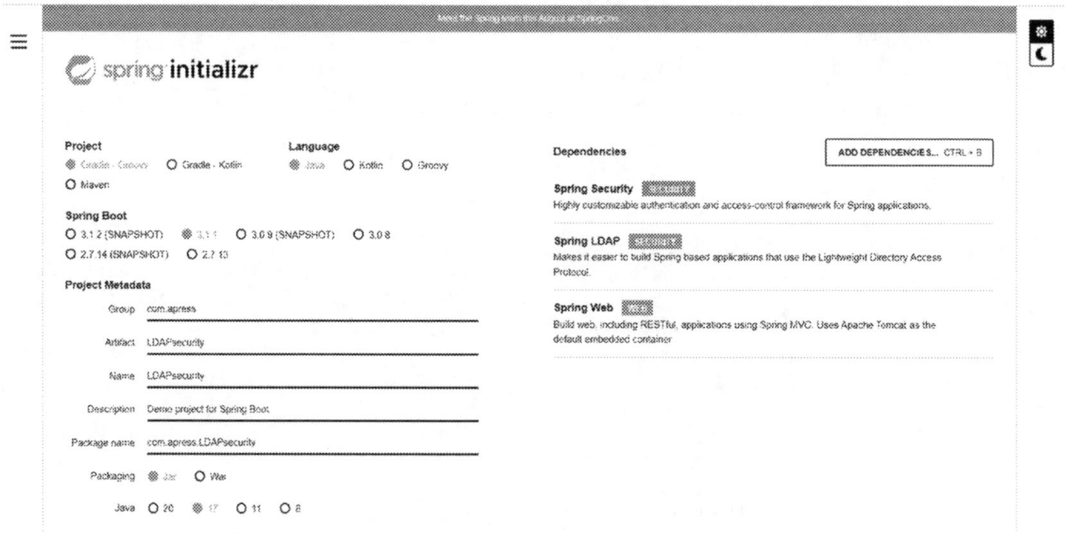

Figure 6-10. *Creating a new LDAP project*

Generate the project and unzip it on your machine.

You must enable and configure the H2 in-memory database console in our application.properties file as follows.

```
spring.thymeleaf.check-template-location=false
spring.ldap.embedded.port=8389
spring.ldap.embedded.ldif=classpath:*.ldif
```

Let's use the same Java classes from the previous example, as shown in Figure 6-11.

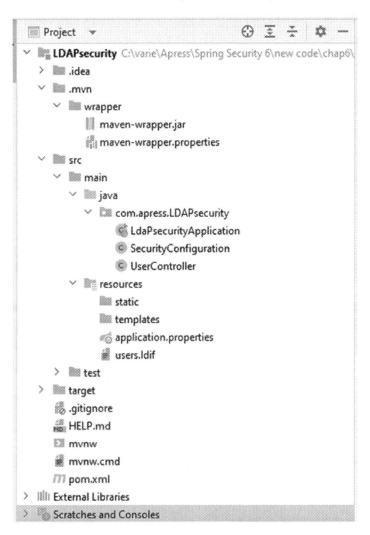

Figure 6-11. *LDAPSecurity project structure*

Listing 6-5 shows the new pom.xml file after generating this new project.

Listing 6-5. Updated pom.xml

```xml
<?xml version="1.0" encoding="UTF-8"?>
<project xmlns="http://maven.apache.org/POM/4.0.0" xmlns:xsi="http://www.
w3.org/2001/XMLSchema-instance"
    xsi:schemaLocation="http://maven.apache.org/POM/4.0.0
    https://maven.apache.org/xsd/maven-4.0.0.xsd">
    <modelVersion>4.0.0</modelVersion>
    <parent>
        <groupId>org.springframework.boot</groupId>
        <artifactId>spring-boot-starter-parent</artifactId>
        <version>3.1.0</version>
        <relativePath/> <!--lookup parent from repository -->
    </parent>
    <groupId>com.apress.LDAPsecurity</groupId>
    <artifactId>LDAPsecurity</artifactId>
    <version>0.0.1-SNAPSHOT</version>
    <name>LDAPsecurity</name>
    <description>Demo project for Spring Boot</description>

    <properties>
        <java.version>17</java.version>
    </properties>
    <dependencies>
        <dependency>
            <groupId>org.springframework.boot</groupId>
            <artifactId>spring-boot-starter-web</artifactId>
        </dependency>
        <!--tag::security[]-->
        <dependency>
            <groupId>org.springframework.boot</groupId>
            <artifactId>spring-boot-starter-security</artifactId>
        </dependency>
        <dependency>
            <groupId>org.springframework.ldap</groupId>
            <artifactId>spring-ldap-core</artifactId>
        </dependency>
```

```
        <dependency>
            <groupId>org.springframework.security</groupId>
            <artifactId>spring-security-ldap</artifactId>
        </dependency>
        <dependency>
            <groupId>com.unboundid</groupId>
            <artifactId>nbounded-ldapsdk</artifactId>
            <version>6.0.9</version>
            <scope>runtime</scope>
        </dependency>          <!--end::security[]-->
        <dependency>
            <groupId>org.springframework.boot</groupId>
            <artifactId>spring-boot-starter-test</artifactId>
            <scope>test</scope>
        </dependency>
        <dependency>
            <groupId>org.springframework.security</groupId>
            <artifactId>spring-security-test</artifactId>
            <scope>test</scope>
        </dependency>
    </dependencies>

    <build>
        <plugins>
            <plugin>
                <groupId>org.springframework.boot</groupId>
                <artifactId>spring-boot-maven-plugin</artifactId>
            </plugin>
        </plugins>
    </build>

</project>
```

The following are the specific Maven dependencies needed in the LDAP Spring Security 6 example.

```
<dependency>
    <groupId>com.unboundid</groupId>
    <artifactId>unboundid-ldapsdk</artifactId>
    <version>6.0.9</version>
    <scope>runtime</scope>
</dependency>
<dependency>
    <groupId>org.springframework.boot</groupId>
    <artifactId>spring-boot-starter-security</artifactId>
</dependency>
<dependency>
    <groupId>org.springframework.ldap</groupId>
    <artifactId>spring-ldap-core</artifactId>
</dependency>
<dependency>
    <groupId>org.springframework.security</groupId>
    <artifactId>spring-security-ldap</artifactId>
</dependency>
```

The next step is to create the LDIF file used as an embedded LDAP server.

An LDIF file is a text file that uses LDIF formatting, a standard format for describing directory entries in LDAP. It allows you to import and export your directory data into or from another LDAP directory in a standard way or just to create new data or modify existing data. You use it here to import the data with your users. Listing 6-6 shows the LDIF file you import. You can name this file whatever you like, but it is users.ldif in this example.

Listing 6-6. LDIF File with the Two Users You Want to Import into the LDAP Directory

```
dn: dc=example,dc=com
objectclass: top
objectclass: domain
dc: example
dn: ou=groups,dc=example,dc=com
objectclass: organizationalUnit
objectclass: top
```

```
ou: groups
dn: cn=administrators,ou=groups,dc=example,dc=com
objectclass: groupOfUniqueNames
objectclass: top
cn: administrators
uniqueMember: uid=mnardone,ou=people,dc=example,dc=com
ou: admin
dn: cn=users,ou=groups,dc=example,dc=com
objectclass: groupOfNames
objectclass: top
cn: users
member: uid=lnardone,ou=people,dc=example,dc=com
ou: user
dn: ou=people,dc=example,dc=com
objectclass: organizationalUnit
objectclass: top
ou: people
dn: uid=lnardone,ou=people,dc=example,dc=com
objectclass: inetOrgPerson
objectclass: organizationalPerson
objectclass: person
objectclass: top
cn: Leo Nardone
sn: Leo
uid: lnardone
userPassword: {SHA}F1OkcxtiioPmVX3tJlIHzZsXkDQ=
dn: uid=mnardone,ou=people,dc=example,dc=com
objectclass: inetOrgPerson
objectclass: organizationalPerson
objectclass: person
objectclass: top
cn: Massimo Nardone
sn: Nardone
uid: mnardone
userPassword: {SHA}xcS5y9TOkjBXDpYijejbhmILFwY=
```

As you can see, this code generated two users, mnardone, part of the administrators group, and lnardone, who is not included in that group.

The SHA password was generated via `http://aspirine.org/htpasswd_en.html`. The passwords are

nardone01 = {SHA}xcS5y9T0kjBXDpYijejbhmILFwY=

nardone02 = {SHA}F1OkcxtiioPmVX3tJlIHzZsXkDQ=

You can see in Listing 6-6 the hierarchical nature of the directory and how everything inherits the DN `dc=example,dc=com`. You can also see how the different entries use different standard object classes. You have created two groups: administrators and users. You also established that *lnardone* is a member of the users group, *mnardone* is a member of the administrators group, and the two SHA passwords.

”””””””””””uccessfuccessfu—>””””””””uccessfully”””‘’”””””””””

The main class is `LdaPsecurityApplication`, as shown in Listing 6-7.

Listing 6-7. LdaPsecurityApplication Java Class

```
package com.apress.LDAPsecurity.LDAPsecurity;

import org.springframework.boot.SpringApplication;
import org.springframework.boot.autoconfigure.SpringBootApplication;

@SpringBootApplication
public class LdaPsecurityApplication {

    public static void main(String[] args) {
        SpringApplication.run(LdaPsecurityApplication.class, args);
    }

}
```

Next, create some needed Java classes. Start with a simple `UserController`, shown in Listing 6-8, which is similar to one used in other projects in this book.

Listing 6-8. UserController Java Class

```
import org.springframework.web.bind.annotation.GetMapping;
import org.springframework.web.bind.annotation.RestController;
```

```java
@RestController
public class UserController {

    @GetMapping("/")
    public String getLoginPage() {
        return "You have successfully logged in Using Spring Security 6
        LDAP Authentication!";

    }
}
```

Listing 6-8 works so that when a login is successful, the user receives a simple message: "You have successfully logged in Using Spring Security 6 LDAP Authentication!".

Next, update the Java class named SecurityConfiguration, shown in Listing 6-9, to take care of the LDAP authentication.

Listing 6-9. SecurityConfiguration Java Class

```java
package com.apress.LDAPsecurity;

import org.springframework.context.annotation.Bean;
import org.springframework.context.annotation.Configuration;
import org.springframework.ldap.core.support.BaseLdapPathContextSource;
import org.springframework.security.authentication.AuthenticationManager;
import org.springframework.security.config.annotation.web.builders.
HttpSecurity;
import org.springframework.security.config.annotation.web.configuration.
EnableWebSecurity;
import org.springframework.security.config.ldap.
LdapPasswordComparisonAuthenticationManagerFactory;
import org.springframework.security.crypto.bcrypt.BCryptPasswordEncoder;
import org.springframework.security.ldap.userdetails.
DefaultLdapAuthoritiesPopulator;
import org.springframework.security.ldap.userdetails.LdapAuthoritiesPopulator;
import org.springframework.security.web.SecurityFilterChain;

import static org.springframework.security.config.Customizer.withDefaults;

@Configuration
@EnableWebSecurity
```

```java
public class SecurityConfiguration {

    @Bean
    public SecurityFilterChain filterChain1(HttpSecurity http) throws
    Exception {
        http
                .authorizeHttpRequests((authorize) -> authorize
                        .anyRequest().fullyAuthenticated()
                )
                .formLogin(withDefaults());
        return http.build();
    }

    @Bean
    AuthenticationManager authenticationManager(BaseLdapPathContextSource
    contextSource) {
        LdapPasswordComparisonAuthenticationManagerFactory factory = new
        LdapPasswordComparisonAuthenticationManagerFactory(
                contextSource, new BCryptPasswordEncoder());
        factory.setUserDnPatterns("uid={0},ou=people");
        factory.setPasswordAttribute("userPassword");
        factory.setUserSearchBase("ou=people");
        factory.setPasswordEncoder(new BCryptPasswordEncoder());
        return factory.createAuthenticationManager();
    }

    @Bean
    LdapAuthoritiesPopulator authorities(BaseLdapPathContextSource
    contextSource) {
        String groupSearchBase = "ou=groups";
        DefaultLdapAuthoritiesPopulator authorities = new
        DefaultLdapAuthoritiesPopulator
                (contextSource, groupSearchBase);
        authorities.setGroupSearchFilter("(member={0})");
        return authorities;
    }

}
```

Let's discuss the Java class.

The following lines force you to request full authentication for any URL via formLogin.

```
http
        .authorizeHttpRequests((authorize) -> authorize
                .anyRequest().fullyAuthenticated()
        )
        .formLogin(withDefaults());
return http.build();
```

This example uses LDAP password authentication, where password comparison is when the password supplied by the user is compared with the one stored in the repository. This can be done by retrieving the value of the password attribute and checking it locally or by performing an LDAP "compare" operation, where the supplied password is passed to the server for comparison, and the real password value is never retrieved. An LDAP comparison cannot be done when the password is properly hashed with a random salt.

The following lines define the LDAP password authentication.

```
authenticationManager(BaseLdapPathContextSource contextSource) {
        LdapPasswordComparisonAuthenticationManagerFactory factory = new
        LdapPasswordComparisonAuthenticationManagerFactory(
                contextSource, new BCryptPasswordEncoder());
        factory.setUserDnPatterns("uid={0},ou=people");
        factory.setPasswordAttribute("userPassword");
        factory.setUserSearchBase("ou=people");
        factory.setPasswordEncoder(new BCryptPasswordEncoder());
        return factory.createAuthenticationManager();
}
```

Finally, to determine which authorities are returned for the user, we used the following LdapAuthoritiesPopulator code.

```
@Bean
LdapAuthoritiesPopulator authorities(BaseLdapPathContextSource
contextSource) {
    String groupSearchBase = "ou=groups";
```

```
DefaultLdapAuthoritiesPopulator authorities = new
DefaultLdapAuthoritiesPopulator
        (contextSource, groupSearchBase);
authorities.setGroupSearchFilter("(member={0})");
return authorities;
}
```

Start the application now with this configuration. You should be able to see the login page via http://localhost:8080/.

Log in and access the Spring Security 6 login page, as shown in Figure 6-12.

Figure 6-12. *Application login page*

In the LDAP, there are two users: mnardone and lnardone. The difference is that mnardone is part of the administrators group, so they can access the successful page.

Log in with the **mnardone** username and the **nardone02** password to access the authorized page, as shown in Figure 6-13.

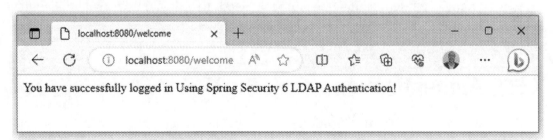

Figure 6-13. *LDAP login page*

The configuration is not that difficult to understand. The login configuration is within the `SpringSecurityConfiguration` Java class.

The `SecurityFilterChain filterChain1(HttpSecurity http)` configures the HTTP for features such as login and logout so that users can only access the URL in the LDAP as part of the administrators group.

```
dn: cn=administrators,ou=groups,dc=example,dc=com
objectclass: groupOfUniqueNames
objectclass: top
cn: administrators
uniqueMember: uid=mnardone,ou=people,dc=example,dc=com
ou: admin
```

In this case, mnardone is part of the administrators LDAP group, so they can access the secure page.

Remember that all your entries are relative to the domain name `dc=example,dc=com`.

As you can see from the example, configuring LDAP's basic support as the authentication solution for your application with Spring Security is not that complex. Thanks to the modular architecture and well-thought-out XML and Java namespace, it is very straightforward. The complexity of LDAP is LDAP itself. Although it is a simple hierarchical system (very much like the file system in your standard Unix box), some of the nomenclature and functionality seem a bit complex and very different from the database-based solution you explored in the previous section.

Using LDAP as your authentication solution makes great sense in the context of corporate intranets, where the company user base is already stored in LDAP-like directories in a centralized manner. Plugins into this already existing user-management infrastructure are a good way to reuse the user information within the company instead of writing a parallel authentication datastore that needs to be kept in sync with the main repository.

X.509 Authentication

X.509 authentication is an authentication scheme that uses client-side certificates instead of username-password combinations to identify the user. Using this approach, a scheme known as *mutual authentication* takes place between the client and the server. In practice, mutual authentication means that, as part of the Secure Sockets Layer (SSL) handshake, the server requests that the client identify himself by providing a certificate. In a production-ready server, a proper certificate-signing authority must issue and sign the incoming client certificate.

To work with client certificates, the application must be configured to use SSL channels in the sections expected to deal with the authenticated user because the X.509 authentication protocol is part of the SSL protocol.

To enable X.509 client authentication in Spring Security 6, you must add the <x509/> element to your HTTP security namespace configuration, as follows.

```
<http>
...

    <x509 subject-principal-regex="CN=(.*?)," user-service-
    ref="userService"/>;
</http>
```

The element has two optional attributes.

- subject-principal-regex. The regular expression used to extract a username from the certificate's subject name. The default value is shown in the preceding listing. This username is passed to the UserDetailsService to load the authorities for the user.

- user-service-ref. This is the bean ID of the UserDetailsService to be used with X.509. It is unnecessary if only one is defined in your application context.

The subject-principal-regex should contain a single group. For example, the default expression (CN=(.*?)) matches the common name field. So, if the subject name in the certificate is "CN=Jimi Hendrix, OU=...", this gives a user name of "Jimi Hendrix". The matches are case-insensitive. So "emailAddress=(.*?)," matches "EMAILADDRESS=jimi@hendrix.org,CN=...", giving a user name "jimi@hendrix.org". If the client presents a certificate and a valid username is successfully extracted, there should be a valid Authentication object in the security context. The security context remains empty if no certificate or corresponding user can be found. You can use X.509 authentication with other options, such as a form-based login.

To set up SSL in Tomcat, you could use the pre-generated certificates in the Spring Security samples repository to enable SSL for testing if you do not want to generate your own. The server.jks file contains the server certificate, the private key, and the issuing authority certificate. Some client certificate files are also for the users from the sample applications. You can install these in your browser to enable SSL client authentication.

To run Tomcat with SSL support, drop the server.jks file into the tomcat conf directory and add the following connector to the server.xml file.

```
<Connector port="8443" protocol="HTTP/1.1" SSLEnabled="true" scheme="https"
secure="true"
                clientAuth="true" sslProtocol="TLS"
                keystoreFile="${catalina.home}/conf/server.jks"
                keystoreType="JKS" keystorePass="password"
                truststoreFile="${catalina.home}/conf/server.jks"
                truststoreType="JKS" truststorePass="password"
/>
```

clientAuth can also be set to want if you still want SSL connections to succeed, even if the client does not provide a certificate. Clients who do not present a certificate cannot access any objects secured by Spring Security unless they use a non-X.509 authentication mechanism, such as form authentication.

OAuth 2.0

OAuth 2.0 is the industry-standard protocol for authorization. You can get more information at `https://oauth.net/2/`.

Since Spring Security 5.0 supports the OAuth 2.0 authorization framework and OpenID Connect 1.0. with Spring Security 5.1. It introduced new Resource Server support as well as additional client support.

The OAuth 2.0 implementation for authentication, which conforms to the OpenID Connect specification and is OpenID Certified, can be used for authentication and authorization via Google's OAuth 2.0 APIs. For more information, please go to `https://developers.google.com/identity/protocols/OAuth2`.

OAuth 2.0 supports

- Client

- Resource server

- Authorization server

The OAuth 2.0 client features support the client role defined in the OAuth 2.0 authorization framework. You can get more information at `https://auth0.com/`.

When developing an OAuth 2.0 Client, the following main features are available.

- Authorization code grant

- Client credentials grant

- The WebClient extension for servlet environments (for making protected resource requests)

Spring Security 5 introduced a new `OAuth2LoginConfigurer` class that you can use to configure an external authorization server.

More information is at `https://docs.spring.io/spring-security/reference/servlet/oauth2/resource-server/jwt.html#oauth2resourceserver-jwt-architecture`,

JSON Web Token

Spring Security 5 supports JSON Web Token (JWT) authentication.

You need to do the following.

- Configure Spring Security for JWT.

- Expose the REST POST API with mapping/authenticate.

- Configure a valid JSON Web Token.

Specifically, to configure Spring Security and JWT, you need to perform two operations.

1. Generate JWT by

   a. Exposing a POST API with mapping/authenticating

   b. Passing the correct username and password

2. Validate JWT by

   a. When trying to access the GET API with a certain mapping like /Testing

   b. Allowing access only if a request is valid

Spring Security and JWT dependencies include the following.

```
<dependency>
<groupId>io.jsonwebtoken</groupId>
<artifactId>jjwt</artifactId>
<version>0.9.1</version>
</dependency>
```

Spring WebSocket

Since Spring Security 5 MVC supports Spring WebSocket. For WebSocket implementation, you want to add the following Maven dependencies.

```
<dependency>
    <groupId>org.springframework</groupId>
    <artifactId>spring-websocket</artifactId>
    <version>6.0.10</version>
</dependency>
<dependency>
    <groupId>org.springframework</groupId>
    <artifactId>spring-messaging</artifactId>
    <version>6.0.10</version>
</dependency>
<dependency>
    <groupId>org.springframework.security</groupId>
    <artifactId>spring-security-messaging</artifactId>
    <version>6.1.1</version>
</dependency>
```

Then, define the configuration of WebSocket-specific security as follows:

```
@Configuration
@EnableWebSocketSecurity
public class WebSocketSecurityConfig {

    @Bean
    AuthorizationManager<Message<?>> messageAuthorizationManager(
    MessageMatcherDelegatingAuthorizationManager.Builder messages) {
```

```
    messages
            .simpDestMatchers("/user/**").hasRole("USER")

    return messages.build();
  }
}
```

For more information on WebSockets, check out the Spring Security 6 reference documentation at `https://docs.spring.io/spring-security/reference/servlet/integrations/websocket.html#page-title`.

Java Authentication and Authorization Service

The Java Authentication and Authorization Service (JAAS) is the standard Java support for managing authentication and authorization. Its functionality overlaps with that of Spring Security.

JAAS is a relatively large standard involving much more than the small amount of information covered here. However, the main concepts are the ones we showed you, and the goal of the section is to show the building blocks for integrating them with Spring Security.

For more information on JAAS, check out the Spring Security 5 reference documentation at `https://docs.spring.io/spring-security/reference/servlet/authentication/jaas.html`.

Central Authentication Service

The Central Authentication Service (CAS) is an enterprise single sign-on solution built in Java and open source. It has a great support community and integrates into many Java projects. CAS provides a centralized place for authentication and access control in an enterprise.

The JA-SIG (`www.ja-sig.org`) CAS a is a simple, open source, independent platform that supports proxy capabilities. Spring Security fully supports CAS for single applications and multiple-application deployments secured by an enterprise-wide CAS server. You can learn more about CAS at `www.apereo.org/projects/cas`.

One important characteristic of CAS is that it is designed to serve as a proxy for different authentication storage solutions. It can be used with LDAP, JDBC, or other user stores containing real user data. This looks a lot like the way Spring Security leverages these same user data stores.

For more information on CAS, check out the Spring Security 6 reference documentation at `https://docs.spring.io/spring-security/reference/servlet/authentication/cas.html`.

Summary

This chapter illustrated how to use Spring Security's modular architecture to integrate different authentication mechanisms relatively easily. We explained some of the authentication mechanisms that come with the framework. We demonstrated how to authenticate your users in a database, an LDAP server, and by using client X.509 certificates. JAAS, OAuth 2.0/OpenID Connect 1.0, WebSocket, JWT, and CAS were also introduced.

This chapter focused on showing how all these different authentication providers relate to each other when used inside the framework. The goal was to show you that integrating new providers into the framework is simple enough for you to try. Of course, how easy it is depends on the authentication scheme that you want to plug in.

Other authentication providers weren't covered in this chapter, but the main ideas remain the same: create a connector into Spring Security that deals with the particulars of the integrating protocol and adapt it to use the Spring Security model of authentication and authorization.

CHAPTER 7

Business Object Security with ACLs

This chapter introduces access control lists (ACLs) in the context of Spring Security.

Access control lists can be considered an extension to the business-level security rules reviewed in Chapter 6. This chapter, however, looks at more fine-grained rules to secure individual domain objects instead of the relatively coarse-grained rules used to secure method calls on services.

This means that ACLs are in charge of securing instances of domain classes (such as a Forum class, a Cart class, and so on), while the standard method-level rules secure entry points determined by methods (like a Service method or a DAO method).

Securing domain objects with ACLs is conceptually simple. The idea is that any user has a certain level of access (read, write, none, and so on) to each domain object. A user's level of access (*permissions*) to a particular domain object depends on the user or the role or group to which the user belongs.

ACL Key Concepts

The source code of the Spring Security ACL module or inside the .jar file itself: spring-security-acl-6.1.3.RELEASE.jar. It is in the src/main/resources folder in the source code, which means it is in the root of the classpath.

Spring Security's domain object instance security capabilities center on the concept of an access control list (ACL). Every domain object instance in our system has its own ACL, and the ACL records details of who can and cannot work with that domain object. Spring Security provides three main ACL-related capabilities to your application.

© Massimo Nardone, Carlo Scarioni 2024
M. Nardone and C. Scarioni, *Pro Spring Security*, https://doi.org/10.1007/979-8-8688-0035-1_7

- A way to retrieve ACL entries for our domain objects

- A way to ensure a given principal is permitted to work with our objects before methods are called

- A way to ensure a given principal is permitted to work with our objects after methods are called

Note that one of the main capabilities of the Spring Security ACL module is providing a high-performance way of retrieving ACLs.

This ACL repository capability is extremely important because every domain object instance in our system might have several access control entries, and each ACL might inherit from other ACLs in a tree-like structure.

Spring Security's ACL capability has been carefully designed to provide high-performance retrieval of ACLs, together with pluggable caching, deadlock-minimizing database updates, independence from ORM frameworks (we use JDBC directly), proper encapsulation, and transparent database updating.

The following are the main abstractions in Spring Security's ACL support.

- **Security identity (SID)** is an abstraction that represents a security identity in the system to be used by the ACL infrastructure. A security identity can be a user, role, group, and so forth. It maps to the `ACL_SID` table.

- **Access control entry (ACE)** represents an individual permission in the ACL, making relationships between objects, SIDs, and permissions. It maps to the `ACL_ENTRY` table.

- **Object identity** represents the identity of an individual domain object instance. They are the entities on which the permissions are set. It maps to the `ACL_OBJECT_IDENTITY` table.

- **Entry** stores the individual permissions assigned to each recipient. Columns include a foreign key to the `ACL_OBJECT_IDENTITY`, the recipient (i.e., a foreign key to ACL_SID), whether auditing or not and the integer bit mask that represents the actual permission being granted or denied.

The ACL system uses integer bit masking so that when you have 32 bits, you can switch on or off. Each of these bits represents a permission. By default, the permissions are read (bit 0), write (bit 1), create (bit 2), delete (bit 3), and administer (bit 4). You can implement your own permission instance so that the ACL framework operates without knowledge of your extensions.

You should understand that the number of domain objects in your system has no bearing on the fact that we have chosen to use integer bit masking. While you have 32 bits available for permissions, there could be billions of domain object instances to avoid mistakenly believing that one is needed for each potential domain object, which is not the case.

Now that you have a basic understanding of what the ACL system does and what it looks like at a table-structure level, you need to understand the ACL key interfaces.

- **ACL**: This is every domain object has one and only one ACL object, which internally holds the AccessControlEntry objects and knows the owner of the ACL, which does not refer directly to the domain object but instead to an ObjectIdentity. It is stored in the ACL_OBJECT_IDENTITY table.

- **AccessControlEntry** holds multiple AccessControlEntry objects, often abbreviated as ACEs in the framework. Each ACE refers to a specific tuple of permission, SID, and ACL. An ACE can also be granting or non-granting and contain audit settings. The ACE is stored in the ACL_ENTRY table.

- **Permission** represents a particular immutable bit mask and offers convenience functions for bit masking and outputting information. The basic permissions (bits from 0 to 4) are contained in the BasePermission class.

- **SID** is the abbreviation for *security identity*. The ACL module must refer to principals and GrantedAuthority instances, and the SID interface provides a level of indirection. Common classes include PrincipalSid, which represents the principal inside an Authentication object, and GrantedAuthoritySid. The SID information is stored in the ACL_SID table.

- **ObjectIdentity** internally represents each domain object within the ACL module. The default implementation is ObjectIdentityImpl.

- **AclService** retrieves the ACL applicable for a given ObjectIdentity. In the included implementation (JdbcAclService), retrieval operations are delegated to a LookupStrategy, which provides a highly optimized strategy for retrieving ACL information, using batched retrievals (BasicLookupStrategy) and supporting custom implementations that use materialized views, hierarchical queries, and similar performance-centric, non-ANSI SQL capabilities.

- **MutableAclService** presents a modified ACL for persistence; this interface is optional.

Note that our AclService and related database classes use ANSI SQL, which should work with all major databases. At the time of writing, the system had been successfully tested with Hypersonic SQL, PostgreSQL, Microsoft SQL Server, and Oracle.

The following is the Maven dependency in our code.

```
<dependency>
    <groupId>org.springframework.security</groupId>
    <artifactId>spring-security-acl</artifactId>
    <version>6.1.3</version>
</dependency>
```

To get started with Spring Security's ACL capability, you must first store your ACL information somewhere. This means that an instantiation of a DataSource in Spring is needed. It is then injected into a JdbcMutableAclService and a BasicLookupStrategy instance.

Next, you need to populate the database with the four ACL-specific tables.

Finally, once you have created the required schema and instantiated JdbcMutableAclService, you need to ensure that our domain model supports interoperability with the Spring Security ACL package like ObjectIdentityImpl proves sufficient because it provides many ways in which it can be used.

If you use domain objects that contain a public serializable getId() method, it returns a type that is long or compatible with long (such as an int), and you may find that you need not give further consideration to ObjectIdentity issues.

In general, many parts of the ACL module rely on long identifiers, and if you do not use long (or an int, byte, and so on), you might need to reimplement several classes.

We avoid using and supporting non-long identifiers in Spring Security's ACL module, as longs are already compatible with all database sequences, are the most common identifier data type, and are of sufficient length to accommodate all common usage scenarios.

Listing 7-1 shows how to create an ACL or modify an existing one.

Listing 7-1. Example of ACL Java Code

```
// Prepare the information to be in the access control entry (ACE)
ObjectIdentity oi = new ObjectIdentityImpl(Foo.class, new Long(44));
Sid sid = new PrincipalSid("Massimo");
Permission p = BasePermission.ADMINISTRATION;

// Create or update the relevant ACL
MutableAcl acl = null;
try {
acl = (MutableAcl) aclService.readAclById(oi);
} catch (NotFoundException nfe) {
acl = aclService.createAcl(oi);
}

// Granting permissions via an access control entry (ACE)
acl.insertAce(acl.getEntries().length, p, sid, true);
aclService.updateAcl(acl);
```

In this simple example, prepare the information you want in the access control entry (ACE) with ObjectIdentityImpl.

Then, retrieve the ACL associated with the Foo domain object with identifier 44.

Next, add an ACE so a principal named "Massimo" can "administer" the object. The code fragment is relatively self-explanatory, except for the insertAce method, where the first argument determines the position in the ACL at which the new entry is inserted.

Then, add code to create or update the relevant ACL.

Finally, grant permissions via an access control entry (ACE) at the end of the existing ACEs. The final argument is a Boolean indicating whether the ACE is granting or denying, which it usually grants (true), but if it denies (false), the permissions are blocked.

Spring Security does not provide any special integration to automatically create, update, or delete ACLs as part of your DAO or repository operations. Instead, you must write code similar to the preceding example for your domain objects. You should consider using AOP on your services layer to automatically integrate the ACL information with your services layer operations. We have found this approach to be effective.

Once you have used the techniques described here to store some ACL information in the database, the next step is to use the ACL information as part of authorization decision logic, which can be done by writing your own AccessDecisionVoter or AfterInvocationProvider that (respectively) fires before or after a method invocation. Such classes would use AclService to retrieve the relevant ACL and then call Acl. isGranted(Permission[] permission, Sid[] sids, boolean administrativeMode) to decide whether permission is granted or denied.

Alternatively, you could use the following classes, which provide a declarative-based approach to evaluating ACL information at runtime, freeing you from needing to write any code.

- AclEntryVoter

- AclEntryAfterInvocationProvider

- AclEntryAfterInvocationCollectionFilteringProvider

Summary

This chapter provided general information on how to use Spring Security's support for ACLs.

## CHAPTER 8

Open Authorization 2.0 (OAuth 2.0) and Spring Security

Spring Security is a very extendable and customizable framework. This is primarily because the framework is built using object-oriented principles and design practices so that it is open for extension and closed for modification. In the previous chapter, you saw one of the major extension points in Spring Security—namely, the pluggability of different authentication providers. This chapter covers the popular Open Authorization 2.0 (OAuth 2.0) framework. It shows how to develop login security applications using Spring Boot, Spring Web, and OAuth 2.0 client (security) toward GitHub and Google providers.

An Introduction to OAuth 2.0

OAuth 2.0 is a widely used authorization framework that allows third-party applications to access users' resources without exposing their credentials (such as usernames and passwords). It provides a secure and standardized way for users to grant limited access to their data or services to other applications or services, often called *clients*.

It operates based on tokens, which are short-lived and revocable access credentials. These tokens authenticate and authorize access between the client application, the resource owner (typically a user), and the resource server (where the protected resources are stored).

© Massimo Nardone, Carlo Scarioni 2024
M. Nardone and C. Scarioni, *Pro Spring Security*, https://doi.org/10.1007/979-8-8688-0035-1_8

The following is a high-level overview of how OAuth 2.0 works.

- **Client registration**: The application registers with the OAuth 2.0 authorization server. During this registration, it receives a client identifier and a client secret (a confidential key).

- **User authentication**: When the user wants to grant the client access to their resources, they are redirected to the authorization server for authentication. This step ensures the user's identity and consent.

- **Authorization grant**: After the user is authenticated, they are prompted to grant the client specific permissions to access their resources. This is often done through an authorization code or other types of grants.

- **Token request**: After obtaining the authorization grant, the client requests the authorization server to exchange the grant for an access token.

- **Access token issuance**: If the authorization server validates the request and grants access, it issues an access token to the client.

- **Accessing protected resources**: The client can now use the access token to access the user's protected resources on the resource server. The access token serves as proof of authorization.

- **Token expiration and refresh**: Access tokens typically have a limited lifespan. When they expire, the client can use a refresh token (if provided) to obtain a new access token without requiring the user to re-authenticate.

OAuth 2.0 is widely used for securing APIs, allowing users to grant selective access to their data on platforms like social media, and enabling single sign-on (SSO) across different services.

Please note that OAuth 2.0 is not a protocol for authentication; it's a framework for authorization. For user authentication, OpenID Connect, an identity layer built on top of OAuth 2.0, is often used in conjunction with OAuth 2.0 to provide both authentication and authorization capabilities.

OAuth 2.0 Security

OAuth 2.0 provides a framework for authorization, but it is essential to implement it securely to protect user data and resources. The following describes some key security considerations and best practices when using OAuth 2.0.

- Use **HTTPS**: Always use HTTPS to protect the communication between the client, authorization server, and resource server. This ensures the confidentiality and integrity of data transmitted during the OAuth flow.

- **Client authentication**: Implement proper client authentication. Depending on the OAuth 2.0 flow, clients should authenticate themselves using client credentials or other methods like client certificates.

- **Authorization Code Flow**: Web applications and confidential clients should use this flow, which involves an authorization code exchanged for an access token, reducing the risk of exposing tokens in the browser.

- **Token storage**: Safely stores and manages access and refresh tokens on the client side. Avoid storing tokens in insecure locations such as browser cookies, and use secure storage mechanisms.

- **Token validation**: When receiving access tokens from the authorization server, validate them properly. Check the token's signature and expiration date to ensure it's valid.

- **Scope permissions**: Ensure that clients only request the minimum necessary scope of permissions (access rights) from the user. This principle is known as the principle of least privilege.

- **User consent**: Always obtain clear and informed consent from the user before granting access to their data. Users should understand what data the client application can access and for what purpose.

- **Refresh token security**: Protect refresh tokens as they have a longer lifespan. Use secure storage and transmission mechanisms for refresh tokens. Only grant refresh tokens to confidential clients when necessary.

- **Token revocation**: Implement token revocation mechanisms. Allow users to revoke access to their data, invalidate access tokens, and refresh tokens when no longer needed.

- **Rate limiting and throttling**: Implement rate limiting and throttling to protect against brute-force and denial-of-service attacks on OAuth endpoints.

- **Cross-site request forgery (CSRF) protection**: Use anti-CSRF tokens or other techniques to protect against CSRF attacks that trick users into making unintended requests.

- **Authorization server security**: Secure the authorization server against common security threats, such as injection attacks, and keep its software and libraries current.

- **Logging and monitoring**: Implement comprehensive logging and monitoring to detect and respond to suspicious activities and security breaches.

- **Token rotation**: Periodically rotate client secrets and access tokens to mitigate the risk of exposure due to unauthorized access or leaks.

- **Security assessments**: Conduct security assessments, code reviews, and penetration testing to identify and address vulnerabilities in your OAuth 2.0 implementation.

The security of an OAuth 2.0 implementation depends on a combination of factors like the OAuth flow being used, the specific use case, and the client and authorization server configurations. Therefore, it's crucial to follow best practices, stay informed about security updates, and adapt your OAuth 2.0 implementation to the unique requirements of your application.

Integrating OAuth 2.0 with Spring Security

OAuth 2.0 can be integrated with Spring Security to secure your Java-based web applications, APIs, and microservices. Spring Security provides robust support for implementing OAuth 2.0 authentication and authorization in a Spring-based application.

Here's a basic overview of implementing OAuth 2.0 using Spring Security.

- **Add dependencies:** Ensure that you have the necessary dependencies in your project. Spring Security OAuth 2.0 module is essential for OAuth 2.0 support. You can include it in your pom.xml or build.gradle file.

- **Configuration:** Configure Spring Security to handle OAuth 2.0 by creating a configuration class that extends AuthorizationServerConfigurerAdapter. This class should provide information about your OAuth 2.0 authorization server, client credentials, and endpoints. Listing 8-1 shows a configuration Java example.

Listing 8-1. Configure OAuth 2.0

```
import org.springframework.context.annotation.*;
import org.springframework.security.oauth2.config.annotation.web.
configuration.*;
@Configuration
@EnableAuthorizationServer
public class OAuth2AuthorizationServerConfig extends
AuthorizationServerConfigurerAdapter {

    @Override
    public void configure(ClientDetailsServiceConfigurer clients) throws
    Exception {
        clients.inMemory()
            .withClient("client-id")
            .secret("client-secret")
            .authorizedGrantTypes("authorization_code", "password",
            "refresh_token")
            .scopes("read", "write")
            .redirectUris("http://localhost:8080/callback");
    }
}
```

- **User authentication:** Configure how your application handles user authentication. You can use the default Spring Security mechanisms or integrate with external identity providers.

- **Resource server configuration (optional):** If you're building an OAuth 2.0 resource server (e.g., an API), you must configure Spring Security to validate access tokens. You can do this by creating a class that extends ResourceServerConfigurerAdapter. Listing 8-2 shows a server configuration Java example.

Listing 8-2. Configure OAuth 2.0 Resource Server

```java
import org.springframework.context.annotation.Bean;
import org.springframework.context.annotation.Configuration;
import org.springframework.security.config.annotation.web.builders.
HttpSecurity;
import org.springframework.security.config.annotation.web.configuration.
EnableWebSecurity;
import org.springframework.security.web.SecurityFilterChain;

@Configuration
@EnableWebSecurity

public class SecurityConfiguration {

    @Bean
    SecurityFilterChain securityFilterChain(HttpSecurity http) throws
    Exception {
        return http
                .authorizeHttpRequests(auth -> {
                    auth.requestMatchers("/api/**").authenticated ();
                    auth.anyRequest().authenticated();
                })
                .oauth2Login(withDefaults())
                .build();
    }

}
```

- **Secure endpoints**: Use Spring Security annotations like @Secured, @PreAuthorize, or @PostAuthorize to secure specific methods or endpoints in your application.

- **User consent and authentication flow**: Implement a user interface for the OAuth 2.0 authentication flow. This includes handling user consent and redirecting users to the OAuth 2.0 authorization endpoint.

- **Token storage and management:** Implement token storage and management, including access tokens, refresh tokens, and their lifecycles. Spring Security OAuth 2.0 provides mechanisms to handle this.

- **Testing and validation**: Thoroughly test your OAuth 2.0 implementation to ensure that the authentication and authorization flows work as expected. You can use tools like Postman or dedicated OAuth 2.0 clients for testing.

- **Logging and monitoring**: Implement logging and monitoring to track security-related events and potential issues.

- **Documentation and error handling**: Provide clear documentation for developers using your OAuth 2.0-protected resources and implement proper error handling to respond to various OAuth 2.0–related errors gracefully.

Remember that OAuth 2.0 implementation can vary depending on your requirements and use cases. Spring Security provides flexibility to adapt OAuth 2.0 to your application's needs while following security best practices.

OAuth 2.0 Login

OAuth 2.0 Login is a secure and standardized way for users to grant permission to third-party applications to access their protected resources or perform actions on their behalf without sharing their login credentials. It is commonly used for single sign-on (SSO) and enabling users to log in to different websites or applications using their existing credentials from a trusted identity provider (IdP).

Here's what is included in OAuth 2.0 Login.

- **User-centric authentication**: OAuth 2.0 Login is user-centric, focusing on the user's consent and authorization. Users grant permission to applications to access specific resources without revealing their usernames and passwords.

- **Role of the user**: When users try to log in to a third-party application, they are redirected to an IdP authentication page. The user authenticates themselves with the IdP, which verifies their identity.

- **Authorization Code Flow**: One of the most common OAuth 2.0 Login flows.

  - The user is redirected to the IdP's login page.

  - After successful authentication, the IdP asks the user for consent to share their data with the requesting application.

  - If the user consents, the IdP generates an authorization code.

  - The application exchanges this authorization code for an access token, which it can use to access the user's resources.

- **Single sign-on (SSO)**: OAuth 2.0 Login is often used for SSO scenarios, where users can log in once and then access multiple applications without re-entering their credentials. This reduces the need for users to remember multiple usernames and passwords.

- **Third-party applications**: OAuth 2.0 Login enables third-party applications to request access to a user's resources without having direct access to their credentials. This enhances security by limiting the exposure of sensitive information.

- **Scoped access**: OAuth 2.0 Login allows users to grant specific permissions (scopes) to applications, ensuring that applications only access the data or perform the actions the user allows.

- **Token-based authentication**: OAuth 2.0 Login relies on access tokens, which are short-lived revocable credentials used to authenticate API requests on behalf of the user. These tokens replace the need for the user's username and password in each API call.

- **Security and authorization**: OAuth 2.0 Login provides a robust framework for securing user data and resources. Users have control over which applications have access to their data, and they can revoke access at any time.

- **Widely adopted**: OAuth 2.0 is widely adopted across various platforms, services, and industries. It is used by many well-known identity providers, including Google, Facebook, and Microsoft, making it a common choice for integrating with their services.

OAuth 2.0 Login is implemented using the authorization code grant, as specified in the OAuth 2.0 authorization framework at `https://datatracker.ietf.org/doc/html/rfc6749#section-4.1`. Similarly, OpenID Connect Core 1.0 is at `https://openid.net/specs/openid-connect-core-1_0.html#CodeFlowAuth`.

The OAuth 2.0 Login feature lets users log in to the application using their existing account at an OAuth 2.0 provider (such as GitHub) or OpenID Connect 1.0 provider (such as Google). OAuth 2.0 Login can also authenticate toward Facebook, Twitter, and so on.

This example seeks to configure the Spring Authorization Server with a social login provider such as Google and GitHub and authenticate the user with OAuth 2.0 Login, replacing the common form login.

Let's build our authentication and login application using Spring Boot 3.x, Spring Security 6, Spring Web, and OAuth 2.0 Client.

The first step is to create the Spring Boot Maven project using the Spring Initializr, the quickest way to generate Spring Boot projects. You just need to choose the language, build system, and JVM version for your project, and it is automatically generated with all the dependencies needed.

Navigate to `https://start.spring.io/` and use the Spring Initializr web-based Spring project generator to create the Spring Boot Maven project named OAuth2SecurityLogin, as shown in Figure 8-1.

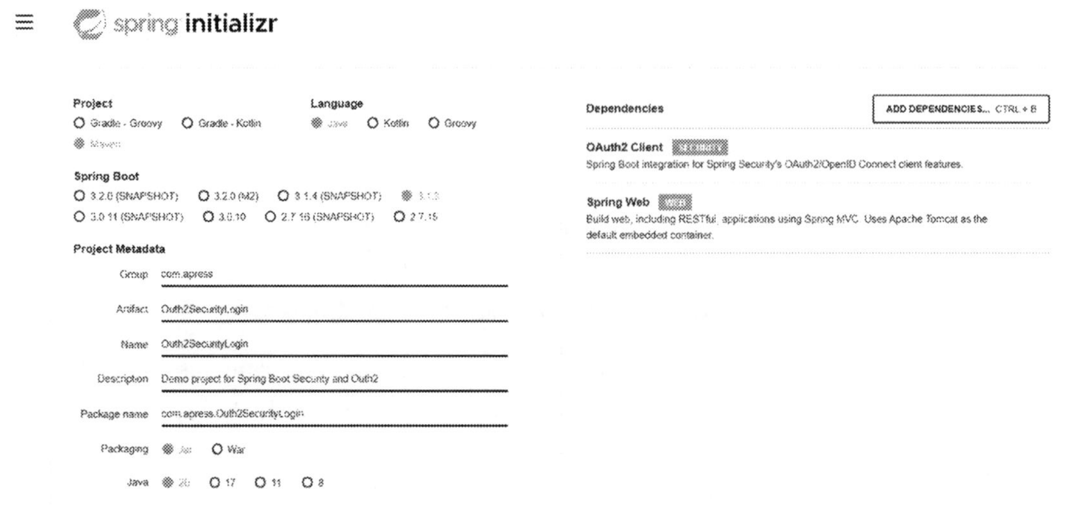

Figure 8-1. *Generate an OAuth 2.0 project using the Initializr web-based Spring project generator*

Select a Java 20 Maven project using Spring Boot version 3.1.3, and add the following dependencies: Spring Web and OAuth 2.0 Client.

Add the Thymeleaf Java library as a dependency to the pom.xml file. It is a template engine used to parse and transform the data produced by the application to template files. It acts just like HTML but provides more attributes used to render data.

Fill in all the required information and then click to generate the project. A project .zip file is automatically generated. Download and unzip the file on your machine.

Figure 8-2 shows the project in IntelliJ IDEA 2023.1.2.

Figure 8-2. *Maven project structure*

The most important dependencies, which are automatically updated in the pom.xml file, are shown in Listing 8-3.

Listing 8-3. Needed Dependencies

```xml
<dependency>
    <groupId>org.springframework.boot</groupId>
    <artifactId>spring-boot-starter-oauth2-client</artifactId>
</dependency>

<dependency>
    <groupId>org.springframework.boot</groupId>
    <artifactId>spring-boot-starter-web</artifactId>
</dependency>
```

The entire generated pom.xml file with the added dependencies is shown in Listing 8-4.

Listing 8-4. *pom.xml File and Dependencies*

```xml
<?xml version="1.0" encoding="UTF-8"?>
<project xmlns="http://maven.apache.org/POM/4.0.0" xmlns:xsi="http://www.
w3.org/2001/XMLSchema-instance"
    xsi:schemaLocation="http://maven.apache.org/POM/4.0.0 https://maven.
    apache.org/xsd/maven-4.0.0.xsd">
    <modelVersion>4.0.0</modelVersion>
    <parent>
        <groupId>org.springframework.boot</groupId>
        <artifactId>spring-boot-starter-parent</artifactId>
        <version>3.1.3</version>
        <relativePath/> <!-- lookup parent from repository -->
    </parent>
    <groupId>com.apress</groupId>
    <artifactId>OAuth2SecurityLogin</artifactId>
    <version>0.0.1-SNAPSHOT</version>
    <name>OAuth2SecurityLogin</name>
    <description>Demo project for Spring Boot Security and OAuth 2.0</
    description>
    <properties>
        <java.version>20</java.version>
    </properties>
    <dependencies>
        <dependency>
            <groupId>org.springframework.boot</groupId>
            <artifactId>spring-boot-starter-oauth2-client</artifactId>
        </dependency>
        <dependency>
            <groupId>org.springframework.boot</groupId>
            <artifactId>spring-boot-starter-web</artifactId>
        </dependency>
        <dependency>
            <groupId>org.thymeleaf.extras</groupId>
            <artifactId>thymeleaf-extras-springsecurity6</artifactId>
            <version>3.1.1.RELEASE</version>
```

```
        </dependency>
        <dependency>
            <groupId>org.springframework.boot</groupId>
            <artifactId>spring-boot-starter-test</artifactId>
            <scope>test</scope>
        </dependency>
    </dependencies>

    <build>
        <plugins>
            <plugin>
                <groupId>org.springframework.boot</groupId>
                <artifactId>spring-boot-maven-plugin</artifactId>
            </plugin>
        </plugins>
    </build>

</project>
```

Let's build our first Java controller class, UserController, in Spring MVC to specify its methods with various annotations of the requests, such as the URLs of the endpoint, the HTTP request method, the path variables, etc.

Listing 8-5 shows the UserController class.

Listing 8-5. UserController Java Class

```
import org.springframework.stereotype.Controller;
import org.springframework.web.bind.annotation.GetMapping;

@Controller
public class UserController {

    @GetMapping("/")
    public String homePage() { return "welcome";
    }

    @GetMapping("/welcome")
    public String welcomePage() {
        return "welcome";
    }
```

```
@GetMapping ("/authenticated")
public String AuthenticatedPage() {
    return "authenticated";
    }

@GetMapping ("/logout")
public String logoutPage() {
    return "redirect:/welcome";
}
}
```

The controller Java class redirects to the welcome.html page for the "/" and "/Welcome" and authenticated.html for "/authenticated" URLs. Logout mapping is used when logging out the user from GitHub or Google authentication.

Let's create two simple HTML pages.

- welcome.html (see Listing 8-6), a simple welcome page permitted to all users to provide the link to the authenticated html page

- authenticated.html (see Listing 8-7), a simple HTML page showing the authenticated (GitHub or Google) username if authenticated

Listing 8-6. welcome.html Page

```
<!DOCTYPE html>
<html xmlns="http://www.w3.org/1999/xhtml" xmlns:th="https://www.
thymeleaf.org">
<html lang="en">
<head>
    <meta http-equiv="Content-Type" content="text/html;
    charset=ISO-8859-1">
    <title>Spring Security 6 and OAuth 2.0 Login authentication
    example!</title>
</head>
<body>

<div th:if="${param.error}">
    Invalid username and password.
```

```
</div>
<div th:if=""${param.logout}">
    You have been logged out.
</div>
```

```
<h2>Welcome to Spring Security 6 and OAuth 2.0 Login authentication
example!</h2>
```

```
<p>Click <a th:href="@{/authenticated}">here</a> to get authenticated to
GitHub or Google with OAuth 2.0 Login!</p>
```

```
</body>
</html>
```

*Listing **8**-**7***. welcome.html Page

```
<!DOCTYPE html>
<html xmlns="http://www.w3.org/1999/xhtml" xmlns:th="https://www.
thymeleaf.org"
      xmlns:sec="https://www.thymeleaf.org/thymeleaf-extras-
      springsecurity6">
<head>
    <title>Spring Security 6 and OAuth 2.0 Login authentication
    example!</title>
</head>
<body>
<h2>Welcome to Spring Security 6 and OAuth 2.0 Login authentication
example!</h2>
```

```
<h2 th:inline="text">You are an authenticated user: <span th:remove="tag"
sec:authentication="name">thymeleaf</span>!</h2>
```

```
<form th:action="@{/logout}" method="post">
    <input type="submit" value="Logout"/>
</form>
```

```
</body>
</html>
```

You now create the most important Java class of the example, SpringSecurityConfiguration, shown in Listing 8-8.

Listing 8-8. SpringSecurityConfiguration Java Class

```
package com.apress.OAuth2SecurityLogin.configuration;

import org.springframework.context.annotation.Bean;
import org.springframework.context.annotation.Configuration;
import org.springframework.security.config.annotation.web.builders.
HttpSecurity;
import org.springframework.security.config.annotation.web.configuration.
EnableWebSecurity;
import org.springframework.security.web.SecurityFilterChain;
import static org.springframework.security.config.Customizer.withDefaults;

@Configuration
@EnableWebSecurity

public class SecurityConfiguration {

    @Bean
    SecurityFilterChain securityFilterChain(HttpSecurity http) throws
    Exception {
        return http
                .authorizeHttpRequests(auth -> {
                    auth.requestMatchers("/", "welcome").permitAll();
                    auth.anyRequest().authenticated();
                })
                .oauth2Login(withDefaults())
                .formLogin(withDefaults())
                .build();
    }

}
```

The Spring Security Java class does the following.

- Allows all users to access routes "/" or "Welcome"

- Makes any other request (e.g., /authenticated) authenticated via GitHub or Google

- Uses OAuth 2.0 Login method to log the listed providers in the application.properties file (in our case, GitHub and Google)

- Uses the Spring Security 6 FormLogin

Next, let's start configuring GitHub and Google to be accessed via OAuth 2.0 Login. The first step is configuring the application properties file, as shown in Listing 8-9.

Listing 8-9. *application.properties Configuration*

```
# GitHub Login
spring.security.oauth2.client.registration.github.client-id= <your-github-
client-id>
spring.security.oauth2.client.registration.github.client-secret= <your-
github-client-secret>

# Google Login
spring.security.oauth2.client.registration.google.client-id= <your-google-
client-id>
spring.security.oauth2.client.registration.google.client-secret= <your-
google-client-secret>

# Configure Spring Security Logging
logging.level.org.springframework.security=TRACE
```

Adding the lines ..`registration.github` and ..`registration.google` tells Spring Security that you want to access those social providers via OAuth 2.0.0.

Let's now look at generating the OAuth 2.0 IDs and secret keys for Google and GitHub.

To use Google's OAuth 2.0 authentication method for login, you must set up a project in the Google API console to obtain OAuth 2.0 credentials (ID and secret) to be added to the application.properties.

Let's follow these steps to generate the OAuth 2.0 ID and secret key for Google.

1. Create a Google OAuth consent project and then link the consent to it. Let's visit the Google Cloud APIs & Services console to create the project and the consent (Figures 8-3 and 8-4) at `https://console.cloud.google.com/projectselector2/apis/credentials/consent`

Figure 8-3. *The Google Cloud console*

Figure 8-4. *The Google Cloud new project page*

2. Create a new consent associated with the project, as shown in
    Figure 8-5.

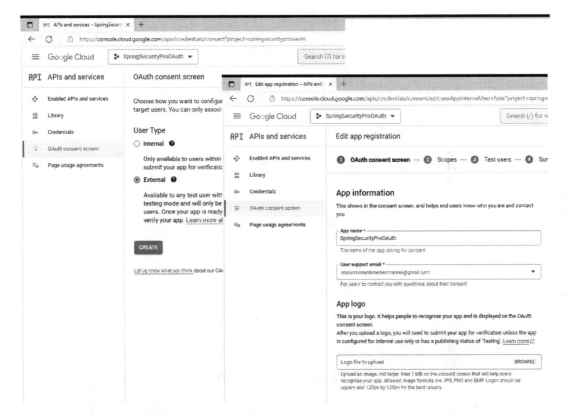

Figure 8-5. *The Google Cloud OAuth consent*

3. Next, go to the Credentials section and select "Create OAuth
    client ID".

    Select "Web application" as the application type and enter an
    application name.

    Add the following as an authorized redirect URI, as shown in
    Figure 8-6.

    http://localhost:8080/login/oauth2/code/google

4. Click the Create button to obtain your client_id and client_secret
    for the application.properties file, as shown in Figure 8-6.

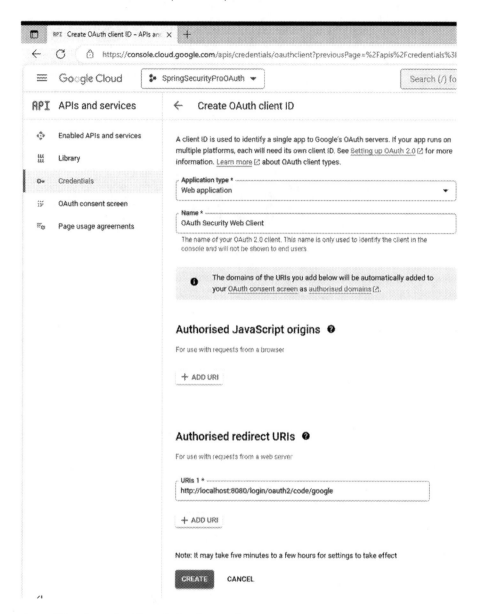

Figure 8-6. *The Google Cloud Credentials page*

Figure 8-7 shows how client_id and client_secret are used in the application.
properties file.

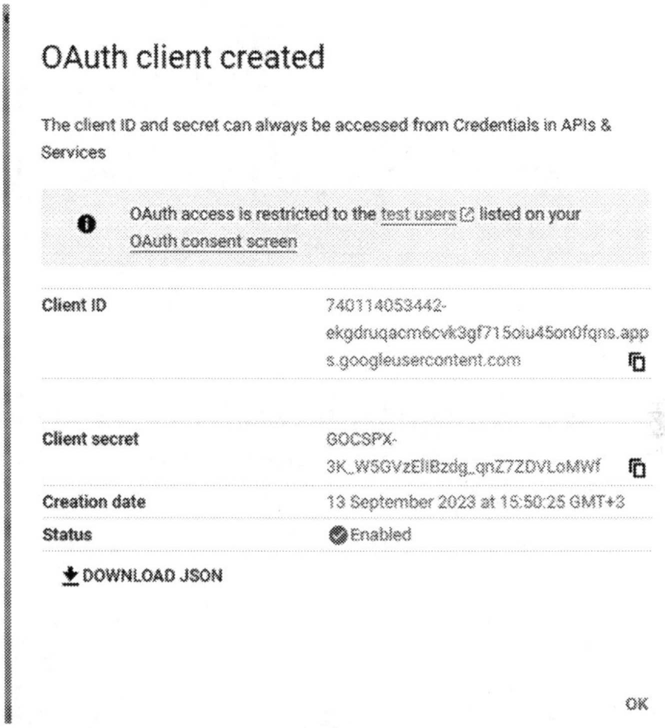

OAuth client created

The client ID and secret can always be accessed from Credentials in APIs & Services

ⓘ OAuth access is restricted to the test users ☑ listed on your OAuth consent screen

Client ID   740114053442-
                   ekgdruqacm6cvk3gf715oiu45on0fqns.app
                   s.googleusercontent.com   ⧉

Client secret   GOCSPX-
                   3K_W5GVzElIBzdg_qnZ7ZDVLoMWf   ⧉

Creation date   13 September 2023 at 15:50:25 GMT+3

Status   ✓ Enabled

⬇ DOWNLOAD JSON

OK

Figure 8-7. *The Google client_id and client_secret*

Copy the generated client ID and secret to our example application.properties.

```
# Google Login
spring.security.oauth2.client.registration.google.client-id=
740114053442-ekgdruqacm6cvk3gf715oiu45on0fqns.apps.googleusercontent.com
spring.security.oauth2.client.registration.google.client-secret= GOCSPX-3K_
W5GVzElIBzdg_qnZ7ZDVLoMWf
```

The application is ready to be tested.

Run the application and visit http://localhost:8080/welcome. You see the welcome.html page shown in Figure 8-8.

Figure 8-8. *The welcome.html page*

Click the "here" link to access the authenticated.html page, which automatically redirects to the Spring login web page. This provides the list (added in application. properties) of the social providers we are trying to access via the OAuth 2.0 Login authentication method, as shown in Figure 8-9.

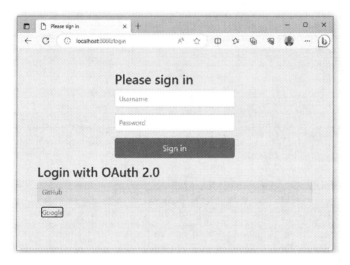

Figure 8-9. *The login page*

Click the Google link to be redirected to Google for authentication.

Next, authenticate (see Figure 8-10) with your Google account credentials. You see the Consent screen, which asks you to allow or deny access to the OAuth Client you created earlier. Click the Allow button to authorize the OAuth Client to access your email address and basic profile information.

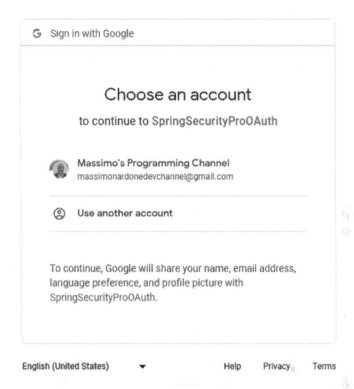

Figure 8-10. *The Google selecting account page*

Finally, the OAuth Client retrieves your email address and all the basic profile information from the UserInfo endpoint you configured in Google and establishes an authenticated session.

If the Google client credential configured in the Spring application matches the Google OAuth configured ID and secret, then the user is authenticated, showing the unique username, as shown in Figure 8-11; otherwise, a message error is displayed.

Figure 8-11. *Google user is authenticated*

Let's configure GitHub as an OAuth 2.0 Login provider.

1. Create a new OAuth app by going to your GitHub account settings and navigating to the Developer settings at `https://github.com/settings/profile`.

2. Go to the OAuth Apps section and click New OAuth App. Complete the required fields, as shown in Figure 8-12.

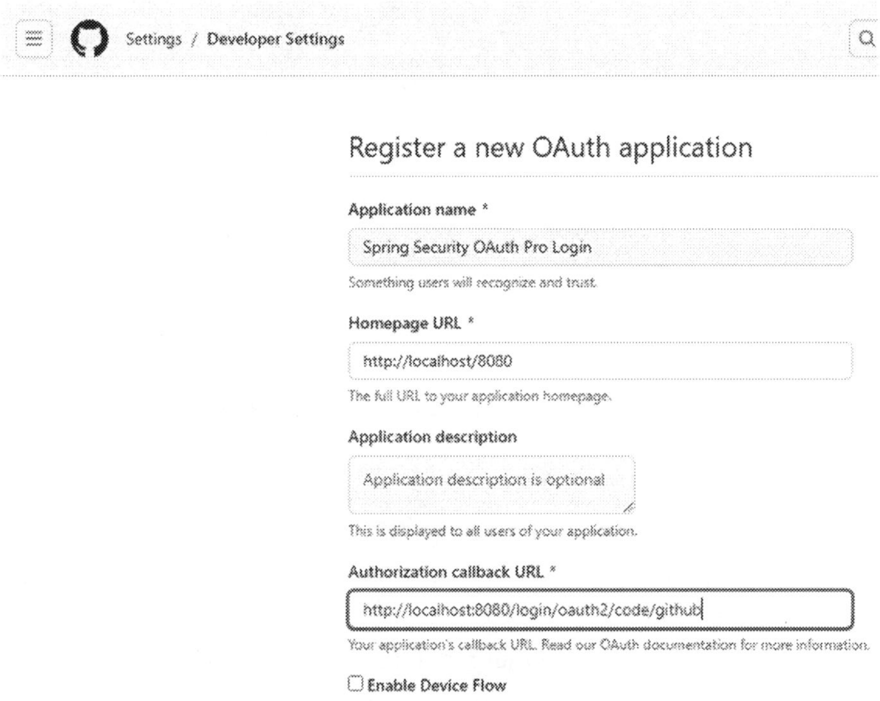

Figure 8-12. *Create a new GitHub OAuth app*

The authorization callback URL is http://localhost:8080/login/oauth2/code/github.

3. Click register the application to receive a client_id and client_ secret to add to the application.properties file, as shown in Figure 8-13.

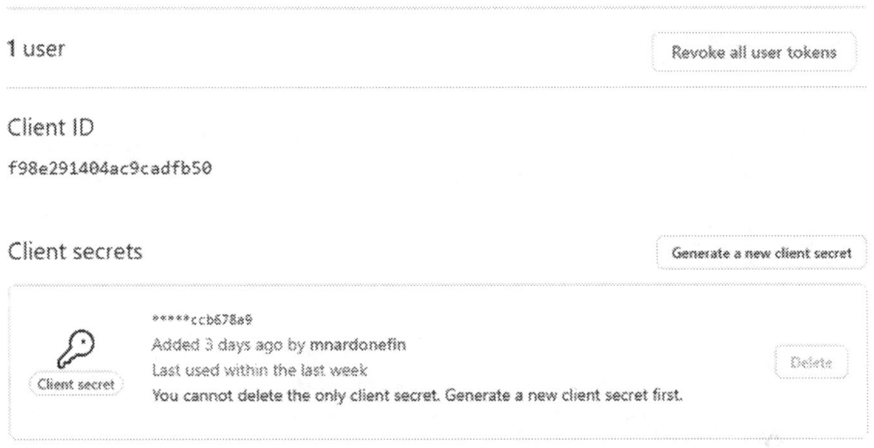

1 user   Revoke all user tokens

Client ID

f98e291404ac9cadfb50

Client secrets   Generate a new client secret

*****ccb678a9
Added 3 days ago by mnardonefin
Last used within the last week   Delete
Client secret
You cannot delete the only client secret. Generate a new client secret first.

Figure 8-13. *New GitHub OAuth app generates ID and secret key*

Copy the ID and secret key into the application.proporties file in our application.

```
# GitHub Login
spring.security.oauth2.client.registration.github.client-
id=f98e291404ac9cadfb50
spring.security.oauth2.client.registration.github.client-secret=e29120
1b5f8f3e368bc7380ecf0e3534ccb678a9
```

Rerun the application and select GitHub as the login method, as shown in Figure 8-14.

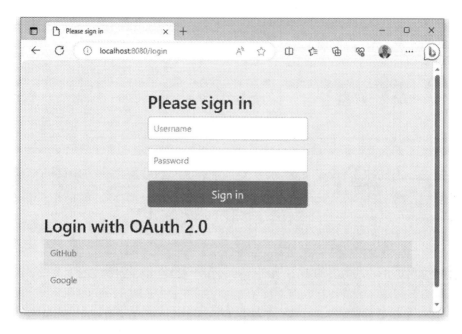

Figure 8-14. *The GitHub account selecting the web page*

If the user has a registered ID and secret key match, you can access the authenticated page, which shows the unique username (see Figure 8-15).

Figure 8-15. *GitHub user is authenticated*

This completes the demonstration on configuring OAuth 2.0 Login for Google and GitHub. Please note that this example is only configured in the application.properties file with some values like ID and secret key. Many other Spring Boot property mappings values can be added as OAuth Client properties to the ClientRegistration properties, including the following.

- `spring.security.oauth2.client.registration.[registrationId]`

- `spring.security.oauth2.client.registration.[registrationId].client-id`

- `spring.security.oauth2.client.registration.[registrationId].client-secret`

- `spring.security.oauth2.client.registration.[registrationId].client-authentication-method`

- `spring.security.oauth2.client.registration.[registrationId].authorization-grant-type`

- `spring.security.oauth2.client.registration.[registrationId].redirect-uri`

- `spring.security.oauth2.client.registration.[registrationId].scope`

- `spring.security.oauth2.client.registration.[registrationId].client-name`

- `spring.security.oauth2.client.provider.[providerId].authorization-uri`

- `spring.security.oauth2.client.provider.[providerId].token-uri`

- `spring.security.oauth2.client.provider.[providerId].jwk-set-uri`

- `spring.security.oauth2.client.provider.[providerId].issuer-uri`

- `spring.security.oauth2.client.provider.[providerId].user-info-uri`

- `spring.security.oauth2.client.provider.[providerId].user-info-authentication-method`

- `spring.security.oauth2.client.provider.[providerId].user-name-attribute`

Summary

This chapter demonstrated how Spring Security can be a very extendable and customizable framework as it is built using object-oriented principles and design practices so that it is open for extension and closed for modification. You learned how to use the Open Authorization 2.0 (OAuth 2.0) framework and how to develop login security applications using Spring Boot, Spring Web, and OAuth 2.0 client (security) to authenticate toward GitHub and Google providers.

CHAPTER 9

JSON Web Token (JWT) Authentication

This chapter explores REST API and JWT authentication and authorization using Spring Boot 3 and Spring Security 6.

In previous chapters, you saw some types of Spring Security authentication methods. First, let's look at the REST API and an example of JWT authentication.

The REST API

REST, which stands for *REpresentational State Transfer*, is an architectural style for designing networked applications. REST has become the predominant way of designing an API (application programming interface) for web-based applications.

REST APIs provide a structured and standardized way for different software applications to communicate over the Internet. They've become the backbone of modern web and mobile applications, enabling seamless integration and interaction between various services and systems.

REST APIs allow different software applications to communicate and interact with each other over the Internet using standard HTTP methods.

The following describes REST API key concepts.

- **Resources**: In REST, everything is considered a resource. A resource can be a data entity, an object, or any other type of information that can be identified by a unique URL (Uniform Resource Locator).

- **HTTP methods**: REST APIs utilize standard HTTP methods to perform operations on resources like the following.

239

- **GET** retrieves data from the server.

- **POST** sends data to the server to create a new resource.

- **PUT** updates an existing resource on the server.

- **DELETE** removes a resource from the server.

- **PATCH** partially updates a resource.

- **Uniform interface**: REST APIs have a uniform and consistent interface. Each resource is identified by a URL, and different HTTP methods are used to interact with those resources.

- **Stateless**: Each API request from a client to a server must contain all the information needed to understand and fulfill the request. The server doesn't store any client state between requests.

- **Client-server architecture**: REST separates the client (the application making the request) from the server (the application fulfilling the request), which allows them to evolve independently.

- **Response format**: REST APIs typically return data in common formats such as JSON (JavaScript Object Notation) or XML (eXtensible Markup Language).

The following are simple examples of a REST API managing a list of cars.

- GET /cars: Retrieve a list of all cars.

- GET /cars/{id}: Retrieve details of a specific car.

- POST /cars: Create a new car record by sending car data.

- PUT /cars/{id}: Update details of a specific car.

- DELETE /cars/{id}: Delete a specific car.

The following describes the most important advantages of REST API.

- **Scalability**: RESTful architectures are scalable due to their stateless nature.

- **Flexibility**: Clients and servers can evolve independently without affecting each other if the API contract remains consistent.

- **Wide adoption**: REST is widely adopted and understood, making it easier for developers to work with.

- **Caching**: REST APIs can use HTTP caching mechanisms to improve performance.

- **Language and platform independence**: Since REST APIs use standard HTTP methods and formats, they can be accessed from various programming languages and platforms.

While REST APIs have numerous advantages, there are also some disadvantages and limitations to consider.

- **Lack of standardization**: Despite being a widely adopted architectural style, REST doesn't provide strict guidelines on how to design APIs. This can lead to inconsistencies in API design and make it challenging to ensure uniformity across different APIs.

- **Overfetching and underfetching**: REST APIs often return fixed data structures, which can lead to overfetching (receiving more data than needed) or underfetching (receiving less data than needed) of information. This can result in wasted bandwidth or additional requests.

- **Limited support for real-time communication**: REST APIs are typically request-response-based and may not be well-suited for real-time communication. Implementing features like instant messaging or live updates can be complex and might require additional technologies.

- **No built-in state management**: REST APIs are stateless, which means the server doesn't store the client state. While this simplifies server design, managing session-related information can lead to challenges.

- **Lack of rich semantics**: REST APIs primarily rely on HTTP methods and status codes, which may not always convey rich semantics about the underlying operations. This can lead to ambiguity in understanding the purpose of certain API endpoints.

- **Performance overhead**: REST APIs may involve additional data parsing and serialization steps due to reliance on formats like JSON or XML. This can introduce performance overhead, especially in high-frequency scenarios.

- **Multiple requests for complex operations**: Complex operations often require multiple requests to the server, leading to additional network overhead and latency. This can be a concern for mobile applications or in situations with limited bandwidth.

- **Lack of flexibility in versioning**: Changing a REST API while maintaining backward compatibility can be challenging. Different versions of the API might need to be managed, which can complicate the development and deployment process.

- **Security considerations**: While REST APIs can be secured using mechanisms like HTTPS and authentication, designing a secure REST API requires careful consideration of authorization, token management, and protection against common security vulnerabilities.

- **Limited discoverability**: Discovering the available endpoints and their functionalities in a REST API might require external documentation, as there's no built-in mechanism for exposing the API structure to clients.

Introduction to JSON Web Token

JWT is an open standard (RFC 7519) that defines a compact and self-contained way for securely transmitting information between parties as a JSON object. JWTs are commonly used for authentication and authorization in web applications and APIs.

A JWT consists of three parts.

- **Header**: The header typically consists of two parts: the type of the token (JWT) and the signing algorithm being used, such as HMAC SHA256 or RSA.

```
{
  "alg": "HS256",
  "typ": "JWT"
}
```

- **Payload**: The second part of the token is the payload, which contains the claims. Claims are statements about an entity (typically the user) and additional metadata and can be categorized into three types.

    - **Registered Claims** are predefined claims with specific meanings, like iss (issuer), exp (expiration time), sub (subject), and more.

    - **Public Claims** are custom claims that you define to convey additional information.

    - **Private Claims** are custom claims meant to be shared between parties that agree on their usage and are not defined in any public specification.

    ```
    {
      "sub": "1234567890",
      "name": "Massimo Nardone",
      "iat": 6723561290
    }
    ```

- **Signature**: To create a signature, you must sign the encoded header, the encoded payload, a secret, and the algorithm specified in the header. The signature is used to verify that the sender of the JWT is who it says it is and to ensure that the message wasn't changed along the way.

The following explains how JWTs work.

- **Authentication**: When a user logs in, the server creates a JWT containing the user's information and signs it with a secret key. This JWT is then sent to the client.

- **Authorization**: The client includes the JWT in the headers of subsequent requests to the server. The server can then verify the JWT's signature and extract the user's information from the payload to grant access to protected resources.

Figure 9-1 shows how JWT works.

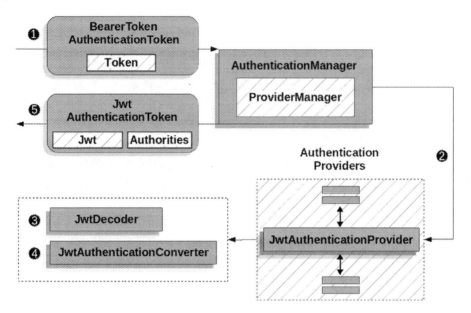

Figure 9-1. *JWT working diagram (source docs.spring.io)*

1. The authentication filter from reading the bearer token passes a
    BearerTokenAuthenticationToken to the AuthenticationManager,
    which is implemented by ProviderManager.

2. The ProviderManager is configured to use an
    AuthenticationProvider of type JwtAuthenticationProvider.

3. JwtAuthenticationProvider decodes, verifies, and validates JWT
    using a JwtDecoder.

4. JwtAuthenticationProvider then uses the
    JwtAuthenticationConverter to convert the Jwt into a Collection of
    granted authorities.

5. When authentication is successful, the authentication returned is
    of type JwtAuthenticationToken and has a principal that is the Jwt
    returned by the configured JwtDecoder. Ultimately, the returned
    JwtAuthenticationToken is set on SecurityContextHolder by the
    authentication filter.

The following are some of the advantages of JWT.

- **Compact**: JWTs are compact and can be sent as URL parameters, in an HTTP header, or in cookies.

- **Self-contained**: The token contains all the necessary information, reducing the need to query a database for user information.

- **Decentralized**: Since JWTs are self-contained, the server doesn't need to keep session information, making it easier to scale and distribute applications.

As per security considerations, JWTs are digitally signed, not encrypted. The information they contain can be decoded by anyone with access to the token, but the signature ensures its integrity. Storing sensitive data in the payload is not recommended, as the payload can be easily decoded.

To prevent tampering, it's important to use strong and secure algorithms for signing the tokens.

Secrets used for signing should be kept secret. If using public-key cryptography, the private key must be kept secure.

JWTs are widely used for building secure authentication and authorization mechanisms in modern web applications, APIs, and single sign-on (SSO) systems.

Here's how JWT and Spring Security can be integrated.

- **Dependency setup**: First, you must add the necessary dependencies to your project. Your project's build configuration should include Spring Security and libraries related to JWT.

- **Authentication and authorization configuration**: Configure Spring Security to manage authentication and authorization. This involves setting up security rules, authentication providers, and user details services. You can define which paths require authentication and which roles are required to access certain resources.

- **Token generation and validation**: Implement logic to generate and validate JWTs. Spring Security provides filters and classes to handle token-based authentication. You must create a mechanism to generate JWTs upon successful authentication and validate incoming JWTs for authorized requests.

- **Token processing filters**: Use Spring Security filters to intercept requests and perform authentication and authorization checks. You might implement a filter that examines the incoming JWT, validates it, and sets up the security context if the token is valid.

- **User details and authorities**: Extract user details and authorities from the JWT payload upon successful token validation. These details can be used to populate the Spring Security authentication context, allowing you to control access based on user roles and permissions.

- **Customizing authentication providers**: Depending on your authentication requirements, you might need to implement custom authentication providers to validate JWTs against your backend services or user databases.

- **Access control configuration**: Define access control rules using Spring Security's configuration. You can specify which roles are required to access different endpoints or resources. Roles and authorities can be derived from the JWT payload.

- **Exception handling**: Implement exception handling for cases where JWT validation fails, or unauthorized access is attempted. Customize error responses based on the security context.

- **Logout and token expiration**: For improved security, handle token expiration and implement a logout mechanism. JWTs can have an expiration time specified in their payload.

- **Testing and documentation**: Thoroughly test your JWT-based Spring Security implementation. Also, provide clear documentation for developers who work with the security system.

Keeping the Spring Security and JWT libraries updated is important because their APIs and best practices evolve. Spring Security's official documentation and online resources often provide detailed guides on integrating JWT-based authentication and authorization.

This chapter features an example showing how to secure a REST API using JWT using Spring Security 6, Spring Boot 3+, and PostgreSQL.

First, download and install PostgreSQL from `https://www.postgresql.org/download/windows/`.

Next, create a new database named "jwtsecuritydb". The username is "postgres" and the password is "postgres".

Figure 9-2 shows that our new PostgreSQL database is up and running.

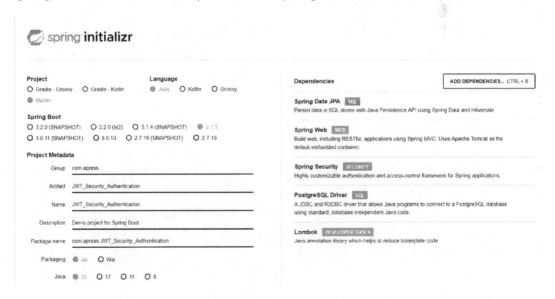

Figure 9-2. *PostgreSQL shell console*

Next, create a new Spring project named JWT_Security_Authentication using the Spring Initializr web tool at `https://start.spring.io/`, as shown in Figure 9-3.

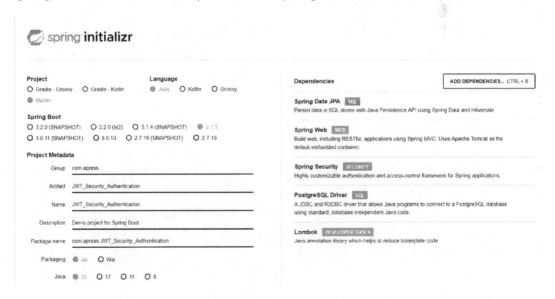

Figure 9-3. *New Spring project using Spring Initializr*

This example uses Java 20, Maven, and JAR, with Spring Web, PostgreSQL Driver, Spring Security, Spring Data JPA, and Lombok as dependencies.

The project's file structure is shown in Figure 9-4.

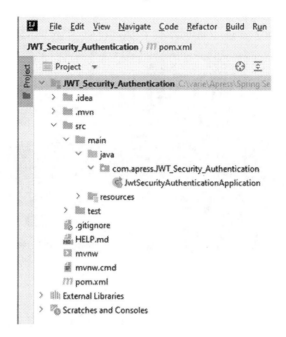

Figure 9-4. *New Spring project structure*

Next, add the needed dependencies in pom.xml files, such as JSON Web Token's io.jsonwebtoken and Jakarta XML Binding's jaxb-api. The entire pom.xml file is shown in Listing 9-1.

Listing 9-1. The pom.xml File

```xml
<?xml version="1.0" encoding="UTF-8"?>
<project xmlns="http://maven.apache.org/POM/4.0.0" xmlns:xsi="http://www.
w3.org/2001/XMLSchema-instance"
    xsi:schemaLocation="http://maven.apache.org/POM/4.0.0
    https://maven.apache.org/xsd/maven-4.0.0.xsd">
    <modelVersion>4.0.0</modelVersion>
    <parent>
        <groupId>org.springframework.boot</groupId>
        <artifactId>spring-boot-starter-parent</artifactId>
        <version>3.1.3</version>
        <relativePath/> <!-- lookup parent from repository -->
    </parent>
```

```xml
<groupId>com.apress</groupId>
<artifactId>JWT_Security_Authentication</artifactId>
<version>0.0.1-SNAPSHOT</version>
<name>JWT_Security_Authentication</name>
<description>Demo project for Spring Boot</description>
<properties>
    <java.version>20</java.version>
</properties>
<dependencies>
    <dependency>
        <groupId>org.springframework.boot</groupId>
        <artifactId>spring-boot-starter-data-jpa</artifactId>
    </dependency>
    <dependency>
        <groupId>org.springframework.boot</groupId>
        <artifactId>spring-boot-starter-security</artifactId>
    </dependency>
    <dependency>
        <groupId>org.springframework.boot</groupId>
        <artifactId>spring-boot-starter-web</artifactId>
    </dependency>
     <dependency>
         <groupId>io.jsonwebtoken</groupId>
         <artifactId>jjwt</artifactId>
         <version>0.9.1</version>
     </dependency>          <dependency>
        <groupId>javax.xml.bind</groupId>
        <artifactId>jaxb-api</artifactId>
        <version>2.3.1</version>
    </dependency>

    <dependency>
        <groupId>org.postgresql</groupId>
        <artifactId>postgresql</artifactId>
        <scope>runtime</scope>
    </dependency>
```

```xml
        <dependency>
            <groupId>org.projectlombok</groupId>
            <artifactId>lombok</artifactId>
            <optional>true</optional>
        </dependency>
        <dependency>
            <groupId>org.springframework.boot</groupId>
            <artifactId>spring-boot-starter-test</artifactId>
            <scope>test</scope>
        </dependency>
        <dependency>
            <groupId>org.springframework.security</groupId>
            <artifactId>spring-security-test</artifactId>
            <scope>test</scope>
        </dependency>
    </dependencies>

    <build>
        <plugins>
            <plugin>
                <groupId>org.springframework.boot</groupId>
                <artifactId>spring-boot-maven-plugin</artifactId>
                <configuration>
                    <excludes>
                        <exclude>
                            <groupId>org.projectlombok</groupId>
                            <artifactId>lombok</artifactId>
                        </exclude>
                    </excludes>
                </configuration>
            </plugin>
        </plugins>
    </build>

</project>
```

Next, configure the application.properties file with information about the database used, the JPA/JWT, and the server configuration, as shown in Listing 9-2.

Listing 9-2. The application.properties File

```
## DB Configuration ##
spring.datasource.url= jdbc:postgresql://localhost:5432/jwtsecuritydb
spring.datasource.username= postgres
spring.datasource.password= postgres

## JPA / HIBERNATE  Configuration ##
spring.jpa.show-sql=true
spring.jpa.hibernate.ddl-auto=create-drop
spring.jpa.properties.hibernate.dialect=org.hibernate.dialect.
PostgreSQLDialect
spring.jpa.generate-ddl=true

## Server Configuration ##
server.servlet.context-path=/api
server.port=8080

## JWT Configuration ##
jwt.jwtsecret = 2b44b0b00fd822d8ce753e54dac3dc4e06c2725f7db930f3b9924
468b53194dbccdbe23d7baa5ef5fbc414ca4b2e64700bad60c5a7c45eaba56880985
582fba4
jwt.jwtExpirationTime = 36000000

## User credentials
# to create user with "USER" Role: http://localhost:8080/api/user/register
#{
#"firstName": "Massimo",
#"lastName": "Nardone",
#"email": "mmassimo@gmail.com",
#"password": "masspasswd",
#"userRole": "user"
#}
```

```
# to login a user: http://localhost:8080/api/user/authenticate
#{
#"email": "mmassimo@gmail.com",
#"password": "masspasswd",
#}

## Admnin credentials
# to create user with "ADMIN" Role: http://localhost:8080/api/user/register
# {
# "firstName": "Neve",
# "lastName": "Nardon",
# "email": "neve@gmail.com",
# "password": "nevepasswd",
# "userRole": "admin"
# }

# to login as admin: http://localhost:8080/api/admin/hello
# {
# "email": "neve@gmail.com",
# "password": "nevepasswd"
# }
```

This Spring Boot JWT authentication example registers a new user and logs in with a username and password. The user's role can be "admin" or "user" to authorize the user to access a certain resource.

The APIs included in our example are shown in Table 9-1.

Table 9-1. *APIs Used in This Example*

Method	URL	Action
POST	/api/user/register	Registers a new account
POST	/api/user/authenticate	Logs into an account
GET	/api/public/welcome	Retrieves public content
GET	/api/admin/hello	Accesses the admin's content

Let's create our user and role models.

First, define the roles and an enum called RoleName, as shown in Listing 9-3.

Listing 9-3. The RoleName Class

```
package com.apress.JWT_Security_Authentication.models;

public enum RoleName {
    USER, ADMIN;

}
```

Next, let's define the role class, as shown in Listing 9-4.

Listing 9-4. The Role Class

```
package com.ons.securitylayerJwt.models;

import jakarta.persistence.*;
import lombok.*;
import lombok.experimental.FieldDefaults;
import org.springframework.security.core.GrantedAuthority;

import java.io.Serializable;

@Entity
@Getter
@Setter
@NoArgsConstructor
@AllArgsConstructor
@FieldDefaults(level = AccessLevel.PRIVATE)
public class Role implements Serializable  {

    @Id
    @GeneratedValue(strategy = GenerationType.IDENTITY)
    Integer id ;
    @Enumerated(EnumType.STRING)
    RoleName roleName ;

    public Role (RoleName roleName) {this.roleName = roleName;}
    public String getRoleName() {
        return roleName.toString();
    }
}
```

The role class creates a table named "Role" with two roles, "USER" and "ADMIN", which define the credentials required to register a new user.

Finally, create the user model class, as shown in Listing 9-5.

Listing 9-5. The User Model Class

```
package com.apress.JWT_Security_Authentication.models;

import jakarta.persistence.*;
import lombok.*;
import lombok.experimental.FieldDefaults;
import org.springframework.security.core.GrantedAuthority;
import org.springframework.security.core.authority.SimpleGrantedAuthority;
import org.springframework.security.core.userdetails.UserDetails;

import java.io.Serializable;
import java.util.ArrayList;
import java.util.Collection;
import java.util.List;

@Entity

@Table(name = "users",
        uniqueConstraints = {
                @UniqueConstraint(columnNames = "firstName"),
                @UniqueConstraint(columnNames = "lastname"),
                @UniqueConstraint(columnNames = "email")
        })

@Getter
@Setter
@AllArgsConstructor
@ToString
@NoArgsConstructor
@FieldDefaults(level = AccessLevel.PRIVATE)
public class User implements Serializable , UserDetails {

    @Id
    @GeneratedValue(strategy = GenerationType.IDENTITY)
```

```
Integer id ;
String firstName ;
String lastName ;
String email;
String password ;
String userRole ;

@ManyToMany(fetch = FetchType.EAGER   , cascade = CascadeType.PERSIST)
List <Role> roles ;

public User (String email , String password , List<Role> roles) {
  this.email= email ;
  this.password=password ;
  this.roles=roles ;}

@Override
public Collection<? extends GrantedAuthority> getAuthorities() {
    List<GrantedAuthority> authorities = new ArrayList<>();
    this.roles.forEach(role -> authorities.add(new
    SimpleGrantedAuthority(role.getRoleName())));
    return authorities;
}

@Override
public String getUsername() {
    return this.email;
}

@Override
public boolean isAccountNonExpired() {
    return true;
}

@Override
public boolean isAccountNonLocked() {
    return true;
}
```

```java
    @Override
    public boolean isCredentialsNonExpired() {
        return true;
    }

    @Override
    public boolean isEnabled() {
        return true;
    }
}
```

The user class is mainly a model to fetch and validate all the user credentials if they are not expired, locked, or enabled.

Next, implement the repositories needed by each model for persisting and accessing data. In the repository package, let's create two repositories.

- UserRepository fetches the user repository information, as shown in Listing 9-6.

- RoleRepository fetches the role repository information, as shown in Listing 9-7.

Listing 9-6. The UserRepository Class

```java
package com.apress.JWT_Security_Authentication.repository;

import com.apress.JWT_Security_Authentication.models.User;
import org.springframework.data.jpa.repository.JpaRepository;

import java.util.Optional;

public interface UserRepository extends JpaRepository<User,Integer> {

    Boolean existsByEmail(String email);
    Optional<User> findByEmail(String email);
}
```

Listing 9-7. The RoleRepository Class

```
package com.apress.JWT_Security_Authentication.repository;

import com.apress.JWT_Security_Authentication.models.Role;
import com.apress.JWT_Security_Authentication.models.RoleName;
import org.springframework.data.jpa.repository.JpaRepository;

public interface RoleRepository extends JpaRepository<Role,Integer> {

    Role findByRoleName(RoleName roleName);
}
```

Let's configure the SpringSecurityConfig class to use the security package, as shown in Listing 9-8.

Listing 9-8. The SpringSecurityConfig Class

```
package com.apress.JWT_Security_Authentication.security;

import lombok.RequiredArgsConstructor;
import org.springframework.context.annotation.Bean;
import org.springframework.context.annotation.Configuration;
import org.springframework.security.authentication.AuthenticationManager;
import org.springframework.security.config.annotation.authentication.
configuration.AuthenticationConfiguration;
import org.springframework.security.config.annotation.web.builders.
HttpSecurity;
import org.springframework.security.config.annotation.web.configuration.
EnableWebSecurity;
import org.springframework.security.config.http.SessionCreationPolicy;
import org.springframework.security.crypto.bcrypt.BCryptPasswordEncoder;
import org.springframework.security.crypto.password.PasswordEncoder;
import org.springframework.security.web.SecurityFilterChain;
import org.springframework.security.web.authentication.
UsernamePasswordAuthenticationFilter;

@Configuration
@EnableWebSecurity
@RequiredArgsConstructor
```

```java
public class SpringSecurityConfig {

    private final JwtAuthenticationFilter jwtAuthenticationFilter ;
    private final CustomerUserDetailsService customerUserDetailsService ;

    @Bean
    public SecurityFilterChain filterChain (HttpSecurity http) throws
    Exception
    { http
            .csrf().disable()
            .sessionManagement(session -> session.sessionCreationPolicy(Ses
            sionCreationPolicy.STATELESS))
            .authorizeHttpRequests(auth ->
            auth.requestMatchers("/public/**", "/user/**").permitAll()
            .requestMatchers("/admin/**").hasAuthority("ADMIN")) ;

        http.addFilterBefore(jwtAuthenticationFilter,
        UsernamePasswordAuthenticationFilter.class);

        return  http.build();
    }

    @Bean
    public AuthenticationManager authenticationManager(AuthenticationConfig
    uration authenticationConfiguration) throws Exception
    { return authenticationConfiguration.getAuthenticationManager();}

    @Bean
    public PasswordEncoder passwordEncoder()
    { return new BCryptPasswordEncoder(); }
}
```

Since this is the most important Spring Security class, let's discuss it in more detail.

- **@EnableWebSecurity**: allows Spring to find and automatically apply the class to the global web security.

- Spring Security loads the user details to perform authentication and authorization. It has customerUserDetailsService interface that you need to implement.

- **PasswordEncoder** used for the AuthenticationProvider if specified, it uses plain text.

- **(HttpSecurity http)** method used from WebSecurityConfigurerAdapter interface to tell Spring Security how to configure CSRF (disabled to send POST API), which filter (jwtAuthenticationFilter) and when you want it to work (filter before UsernamePasswordAuthenticationFilter), which Exception Handler is chosen (JwtUtilities).

- The implementation of customerUserDetailsService configures AuthenticationProvider with the **AuthenticationManagerBuilder. userDetailsService()** method.

- The "/public/**" path as a simple GET API is permitted to everyone so that you can test a simple GET API with public content.

- The "/users/**" path as a POST API is permitted to everyone so that all users can register and log in.

- The "/admin/**" path as a GET API is permitted only to users with hasAuthority("ADMIN"))

Listing 9-9 shows the CustomerUserDetailsService class.

Listing 9-9. The CustomerUserDetailsService Class

```
package com.apress.JWT_Security_Authentication.security;

import com.apress.JWT_Security_Authentication.models.User;
import com.apress.JWT_Security_Authentication.repository.UserRepository;
import lombok.RequiredArgsConstructor;
import org.springframework.security.core.userdetails.UserDetails;
import org.springframework.security.core.userdetails.UserDetailsService;
import org.springframework.security.core.userdetails.
UsernameNotFoundException;
import org.springframework.stereotype.Component;

@Component
@RequiredArgsConstructor
public class CustomerUserDetailsService implements UserDetailsService {
```

```java
    private final UserRepository UserRepository ;

    @Override
    public UserDetails loadUserByUsername(String email) throws
    UsernameNotFoundException {
        User user = UserRepository.findByEmail(email).orElseThrow(()-> new
        UsernameNotFoundException("User not found !"));
        return  user ;

    }

}
```

Now let's create the JWT authentication filter and the authentication provider to make the security filter chain work.

The JwtAuthenticationFilter class is a filter that executes once per request (see Listing 9-10).

Listing 9-10. The JwtAuthenticationFilter Class

```java
package com.apress.JWT_Security_Authentication.security;

import jakarta.servlet.FilterChain;
import jakarta.servlet.ServletException;
import jakarta.servlet.http.HttpServletRequest;
import jakarta.servlet.http.HttpServletResponse;
import lombok.RequiredArgsConstructor;
import lombok.extern.slf4j.Slf4j;
import org.springframework.lang.NonNull;
import org.springframework.security.authentication.
UsernamePasswordAuthenticationToken;
import org.springframework.security.core.context.SecurityContextHolder;
import org.springframework.security.core.userdetails.UserDetails;
import org.springframework.stereotype.Component;
import org.springframework.web.filter.OncePerRequestFilter;

import java.io.IOException;

@Slf4j
@Component
```

```java
@RequiredArgsConstructor
public class JwtAuthenticationFilter extends OncePerRequestFilter {

    private  final JwtUtilities jwtUtilities ;
    private final CustomerUserDetailsService customerUserDetailsService ;

    @Override
    protected void doFilterInternal(@NonNull HttpServletRequest request,
                                    @NonNull HttpServletResponse response,
                                    @NonNull FilterChain filterChain)
                                    throws ServletException, IOException {

        String token = jwtUtilities.getToken(request) ;

        if (token!=null && jwtUtilities.validateToken(token))
        {
            String email = jwtUtilities.extractUsername(token);

            UserDetails userDetails = customerUserDetailsService.
            loadUserByUsername(email);
            if (userDetails != null) {
            UsernamePasswordAuthenticationToken authentication =
                    new UsernamePasswordAuthenticationToken(userDetails.
                    getUsername() ,null , userDetails.getAuthorities());
                log.info("authenticated user with email :{}", email);
            SecurityContextHolder.getContext().setAuthentication(authen
                tication);
        }
        }

            filterChain.doFilter(request,response);
    }

}
```

Let's go over the JwtAuthenticationFilter class.

Create the JWT service class used in the JwtAuthenticationFilter class.

First, make sure the authorization header from our request is not null and that it starts with the word *bearer*.

Next, if the request has JWT, validate it and parse the username from it. Extract our JWT from the authorization header and use a function from the JwtSecvice class called extractUsername to extract the value of the user email from the JWT.

Next, from the username, use UserDetails to create an Authentication object and set the current UserDetails in SecurityContext using the setAuthentication(authentication) method.

Finally, send to get UserDetails.

```
UserDetails userDetails = customerUserDetailsService.loadUserByUsername(email);
```

Let's create the JwtUtilities class in the .security.jwt package, where you do the following.

- extract username from JWT: `extractUsername(String token)`

- generate a JWT from email, date, expiration, secret

- validate a JWT: invalid signature, expired JWT token, unsupported JWT token, and so on

Listing 9-11 shows the JwtUtilities class.

Listing 9-11. The JwtUtilities Class

```
package com.apress.JWT_Security_Authentication.security;

import io.jsonwebtoken.*;
import jakarta.servlet.http.HttpServletRequest;
import lombok.extern.slf4j.Slf4j;
import org.springframework.beans.factory.annotation.Value;
import org.springframework.security.core.userdetails.UserDetails;
import org.springframework.stereotype.Component;
import org.springframework.util.StringUtils;

import java.time.Instant;
import java.time.temporal.ChronoUnit;
import java.util.Date;
import java.util.List;
import java.util.function.Function;

@Slf4j
@Component
public class JwtUtilities{
```

```java
@Value("${jwt.jwtsecret}")
private String jwtsecret;

@Value("${jwt.jwtExpirationTime}")
private Long jwtExpirationTime;

public String extractUsername(String token) {
    return extractClaim(token, Claims::getSubject);
}

public Claims extractAllClaims(String token) {return Jwts.parser().
setSigningKey(jwtsecret).parseClaimsJws(token).getBody();}

public <T> T extractClaim(String token, Function<Claims, T>
claimsResolver) {
    final Claims claims = extractAllClaims(token);
    return claimsResolver.apply(claims);
}

public Date extractExpiration(String token) { return
extractClaim(token, Claims::getExpiration); }

public Boolean validateToken(String token, UserDetails userDetails) {
    final String email = extractUsername(token);
    return (email.equals(userDetails.getUsername()) &&
    !isTokenExpired(token));
}

public Boolean isTokenExpired(String token) {
    return extractExpiration(token).before(new Date());
}

public String generateToken(String email , List<String> roles) {

    return Jwts.builder().setSubject(email).claim("role",roles).
    setIssuedAt(new Date(System.currentTimeMillis()))
            .setExpiration(Date.from(Instant.now().
            plus(jwtExpirationTime, ChronoUnit.MILLIS)))
            .signWith(SignatureAlgorithm.HS256, jwtsecret).compact();
}
```

```java
public boolean validateToken(String token) {
    try {
        Jwts.parser().setSigningKey(jwtsecret).parseClaimsJws(token);
        return true;
    } catch (SignatureException e) {
        log.info("Invalid JWT signature.");
        log.trace("Invalid JWT signature trace: {}", e);
    } catch (MalformedJwtException e) {
        log.info("Invalid JWT token.");
        log.trace("Invalid JWT token trace: {}", e);
    } catch (ExpiredJwtException e) {
        log.info("Expired JWT token.");
        log.trace("Expired JWT token trace: {}", e);
    } catch (UnsupportedJwtException e) {
        log.info("Unsupported JWT token.");
        log.trace("Unsupported JWT token trace: {}", e);
    } catch (IllegalArgumentException e) {
        log.info("JWT token compact of handler are invalid.");
        log.trace("JWT token compact of handler are invalid trace:
        {}", e);
    }
    return false;
}

public String getToken (HttpServletRequest httpServletRequest) {
    final String bearerToken = httpServletRequest.
    getHeader("Authorization");
    if(StringUtils.hasText(bearerToken) && bearerToken.
    startsWith("Bearer "))
    {return bearerToken.substring(7,bearerToken.length()); } // The
    part after "Bearer "
    return null;
}
}
```

Let's create the TDO classes, including the following.

- BearerToken sets the JWT bearer token used in our example (see Listing 9-12).

- LoginDto is the data transfer object for user login (see Listing 9-13).

- RegisterDto is the data transfer object for user registration (see Listing 9-14).

Listing 9-12. The BearerToken Class

```
package com.ons.securitylayerJwt.dto;

import lombok.Data;

@Data
public class BearerToken {

    private String accessToken ;
    private String tokenType ;

    public BearerToken(String accessToken , String tokenType) {
        this.tokenType = tokenType ;
        this.accessToken = accessToken;
    }
}
```

Listing 9-13. The LoginDto Class

```
package com.ons.securitylayerJwt.dto;

import lombok.AccessLevel;
import lombok.Data;
import lombok.experimental.FieldDefaults;

@Data
@FieldDefaults(level = AccessLevel.PRIVATE)
public class LoginDto {

    private String email ;
    private String password ;
}
```

Listing 9-14. The RegisterDto Class

```
package com.ons.securitylayerJwt.dto;

import lombok.AccessLevel;
import lombok.Data;
import lombok.experimental.FieldDefaults;
import java.io.Serializable;

@Data
@FieldDefaults(level = AccessLevel.PRIVATE)
public class RegisterDto implements Serializable {

    String firstName ;
    String lastName ;
    String email;
    String password ;
    String userRole ;
}
```

Let's create the Spring REST API Controller classes, including the following.

- PublicRestController is a simple REST GET API with a "/public/welcome" link to return a welcome message (see Listing 9-15).

- AdminRestController is a REST GET API with the "/admin/hello" link to return a Welcome admin message in case the email/password are the admin's correct credential, the user has an "ADMIN" role, and the valid JWT is provided (see Listing 9-16).

- UserRestController is two REST POST APIs to register and log in a user. This is discussed more in Listing 9-17.

Listing 9-15. The PublicRestController Class

```
package com.apress.JWT_Security_Authentication.presentation;

import lombok.RequiredArgsConstructor;
import org.springframework.web.bind.annotation.GetMapping;
import org.springframework.web.bind.annotation.RequestMapping;
import org.springframework.web.bind.annotation.RestController;
```

```java
@RestController
@RequestMapping("/public")
@RequiredArgsConstructor
public class PublicRestController {

    @GetMapping("/welcome")
    public String welcome ()
    { return "Welcome! This is a public content!" ;}
}
```

Listing 9-16. The AdminRestController Class

```java
package com.apress.JWT_Security_Authentication.presentation;

import lombok.RequiredArgsConstructor;
import org.springframework.web.bind.annotation.GetMapping;
import org.springframework.web.bind.annotation.RequestMapping;
import org.springframework.web.bind.annotation.RestController;

@RestController
@RequestMapping("/admin")
@RequiredArgsConstructor
public class AdminRestController {

    @GetMapping("/hello")
    public String sayHello ()
    { return "Welcome you are authenticated as Admin!" ;}
}
```

Listing 9-17. The UserRestController Class

```java
package com.apress.JWT_Security_Authentication.presentation;

import com.apress.JWT_Security_Authentication.controllers.IUserService;
import com.apress.JWT_Security_Authentication.dto.LoginDto;
import com.apress.JWT_Security_Authentication.dto.RegisterDto;

import lombok.RequiredArgsConstructor;
import org.springframework.http.ResponseEntity;
import org.springframework.web.bind.annotation.PostMapping;
```

```java
import org.springframework.web.bind.annotation.RequestBody;
import org.springframework.web.bind.annotation.RequestMapping;
import org.springframework.web.bind.annotation.RestController;

@RestController
@RequestMapping("/user")
@RequiredArgsConstructor
public class UserRestController {

    private final IUserService iUserService ;

    @PostMapping("/register")
    public ResponseEntity<?> register (@RequestBody RegisterDto
    registerDto)
    { return  iUserService.register(registerDto);}

    @PostMapping("/authenticate")
    public String authenticate(@RequestBody LoginDto loginDto)
    { return  iUserService.authenticate(loginDto);}
}
```

The REST API UserService controller and its IUserService interface register a new user in the database and log in the user.

Finally, let's create the Spring REST APIs controller (see Listings 9-18 and 9-19) for authentication, providing APIs for register and login actions, such as the following.

- api/user/register

    - checks existing username/email

    - creates a new user (with "USER" or "ADMIN" role based on register input)

    - saves User to database using UserRepository

- api/user/authenticate

    - authenticates email, password

    - updates SecurityContext using the Authentication object

    - generates JWT

- gets UserDetails from the Authentication object
- response contains JWT and UserDetails data

Listing 9-18. The IUserService Class

```
package com.apress.JWT_Security_Authentication.controllers;

import com.apress.JWT_Security_Authentication.dto.LoginDto;
import com.apress.JWT_Security_Authentication.dto.RegisterDto;
import com.apress.JWT_Security_Authentication.models.User;
import com.apress.JWT_Security_Authentication.models.Role;
import org.springframework.http.ResponseEntity;

public interface IUserService {

    String authenticate(LoginDto loginDto);
    ResponseEntity<?> register (RegisterDto registerDto);
    Role saveRole(Role role);

    User saverUser (User user) ;
}
```

Listing 9-19. The IUserService Class

```
package com.apress.JWT_Security_Authentication.controllers;

import com.apress.JWT_Security_Authentication.dto.LoginDto;
import com.apress.JWT_Security_Authentication.dto.RegisterDto;
import com.apress.JWT_Security_Authentication.dto.BearerToken;
import com.apress.JWT_Security_Authentication.models.User;
import com.apress.JWT_Security_Authentication.models.Role;
import com.apress.JWT_Security_Authentication.models.RoleName;
import com.apress.JWT_Security_Authentication.repository.RoleRepository;
import com.apress.JWT_Security_Authentication.repository.UserRepository;
import com.apress.JWT_Security_Authentication.security.JwtUtilities;
import jakarta.transaction.Transactional;
import lombok.RequiredArgsConstructor;
import org.springframework.http.HttpStatus;
import org.springframework.http.ResponseEntity;
```

```java
import org.springframework.security.authentication.AuthenticationManager;
import org.springframework.security.authentication.
UsernamePasswordAuthenticationToken;
import org.springframework.security.core.Authentication;
import org.springframework.security.core.context.SecurityContextHolder;
import org.springframework.security.core.userdetails.
UsernameNotFoundException;
import org.springframework.security.crypto.password.PasswordEncoder;
import org.springframework.stereotype.Service;

import java.util.ArrayList;
import java.util.Collections;
import java.util.List;

@Service
@Transactional
@RequiredArgsConstructor
public class UserService implements IUserService{

    private final AuthenticationManager authenticationManager ;
    private final UserRepository userRepository ;
    private final RoleRepository roleRepository ;
    private final PasswordEncoder passwordEncoder ;
    private final JwtUtilities jwtUtilities ;

    @Override
    public Role saveRole(Role role) {
        return roleRepository.save(role);
    }

    @Override
    public User saverUser(User user) {
        return userRepository.save(user);
    }

    @Override
    public ResponseEntity<?> register(RegisterDto registerDto) {
        if(userRepository.existsByEmail(registerDto.getEmail()))
```

```
    { return  new ResponseEntity<>("email is already taken !",
    HttpStatus.SEE_OTHER); }
    else
    { User user = new User();
        user.setEmail(registerDto.getEmail());
        user.setFirstName(registerDto.getFirstName());
        user.setLastName(registerDto.getLastName());
        user.setPassword(passwordEncoder.encode(registerDto.
        getPassword()));
        String myrole = "user";

        if (registerDto.getUserRole().equals("") || registerDto.
        getUserRole().equals("user")) {
            myrole = "USER";
        }

        if (registerDto.getUserRole().equals("admin")) {
            myrole = "ADMIN";
        }

        Role role = roleRepository.findByRoleName(RoleName.valueOf
        (myrole));

        user.setUserRole(registerDto.getUserRole());

        user.setRoles(Collections.singletonList(role));
        userRepository.save(user);
        String token = jwtUtilities.generateToken(registerDto.getEmail(
        ),Collections.singletonList(role.getRoleName()));
        return new ResponseEntity<>(new BearerToken(token , "Bearer
        "),HttpStatus.OK);
    }
    }

@Override
public String authenticate(LoginDto loginDto) {
  Authentication authentication= authenticationManager.authenticate(
          new UsernamePasswordAuthenticationToken(
                  loginDto.getEmail(),
```

271

```
                    loginDto.getPassword()
            )
    );
    SecurityContextHolder.getContext().setAuthentication(authen
    tication);
    User user = userRepository.findByEmail(authentication.getName()).
    orElseThrow(() -> new UsernameNotFoundException("User not found"));
    List<String> rolesNames = new ArrayList<>();
    user.getRoles().forEach(r-> rolesNames.add(r.getRoleName()));
    String token = jwtUtilities.generateToken(user.
    getUsername(),rolesNames);

    return "User login successful! Token: " + token;
    }
}
```

The last Java class to update is JwtSecurityAuthenticationApplication, shown in
Listing 9-20, where the user and admin roles are populated automatically into the roles
database table, as shown in Figure 9-5.

Listing 9-20. The JwtSecurityAuthenticationApplication Class

```
package com.apress.JWT_Security_Authentication;

import org.springframework.boot.CommandLineRunner;
import org.springframework.boot.SpringApplication;
import org.springframework.boot.autoconfigure.SpringBootApplication;
import org.springframework.context.annotation.Bean;
import org.springframework.security.crypto.password.PasswordEncoder;

import com.apress.JWT_Security_Authentication.controllers.IUserService;
import com.apress.JWT_Security_Authentication.models.Role;
import com.apress.JWT_Security_Authentication.models.RoleName;
import com.apress.JWT_Security_Authentication.repository.RoleRepository;
import com.apress.JWT_Security_Authentication.repository.UserRepository;
```

```
@SpringBootApplication
public class JwtSecurityAuthenticationApplication {

    public static void main(String[] args) {
        SpringApplication.run(JwtSecurityAuthenticationApplication.
        class, args);
    }

    @Bean
    CommandLineRunner run (IUserService iUserService , RoleRepository
    roleRepository , UserRepository userRepository , PasswordEncoder
    passwordEncoder)
    {return  args ->
    {   iUserService.saveRole(new Role(RoleName.USER));
        iUserService.saveRole(new Role(RoleName.ADMIN));
    };}

}
```

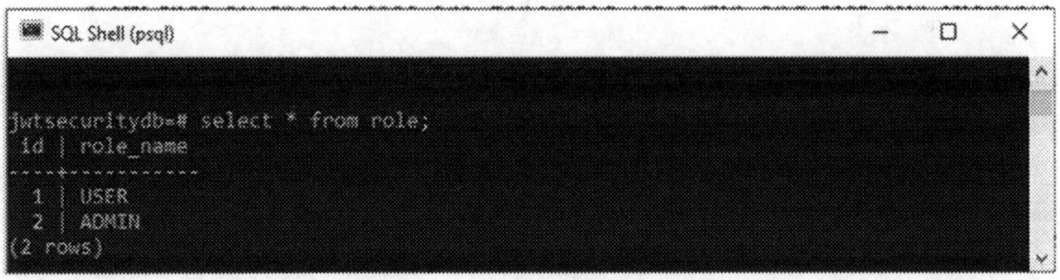

Figure 9-5. *Spring user roles added into database*

The new project structure should look like Figure 9-6.

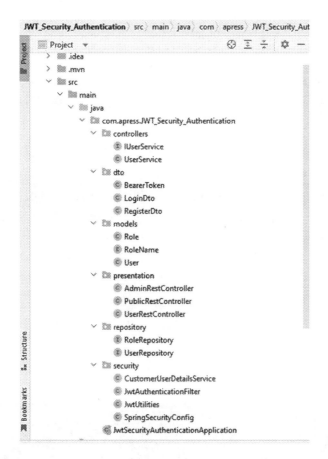

Figure 9-6. *Final Spring project structure*

Now that all the classes are generated, let's run and test our example: `mvn spring-boot:run`

Let's test the http://localhost:8080/api/public/welcome to see that the public REST GET API works properly. Figure 9-7 shows the result using the Postman testing tool.

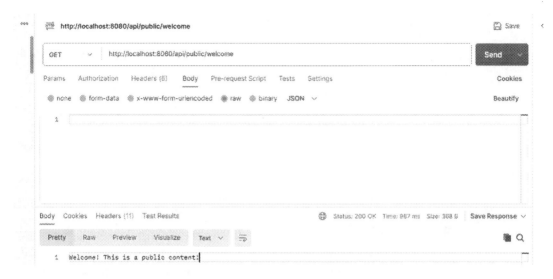

Figure 9-7. *Testing public REST GET API*

Next, let's register, via http://localhost:8080/api/user/register, a new user with the "USER" role and the following credentials.

```
{
"firstName": "Massimo",
"lastName": "Nardone",
"email": "mmassimo@gmail.com",
"password": "masspasswd",
"userRole": "user"
}
```

Figure 9-8 shows the result in Postman.

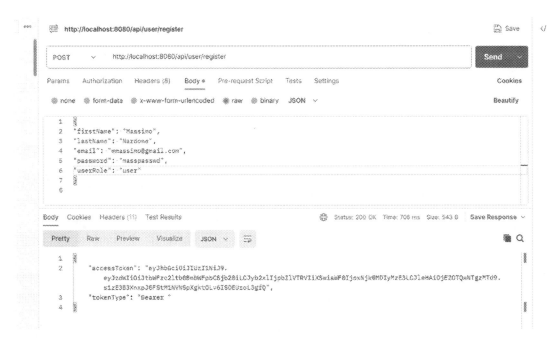

Figure 9-8. *Registered new user with "user" role*

A new user is registered with status 200 OK, and an access JSON web token is generated. The token type is Bearer. You can use that token to log in, providing an email/password and the newly created JSON token, via http://localhost:8080/api/user/authenticate. Figures 9-9 and 9-10 show the results.

Figure 9-9. *Log in user with valid email/password*

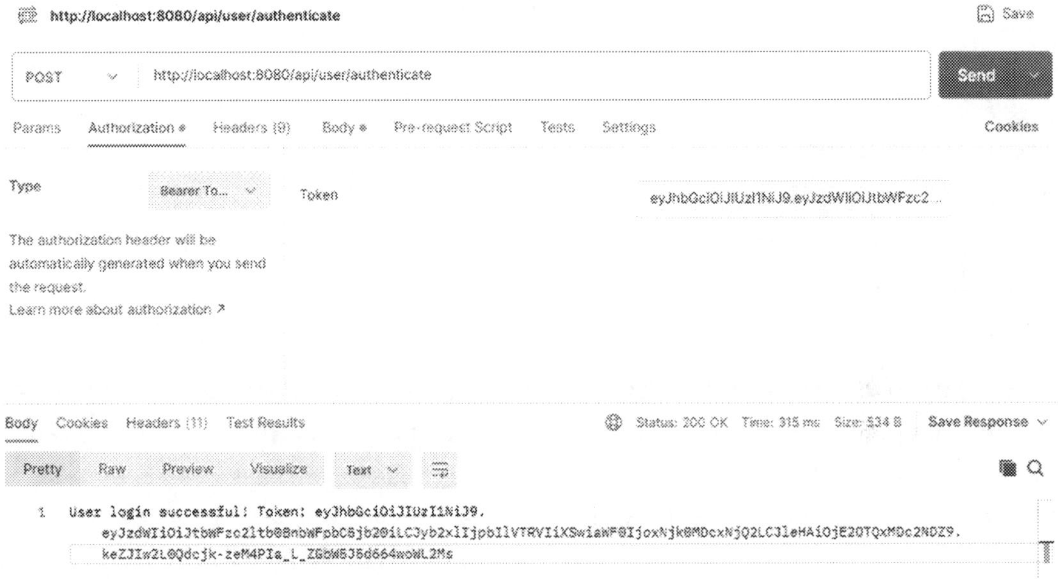

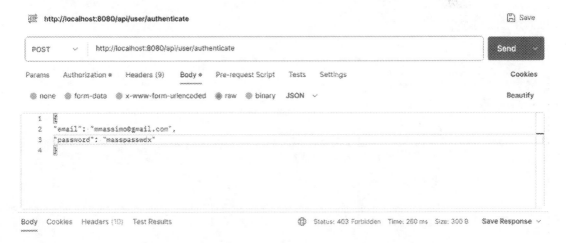

Figure 9-10. *Log in user with valid JWT*

Status 200 OK validates the user login. Figure 9-11 shows the result when a wrong password is entered.

Figure 9-11. *Forbidden login for user providing wrong password*

Let's create another user with the "ADMIN" role.

```
{
"firstName": "Neve",
"lastName": "Nardon",
"email": "neve@gmail.com",
"password": "nevepasswd",
"userRole": "admin"
}
```

If you try to log in using http://localhost:8080/api/admin/hello to the user API using the admin credential, it fails because we defined that only users with an admin role can access the admin URL. If instead you log in providing valid email/password credentials and a valid JWT, you see what is shown in Figure 9-12.

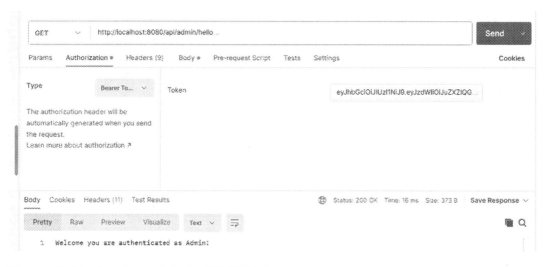

Figure 9-12. *Log in to Admin REST API*

The users and roles created in the database are shown in Figure 9-13.

Figure 9-13. *Created users in the database*

Summary

This chapter showed you how to secure a REST API using JWT and Spring Security 6, Spring Boot 3+, and PostgreSQL.

Index

A

Access control entry (ACE), 206, 207, 209
Access control list (ACL), 9, 24, 115, 205
    capability, 208
    concept, 205
    database classes, 208
    domain classes, 205
    domain objects, 207
    evaluating, 210
    getId() method, 208
    Java Code, 209
    key interfaces, 207
    Spring Security, 205, 206
    support, 206
AccessDecisionManager, 108, 109
    AffirmativeBased, 109
    ConsensusBased, 110
    implementations, 108, 109
    informations, 109
    interface, 108
    reference, 109
    UnanimousBased, 110
Acegi Security System for Spring, 28
AccessDecisionVoter, 110, 111, 113
Admin REST API, 278
AdminRestController Class, 267
Application security, 3
Application security layer, 5, 6
    authentication, 6, 7
    authorization, 7
Aspect-oriented programming (AOP), 22,
    34, 36–38

Asymmetric encryption
    encryption/decryption, 13
    key, 13
    security, 13
    use case, 13
Attribute-based access control (ABAC), 7
Authentication, 6, 7
Authentication interface, 100
Authentication mechanisms, 169, 170,
    200, 204
Authentication object
    creation, 101
    framework, 101
    implementations, 102, 103
    interface, 101, 102
    uses, 101
AuthenticationProvider, 106, 108, 204
AuthenticationUserDetailsService, 114
Authorization, 7–9, 132

B

<bean>-based configuration, 87
BearerToken Class, 265
Biometric authentication, 6

C

Central Authentication Service
    (CAS), 60, 203
Cloud security, 17
Comprehensive security, 2
Confidentiality, 13

CookieCsrfTokenRepository.saveToken
 method, 133
Cross-site request forgery (CSRF), 23,
 133, 214
Cross-site scripting (XSS), 15, 23
CustomerUserDetailsService Class, 259
Custom login form, 146
 authenticated.html file, 145
 authenticated page, 146
 AuthenticationFailureHandler, 148
 AuthenticationSuccessHandler, 148
 CustomAuthenticationFailureHandler
  class, 149, 150
 custom error, 147, 148
 DefaultLoginPageGeneratingFilter, 143
 <form-login>, 147
 404 error, 143, 144
 http.authorizeHttpRequests ()
  method, 143
 http.authorizeRequests() method, 143
 login controller, 144
 login.html, 144–146
 login.jsp, 147
 SecurityConfiguration file, 144

D

Data breaches, 16
Data definition language (DDL), 115
Data encryption, 3
Decorator pattern, 36, 117
Defense in depth (DiD)
 application security, 3
 awareness/training, 3
 combination of measures, 2
 data encryption, 3
 defensive mechanisms, 2
 failing/weak, 2

goal, 2
IAM, 3
IT infrastructure layers, 4
monitoring/incident response, 3
multi-layered, 4
network security, 3
perimeter security, 2
physical controls, 2
Defensive mechanisms, 2
Demilitarized zones (DMZs), 2
Denial-of-service attacks, 15, 214
Dependency injection (DI), 22, 34–36, 118
Digest authentication, 98, 152–154
Domain-specific language (DSL),
 87, 88

E

Embedded LDAP server, 186, 191
Encryption algorithms
 one-way encryption, 10
 symmetric encryption, 11, 12
Environment set up, Spring Security
 6 project
 Apache Tomcat 10, 50, 51
 IntelliJ IDEA 2023.1.2
  dashboard, 49
  directory, 48
  installation, 48
 JAVA_HOME system
  variable, 46, 47
 Java installation, testing, 47
 JDK
  compiler, 52
  configuration, 51, 52
  download/installation, 46
 Maven 3.9.2, 49, 50
 software lists, 45

F

Filter chain, 94
    configuration, 97
    overview, 96
    Spring beans, 95
Filters, 137–139
    configuration, 96
    DelegatingFilterProxy filter, 96
    documentation, 140
    enums, 97
    HTTP request, 94, 95
    overview, 95
    security filter, 96
    servlet filter, 96
    types, 97–99
Forbidden login, 277

G

GitHub, 58, 219, 234–236, 238
Groovy, 23

H

Hashing algorithms, 10
H2 console
    authorities, 184
    authorities table, 184
    autnenticated.html page, 181
    login page, 180–182
    securitydb tables, 182, 183
    users, 185
    users table, 184, 185
    welcome.html page, 180
H2 Database project
    application.properties file, 171
    authenticated.html file, 174
    dependencies, 170
    frame options, 180
    Java classes and HTML files, 171
    pom.xml file, 172, 173
    requestMatchers, 180
    SecurityConfiguration Java
        class, 174–177
    settings, 170
HTTP Basic authentication, 150, 151
HttpSecurity instance, 132, 133
Hybrid encryption, 14

I

Identity and access management (IAM), 3
Identity management, 14
Information technology (IT), 1
Insider threats, 16
Integrated development environment
    (IDE), 88
Integrity, 14
IntelliJ IDEA 2023.1.2., 220
Internet of Things (IoT), 1
Intrusion detection systems (IDS), 2, 3
Intrusion prevention systems (IPS), 2
Inversion of Control (IoC), 34, 36
IoT security, 1, 17

J

Jasypt cryptography, 22
Java Authentication and Authorization
    Service (JAAS), 18, 19, 203
Java Certification Path API
    (CertPath), 17, 19
Java Cryptographic Extensions
    (JCE), 17, 19
Java Cryptography Architecture
    (JCA), 17

Java Generic Security Services (Java GSS-API), 18
Java Secure Socket Extension (JSSE), 17
Java SE Runtime Environment (JRE), 46, 51
Java web application, 121
Java web application project
    configuration, 54
    index.jsp file, 56
    Package Explorer, 54
    pom.xml file, 55, 56
    Pss01, 52, 53
    run, Tomcat Server 10, 56, 57
    structure, 54, 55
    updation, 55
    web browser, 57
JDBC project
    DataSource, 178
    dependencies, 170
    Java classes and HTML files, 171
    JdbcDaoImpl, 177
    JdbcUserDetailsManager bean, 178
    SecurityFilterChain bean, 179
    settings, 170
JDK, 18
JSON Web Token (JWT), 201, 202
    advantages, 245
    application.properties file, 251
    Authentication object, 262
    BearerToken Class, 265
    Controller classes, 266
    definition, 242
    header, 242, 243
    IUserService Class, 269
    JwtSecurityAuthenticationApplication Class, 272
    JwtUtilities class, 262
    payload, 243

PostgreSQL database, 247
project's file structure, 248
project structure, 273
ProviderManager, 244
PublicRestController Class, 266
RoleRepository Class, 257
secret key, 243
sensitive data, 245
signature, 243
Spring Boot, 252
Spring Security, 245
user class, 256
user model class, 254
The UserRestController Class, 267
JSP taglib, 115
JwtAuthenticationFilter Class, 260

K

Kotlin, 23, 30, 34

L

Lightweight Directory Access Protocol (LDAP), 6, 22, 92
    application login page, 197
    application.properties file, 188
    attributes, 186
    complexity, 198
    definition, 185
    dependencies, 187
    directory, 185, 186
    entry, 186
    formLogin, 196
    groups, 193
    LdapAuthoritiesPopulator code, 196, 197
    LdaPsecurityApplication, 193

LDIF file, 191, 192
login page, 197
Maven dependencies, 186, 187
password authentication, 196
plugins, 198
pom.xml file, 188–191
project, 187
project structure, 188
SecurityConfiguration Java class, 194, 195
SHA password, 193
storage, 185
TV Guide, 185
UserController Java class, 193, 194
users, 193, 197, 198
values, 186
Logging out, 158
   cookies, 159, 160
   flow, 160
   invalidate method, 160
   movies.jsp page, 159
   remember-me functionality, 159, 160
   SecurityConfiguration file, 159
   TokenBasedRemember
      MeServices, 161
   UserController file, 159
Login authentication method, 232
LoginDto Class, 265

M

Malware, 16
Maven web application, 121
   authenticated.html page, 127, 128
   HTML files, 126
   Java classes, 128
   Java packages, 128
   tools and directories, 126
   UserController Java class, 128, 129
   welcome.html page, 126, 127
Maven web application project, 52, 61
Message digest, 10
Microsoft Windows Active
      Directory system, 185
Multi-factor authentication (MFA), 3, 6
Mutual authentication, 25, 198
MVC applications, 130

N

Network security, 3
Network security layer, 4, 5

O

One-way encryption, 10, 11
Open Authorization 2.0 (OAuth 2.0), 22, 40, 43, 200–201
   access tokens, 212
   application properties, 227
   application registers, 212
   authentication, 225
   authorization capabilities, 212
   authorization code, 213
   authorization server, 212
   Client, 232
   client authentication, 213
   ClientRegistration properties, 236
   consent, 213
   CSRF, 214
   dependencies, 221
   generated client ID, 231
   GitHub, 234
   Google authentication, 224
   Google client credential, 233
   Google Cloud, 229, 230

Open Authorization 2.0 (OAuth 2.0) (*cont.*)
grant, 212
HTTPS, 213
ID and secret key, 235
implementation, 217
logging and monitoring, 214, 217
Login, 217–219
overview, 212, 215
refresh tokens, 213
resource, 216
scope of permissions, 213
secret key match, 236
security, 214
Spring Security, 214, 227
Spring Security annotations, 217
steps, 228
template files, 220
third-party applications, 211
token revocation, 214
tokens, 213
token storage and
management, 217
unauthorized access, 214
UserController class, 223
user's protected resources, 212
Open source software, 23, 58, 116
Operating system layer, 5
Operating system (OS), 5
Operational technology (OT), 1
Output sanitation, 15

P, Q

PasswordEncoder bean, 177
Password security, 16
Pattern matching, 33
Perimeter security, 2
Phishing, 16

PKI encryption, *see* Asymmetric
encryption
PostgreSQL shell console, 247
Postman testing tool, 274
Private key, 12
Public key, 12
Public key cryptography, 12, 13

R

Ransomware, 16
RegisterDto Class, 266
Remember-me authentication
Amazon.com, 155
autoLogin method, 158
check box, 156
cookie, 155–157
functionality, 155
login.html file, 156
problem, 155
RememberMeAuthenticationFilter,
155, 157, 158
SecurityConfiguration configuration
file, 156
TokenBasedRemember
MeServices, 155, 156, 158
UserDetails, 158
UsernamePassword
AuthenticationFilter, 155, 156
REpresentational State Transfer (REST)
advantages, 240–41
APIs, 239
authorization, 242
client state, 240
disadvantages, 241
functionalities, 242
HTTP methods, 239
JWT authentication, 239

list of cars, 240

performance overhead, 242

resource, 239

session-related information, 241

software applications, 239

uniform and consistent interface, 240

Resilient security, 2

RESTful applications, 130

Role-based access control (RBAC), 7, 8

S

Secured connections, 14

Secure Sockets Layer (SSL), 5, 94, 198–200

Security, 1

credentials, 9

encryption, 10

permissions, 10

resource, 10

role, 9

user, 9

SecurityConfiguration Java class, 130–132

SecurityContext class, 103, 104

SecurityContextHolder Class, 103–106

SecurityContext Interface class, 104

Security information and event
management (SIEM), 3

Security Interceptor, 78

AbstractSecurityInterceptor,
81–83, 85, 86

AccessDecisionManager, 80

AfterInvocationManager, 81

AuthenticationManager, 79, 80

FilterSecurityInterceptor, 79

InterceptorStatusToken, 80

MethodSecurityInterceptor, 79

preprocessing step, 79

ProviderManager, 79

RunAsManager, 80

Spring Security 6 class, 81

UML class diagram, 85, 86

Sensitive data protection, 15

Servlet filter, 94, 96, 126, 129, 167

Session management

configuration, 162

HttpSessionEventPublisher, 162

new session ID, 161

SecurityConfiguration file, 163

SecurityConfiguration Java class,
161, 163–166

SessionAuthenticationStrategy, 161

SessionFixationProtectionStrategy
class, 161

Single-responsibility principle
(SRP), 81, 118

Single sign-on (SSO), 212, 217

Social engineering, 16

Software exploits, 16

Spring Boot, 108

definition, 28

Spring Security, 170

versions, 34

Spring Boot project, 170

Spring Data JPA, 247

Spring Expression Language (SpEL), 25

Spring Framework 4.3, 129

Spring Framework 5, 29

Spring Framework 6

core container, 30

core revision, 30

data access and transaction, 31

Jakarta EE 9+ Baseline, 30

JDK 17+, 30

MVC, 32

observability, 33

pattern matching, 33

Spring Framework 6 (*cont.*)
    spring messaging, 32
    testing, 34
    WebFlux, 32
    web revision, 32
Spring project
    login message, 124
    login page, 123
    pom.xml file, 124, 125
    pss01_Security, 121, 122
    run, 123
    simple controller, 124
    structure, 122, 248, 274
    web application, 124
Spring Security, 210
    built-in exception-handling
        mechanism, 25
    code, 116
    concepts/components, 77, 78
    default configuration, 134
    definition, 21
    features, 23, 38, 39
    file structure, 89
    100-Foot View, 77
    1,000-Foot View, 76, 77
    10,000-Foot View, 75, 76
    functionalities, 39
    fundamentals, 41
    implementation, 61
    internal architecture core
        modules, 77
    JAR files, 42
    Java developers, 21, 23
    Java EE, 26
    projects, 26, 27
    public/private key, 25
    reasons, 23

    released dates, 29
    role-based authentication/
        authorization, 23
    URLs, 24
Spring Security 6, 81
    functionalities, 42
    JAR files, 43
    new, 38
Spring Security 6.1.0, 58–60
Spring Security 6 project
    AffirmativeBased, 141
    authentication process, 141, 142
    authorization process, 141, 142
    configuration
        admin login iteration flow, 73
        AppInitializer Java class, 68, 69
        @EnableWebSecurity
          annotation, 66
        index.jsp page, 69
        JAR file, 71
        Java classes, 66
        Java package, 65
        login web page, 71, 72
        SecurityConfiguration
          class, 66–68
        SpringSecurityInitializer
          class, 68
        user/admin credentials, 73
        wrong credentials, 72
    creation, 58
    DaoAuthenticationProvider, 140
    @EnableWebSecurity, 130
    environment set up (*see* Environment
        set up, Spring Security 6 project)
    filters, 137–139
    FilterSecurityInterceptor, 141
    HTTP request filter, 137

JAR file, 135
JARs dependencies, 61
login message, 65
login page, 64, 65, 140
login web page, 135
logout page, 136, 137
Maven dependencies, 61, 62
pom.xml file, 62, 63
Pss02, 60
right admin credentials, 136
running configuration,
    Tomcat 10, 71
security password, 64
SpringSource, 58
steps, 45
structure, 70, 134
UsernamePasswordAuthentication
    Filter, 139
web browser, 135
wrong credentials, 135, 136, 139
Spring Security web project, 126
Spring WebSocket, 202, 203
SQL injection, 15
Strategy pattern, 117
Symmetric encryption, 12
    key, 11
    speed, 12
    use case, 12

T

Thymeleaf Java library, 220
Token revocation mechanisms, 214
Two-factor authentication (2FA), 3

U

Unauthorized access, 10, 16
Unified modeling language (UML),
    85, 86, 108
URLs, 10, 22, 142
UserController Java class, 130
UserDetails, 114, 115
UserDetailsService, 113

V

Virtual private networks (VPNs), 3
Vulnerabilities, 16

W

Weak authentication, 16
Web application firewalls (WAFs), 3
Web security, 23, 81, 129

X, Y, Z

X.509 authentication, 198–200
XML namespace, 87, 118
    config module, 88, 89
    constants, 90–92
    elements, 92, 94
    load-up sequence, 90
    reference, 90
    requirements, 88
    SecurityNamespaceHandler, 90
    spring.handlers, 89, 90
    spring.schemas, 89
    .xsd file, 87